Managing Money

Child care Information
20.00

P.O. 63195

Maney

A Cook

""

Child Care Information Exchange

PO Box 2890   •   Redmond, WA 98073-2890   •   (800) 221-2864

"The Best of Exchange"

Article Collection #11

This is a Best of Exchange Collection of Articles originally published in *Child Care Information Exchange*. The issues in which these articles originally appeared are noted in the Table of Contents on the following pages.

Every attempt has been made to update information on authors and other contributors to these articles. We apologize for any biographical information that is not current.

Child Care Information Exchange is a bimonthly management magazine for directors and owners of early childhood programs. For more information about *Child Care Information Exchange* and other *Exchange* publications for directors and teachers, contact:

Child Care Information Exchange
PO Box 2890
Redmond, WA 98073-2890
(800) 221-2864

ISBN 0-942702-21-2

Cover Photograph:
Subjects & Predicates

Printed in the United States of America

Managing Money
A Center Director's Guidebook

Table of Contents

Basic Money Management Tools

7   Managing Money As If Your Center Depended Upon It by Roger Neugebauer (March 1986)

12   Step-by-Step Guide to the Budget Process by Thomas Wolf (March 1984)

19   Preparing and Using Monthly Financial Status Reports by Roger Neugebauer (March 1981)

22   How to Perform Cash Flow Analysis by Roger Neugebauer (May 1981)

25   Step-by-Step Guide to Break Even Analysis by Keith Stephens (March 1991)

29   Child Care Center Management Software Buying Guide by Roger Neugebauer (July 1995)

Financial Evaluation Tools

35   Financial Management Assessment Guide by Roger Neugebauer (November 1980)

37   Number Crunching: Monitoring Your True Enrollment by L. Steven Sternberg (July 1993)

40   Financial Reports Every Director Needs by Teresa P. Gordon (January 1985)

44   When You Think You Need an Audit — Points to Consider by Teresa P. Gordon (October 1984)

Financial Policies and Procedures

49   Is Your Salary Schedule Up to Speed? by Roger Neugebauer (March 1994)

53   Guidelines for Fine Tuning Your Salary Schedule by Roger Neugebauer (May 1994)

62   State-of-the-Art Thinking on Parent Fee Policies by Roger Neugebauer (November 1993)

68   Implementing a Sliding Fee Scale System for Your Center by Roger Neugebauer (June 1984)

74   Tried and True Techniques for Collecting Fees — Ideas from center directors (May 1986)

78   How Centers Spend Money on Quality by John Morris and Suzanne Helburn (July 1996)

Managing Money

Fundraising Strategies

85   Where the Bucks Are: Sources for Funds to Grow Your Child Care Business by Keith Stephens (May 1987)

92   Keys to Success in Raising Funds by Roger Neugebauer (March 1981)

95   Circles of Support by Kathy Hines (January 1997)

98   Have You Looked Under Every Rock? Multi-Source Funding for Child Care Programs by Harriet Alger and Judith B. Fountain (November 1981)

101   Developing a Proposal: When Opportunity Knocks, Will You Be Prepared? by Craig Boswell (May 1995)

105   Fishing for Dollars in Philanthropic Waters by Anne Mitchell (September 1996)

109   Keys to Maintaining a Good Banking Relationship by Keith Stephens (May 1988)

Fundraising Success Stories

115   Directors' Fundraising Hits — Ideas from center directors (March 1981)

126   Fundraising Ideas that Work by Roger Neugebauer (May 1995)

130   Ask and Ye Shall Receive: A Primer for Large-Scale Fundraising by Patricia Berl (December 1988)

133   People Giving to People: Executing an Annual Giving Campaign by Patricia Berl (March 1987)

137   Step by Step to a Successful Annual Giving Telephone Campaign by Jane Ewing and Susan Morris (February 1989)

142   Losing Money/Making Money by Lynne Meservey (December 1990)

Long Range Planning

147   How to Prepare a Business Plan by Keith Stephens (July 1987)

152   Guidelines for Selling Your Child Care Business (Part I) by Keith Stephens (March 1997)

156   Selling Your Child Care Business: Determining Its Value (Part II) by Roger Neugebauer (May 1997)

Basic Tools

*"Financial management tools,
all based on
a sound
budgeting process,
enable the director
to keep a
finger on the pulse
of the organization's
financial health."*

Managing Money As If Your Center Depended Upon It

by Roger Neugebauer

Directors of child care centers must be as effective at managing money as they are at caring for children. This lesson, had it not been learned too late, would have saved a local nursery school. This school provided a wonderful environment for children — the staff were creative and nurturing, and the parents loved the experiences their children were having. However, the school was closed shortly after the original director left. Her replacement was an outstanding curriculum planner, but she was totally unable to come to grips with managing money. After a few minor financial crises, the school was forced to close its doors.

Unfortunately, this scenario is not rare. Many child care centers and nursery schools are plagued by faulty money management.

If child care centers were highly profitable or generously funded, the consequences of ineffective money management would not be severe. Most centers, however, operate painfully close to the red ink on a daily basis.

The waste of a few dollars here and the loss of some expected income there can cause a center to delay or even cancel a pay day. If income and expenses are not carefully planned and controlled, a center can go out of business in a remarkably short period of time.

In helping centers with financial difficulties, I have noticed that a few problems tend to pop up time and again. I have described below the five most common money management pitfalls as well as some proposed remedies.

1. The Programmed-to-Fail Budget

A director draws up a budget for which projected income equals projected expenses. However, the budget will inevitably fail because faulty assumptions were made in projecting both income and expenses.

The most common mistake here is to project income by multiplying weekly fees by the number of spaces in the center by the number of weeks the program is open. This does project a center's maximum potential income if every space is filled for every week. But this will never happen! Inevitably, a few children will leave the school in the middle of the year, and a lag of a week or more will occur before they are replaced; or a child will leave with two months remaining in the school year, and the space won't be filled; or a family will move out of town and neglect to pay their past due fees; or the welfare department will refuse to provide reimbursement for several snow days. A center that fails to account for shortfalls such as these in planning its budget will find that it never quite has enough money to pay all of its bills.

For a new center, it is difficult to predict what the shortfall in income will be. It might be risky to expect more than 60% of potential income in the first year.

For an older center, the shortfall can probably be reasonably estimated based on previous years' experiences. This can be done by calculating the maximum potential income the center could have received in the past 12 months and dividing this amount into the amount of income the center actually received for the 12 months. For example, if a center had a maximum potential income of $50,000 for last year, but only received $45,000, this means it only received 90% of its potential income ($45,000 ÷ $50,000 = .90 or 90%). For the coming year, this center should set its budget no higher than 90% of its potential income.

Centers often under project expenses by failing to include certain line items altogether. Most frequently neglected are expenses for staff training, leave time, salary increases, fuel cost increases, and major appliance repairs. Certain of these expenses (such as fuel and repairs) cannot be ignored — money must be found to pay for them. Others (such as training and salary increases) can be ignored, and frequently are, but only at the cost of severely undermining staff morale and program quality.

2. Penny Wise and Dollar Foolish Cost Cutting

A center short of funds responds by vigorously cracking down on expenditures for supplies. Napkins are cut in half, drawing is done on recycled computer paper, and free materials are scrounged everywhere.

Such a response is typical, and typically it is ineffective. Even if the average center cut its supply costs in half (which would begin to have a noticeable impact on curriculum quality), the net effect would be to only reduce the center's overall costs by about 1%.

This does not mean that centers shouldn't try to save money on supplies. Certainly all centers have an obligation to parents to keep costs as low as possible. The danger, however, is that the director and teachers will work so hard on scrounging materials and other similar activities that they will begin to think they are doing all they can to solve their money problem. In other words, they will be distracted from effectively addressing the problem.

To put cost cutting efforts into perspective, it is helpful to analyze the savings potential of each budget item (such as in the example in Exhibit A). First, the annual amount allocated for each line item in the budget should be listed. Then, the percent that each line item would have to be cut in order to save $1,000 per year should be calculated. This is done by dividing $1,000 by the amount of each line item. For example, in Exhibit A, the line item teachers' salaries would have to be cut by 2.9% ($1,000 ÷ $34,500) to save $1,000.

A quick review of the resulting figures will identify those areas where significant cuts can be made without having a dramatic negative impact on the program. For example, the Hippy Dippy Child Care Center would have to cut the social services line item by 50%, the training line item by 40%, or the health line item by 67% to save $1,000. Obviously, cuts of this magnitude would dramatically alter these aspects of the program. On the other hand, there are four line items — teachers' salaries, administrative salaries, nutrition, and occupancy — which would be reduced by less than 7% if $1,000 were cut from them. These are clearly areas where Hippy Dippy Child Care staff should concentrate cost savings efforts in order to have the least adverse impact on the program.

By going through this process, a program will quickly be able to identify three or four areas where attention should be focused in cutting costs. Unfortunately, it will not provide directions on how to make the actual cuts. No charts or formulas can relieve the pain from these decisions.

3. The Fruitless Fundraiser

A center pours considerable time and energy into a fundraising project which generates only limited funds. For example, a local nursery school sponsors a fair every year. One year the school netted $725 after expenses. To earn this amount, parents and staff donated over $100 in cash and 500 hours in labor. If, instead, each parent had donated only $7, the center would have raised as much money with no effort.

Before engaging in any fundraising project, a center should perform a cost-benefit analysis. First, estimate the maximum amount of money the project could yield after expenses. Then, estimate the number of staff and volunteer hours required to carry out the project. Finally, divide the dollars by the hours. If the result is less than $10 per hour, the project is probably not worth the effort. From $10-25 per hour, it is of marginal value. Above $25 per hour, it is clearly worthwhile. Really successful fundraisers have been known to yield over $100 per hour.

4. Checkbook Balance Money Management

A center's director controls income and expenses solely by observing the checkbook balance. If the checkbook balance is high, the director freely spends money. If the balance is low, the director spends money cautiously and works hard to cut costs. If the balance is in the red, the director launches a fundraising project.

Such a casual day-to-day form of money management could have disastrous consequences for the average child care center. A center could be deeply in debt but still have a positive checkbook balance because several major purchases were made on credit to be paid 30 days later. It could be forced to raise fees in the middle of the year because no funds were set aside in the fall to cover high heating costs in the winter, or it could simply run short of money at the end of every month and not know why or what to do about it.

To effectively keep a handle on a center's financial status, a director must know much more than how much money is in the checking

Exhibit A
Hippy Dippy Child Care — Cost Savings Analysis

Budget Item	Annual Budget Amount	Percent of Reduction to Save $1,000
Teachers' Salaries	$34,500	3%
Administrative Salaries	20,000	5
Program Supplies/Equipment	3,000	33
Office Supplies/Equipment	2,000	50
Nutrition	15,500	7
Occupancy	15,000	7
Health	1,500	67
Transportation	4,000	25
Training	2,500	40
Social Services	2,000	50
Miscellaneous	1,000	100

account. She must know how much money has been expended on each budget item, how much income has been received, whether these expense and income amounts are in line with what was budgeted, and whether sufficient funds are available for upcoming major expenses. This information can all be obtained by preparing a *monthly status report.*

The monthly status report can be relatively easy to prepare and interpret, yet it provides invaluable information. The report format has all of the income and expense line items from the budget listed vertically on the left hand side, followed by three columns of figures. In the first column, headed *Actual Activity to Date,* is recorded the total of all income or expenses incurred for each budget item as of the last day of the month being reviewed (the closing date). For example, in the report in Exhibit B, $15,000 in parent fees had been received and $20,810 in staff salaries had been expended as of

June 30. These figures should be readily available from the center's accounting records. (To simplify the preparation of status reports, one account or group of accounts in these records should be set up for each budget item.)

In the second column, headed *Projected Activity to Date,* is recorded the cumulative amount the center had planned in the budget to have received or expended as of the closing date. Hippy Dippy Child Care had projected receiving $14,500 in parent fees and expending $20,600 in staff salaries as of June 30. These projections are derived from the budget. The easiest way to do this is to divide each budget item by 12 to arrive at a monthly figure. This figure is then multiplied by the number of months that have passed in the budget year. In the example, the *Projected* figure for rent is $2,550, or $425 per month times 6 months.

For certain budget items, projections cannot be made so easily. For centers in the north, utility expenses are seldom the same every month as heating costs soar in the winter. Similarly, parent fees and staff salaries may dip in the summer months when enrollments decline. For variable items such as these, it may be necessary to project income or expenses month by month, based on previous years' experiences.

In the third column, headed *Percent of Target Achieved*, is recorded the percent of the projected amount that the center actually received or expended for each budget item. As of June 30, Hippy Dippy Child Care had received only 89% of its projected Title XX income and had spent 101% of its projected salary expenses. The percentage figure is computed by dividing the *Actual* amount by the *Projected* amount (for example, $11,760 \div $13,250 = 89\%$).

There are a number of points to check in reviewing the monthly status report. First, of course, one should check the bottom line — the *Balance* (calculated by subtracting *Total Expenses* from *Total Income*). In the example, there is a positive balance of $200 as of June 30. This is bad news since the projected balance was $2,000.

This means that not enough money has been set aside to cover future expenses. Once a problem is found, the next step is to trace the cause by reviewing the *Percent* column. The objective here is to find income items that are significantly below 100% of the projected amounts and expense items that are significantly above 100%. In the example, Title XX income (89%) and fundraising income (10%) are both far too low and sub-

Exhibit B **Hippy Dippy Child Care Monthly Status Report** **As of June 30**			
	Actual Activity to Date	Projected Activity to Date	Percent of Target Achieved
Income			
Parent Fees	$15,000	$14,500	103%
Title XX	11,760	13,250	89
Food Program	5,550	5,700	97
United Way	5,250	5,250	100
Fundraising	40	400	10
Total Income	$37,600	$39,100	96%
Expenses			
Salaries	$20,810	$20,600	101%
Substitutes	1,680	1,400	120
Fringe	3,260	3,200	102
Legal	600	800	75
Training	150	300	50
Rent	2,550	2,550	100
Utilities	300	350	86
Food	5,700	5,600	102
Supplies	1,200	1,150	104
Insurance	250	250	100
Loan	900	900	100
Total Expenses	$37,400	$37,100	101%
Balance	+ $ 200	+ $ 2,000	10%

stitute expenses (120%) are running far too high.

With this report the director has discovered that even though there is money in the checkbook, there is a serious problem developing. She also knows that to correct it she must focus her attention on the problems with Title XX, fundraising, and substitutes. In addition, she can see that small surpluses are accumulating in certain

expense items (legal and audit, training, and utilities) which could be shifted over to partially offset the substitute deficit.

5. The False Sense of Security

A center's board of directors requires that every expenditure be approved by the board and that every check be signed by two designated individuals. The board has adopted these requirements in order to safeguard the center's funds.

Controls such as these may seem to be foolproof. In practice, they are often foolhardy. To be effective, the two signature procedure requires that both individuals signing any check review background documentation to be satisfied that the expenditure is appropriate. More often than not, the second person signing the checks automatically signs them, assuming that the first person has already checked them out.

The two signature procedure can also be inefficient. If both signers are not located in the center, much time can be wasted chasing after the second person. In cases where potential signers are unavailable, major payments or a payroll can be delayed. Some centers circumvent this problem by having one party sign a number of blank checks in advance. This, of course, undermines the safeguarding aspect of the system.

In a non profit center, having all expenditures approved by the board can also be counterproductive. It drains valuable board time and energy away from crucial policymaking and evaluative functions. Instead of developing a sliding fee scale policy, the board debates what brand of construction paper to purchase. Just as importantly in retaining decision-making of this detail, the board can undermine the staff commitment and leadership. The message conveyed to the director and teachers is that they are not trusted and that their function is simply to carry out orders from above.

The biggest danger of both of these safeguards is that they provide a false sense of security. They give the appearance of security without providing it in reality.

To provide effective security, a number of approaches can be implemented:

• All money coming into the center should be documented with duplicate copies of prenumbered receipts.

• All expenditures should be made with prenumbered checks and a file maintained with backup invoices, receipts, or explanations for each check.

• The check writing function should be separated from the bookkeeping and checkbook balancing functions.

• In a larger center in which responsibility for purchasing is delegated by an owner, executive director, parent agency, or board of directors, two signatures should be required on all large purchases with the limit clearly established by the delegator. (Some public and private funding organizations may, of course, require two signatures on all checks.) In addition, two signatures should be required on all withdrawals from savings accounts.

• Someone in a position of authority should regularly review monthly status reports to seek explanations for any expense items that are exceeding budgeted amounts or income items that are lagging behind projections.

References and Resources

Gross, Malvern J., Jr., et al. *Financial and Accounting Guide for Not-for-Profit Organizations* (Fifth Edition). New York: John Wiley and Sons, Inc., 1995.

Morgan, Gwen. *Managing the Day Care Dollars: A Financial Handbook.* Cambridge, MA: Steam Press, 1982. Distributed by Gryphon House, PO Box 207, Beltsville, MD 20704-0207.

Step-by-Step Guide to the Budget Process

by Thomas Wolf

When Mary Phillips accepted the position of director of the Hippety Hop Child Care Center, she focused her attention on the problems of full enrollment and teacher recruitment. Any worries she might have had about the budget were secondary. "Last year we had full enrollment and ended with some money left over," she reasoned. "If we can just fill all the slots again this year, money should not be a problem." Mary knew that child care directors are supposed to work on budgets, but she never seemed to have enough time. Four months into the year, she had only managed to produce some hastily scribbled estimates.

In late January, Mary Phillips discovered that the center's bank balance was getting dangerously low. She was surprised since the center was fully enrolled and tuition was coming in promptly. One night she went over the books and was amazed to find that the center had spent more on supplies in the first four months of the year than had been spent during the entire previous year. As she looked at other categories of expenditure, she began to panic. Money was being spent at an alarming rate. Worse yet, Mary had no way of know what a reasonable rate should be. The figures began to swim around on the page, and she was no longer sure she was adding them correctly.

Mary Phillips' case is not unusual. Many child care directors and other key decisionmakers do not take the budgeting process seriously. Many live to regret it. A budget is an important financial planning tool which can help an organization control expenditures and diagnose problems *before* they occur.

The purpose of this article is to demystify the process of budgeting so that those who identify with Mary Phillips need not repeat her mistakes. For others, this article may suggest new techniques for developing budgets which will facilitate more accurate forecasting and better methods of evaluating cost effectiveness.

The Budgeting Process

If budgeting is a form of financial planning, then it is important to know what specific procedures are involved in doing it effectively. There are two important considerations:

• Budgeting should always be related to overall planning in a child care center. No one is in a position to plan for the future without a clear sense of what the available resources are. Conversely, sensible budgets, or financial plans, cannot be put together without knowing where the organization is going, what its programs will consist of, and who its clients will be. Simply allocating money is not enough. Using it strategically is what the budgeting process should be about.

• The key decisionmakers in a center (whether they be the owners, the board of directors, the representatives from a parent organization, or the director and head teachers) should be involved in every step of both the budgeting and general planning process. Because these leaders must set long-range goals for the organization, decide on program priorities, and ultimately assume fiscal accountability, it is important that they be involved in the budgeting process both in the forecasting stages and later when the budget must be monitored.

Beyond these general considerations, there are eight steps that an organization should take to complete a successful budgeting cycle:

Step 1:
Make a Wish List

The first step in budgeting has nothing to do with numbers or dollars. It concerns an annual review of what the center wishes to accomplish in the year to come. At the beginning of the budget cycle, center leaders should consider objectives for the upcoming year. What should we be doing? What would we like to do if cost was not an object? This step is essential because it forces the people to think systematically about the center's activities, its mission, and its programs. It provides an opportunity to review the purposes for which the organization

was formed, its long-range goals and plans, and its short-term objectives. Making a wish list is fun because it does not require a close monitoring of costs. It is the last time in the budgeting process that such an opportunity presents itself.

Step 2:
Cost Out the List

How much will it cost to carry out the activities listed in Step 1? Obviously, there are some basic costs that have to be covered just to keep the center going. There is the cost of the programs you operated last year and plan to continue. Each of these must be carefully *costed*. In addition, the costs of new activities will also have to be estimated.

Costing is not an easy process. Traditionally, there have been two methods. The first, called the *incremental budgeting* method, leans heavily on information contained in previous years' budgets. If an organization is carrying out an activity that it has done for several years, then the easiest way to prepare a budget for the coming year is to add a percentage increment for inflation and other factors to the figures contained in the previous year's budget.

The other costing method, called *zero-based budgeting*, requires that each line item of a budget be calculated anew; staff members are told that any item in the budget will be zero unless they can provide a full justification for some other figure.

Obviously, some combination of these two approaches is desirable in the budgeting process. The previous year's budget figures will be immensely helpful in estimating

the coming year's. It is also important to look at financial statements from the current year to see how accurate the original budget projections were. However, each item in the budget should also be examined carefully without reference to another year's figures. An assessment should be made, item by item, of whether the expenditure is required and, if so, how large it should be. In addition, new projects and activities require estimates for which the previous year's budget is not very helpful.

In costing out the *wish list* developed in Step 1, two things are important to remember:

• Costs should always be estimated on the high side. Add at least 10% to all expense figures. Those people who budget expenses at a level they think will be correct have almost always under budgeted.

• As you consider the costs of added programs and activities, remember that they will add to your central administrative costs. It is not enough simply to estimate how much you will actually spend on a new program. The simple addition of the program puts an added burden on the core staff, on space, on the typewriter, xerox machine, and so on.

For example, when a director of an existing center is drawing up a budget for a new infant care component, she may neglect to consider the impact this new activity will have on her own workload. Subconsciously, she may assume that she will be able to squeeze the additional work into her regular schedule. Inevitably, however, such a major undertaking places

Table 1
Annual Budget for Hippety Hop Child Care Center
(in $1,000s)

Number of Children	Infants (27)	Toddlers (40)	Middle (36)	Preschool (45)	Total (148)
Projected Expenses					
Teachers' Salaries	90	80	60	50	280
Administrative Salaries	4	6	5	7	22
Support Salaries	8	12	10	13	43
Fringe (15%)	15	15	11	11	52
Consultants	1	1	1	2	5
Rent	18	26	23	30	97
Utilities	6	8	7	9	30
Maintenance	3	4	4	5	16
Food	7	11	10	12	49
Educational Supplies	2	3	3	4	12
Other Supplies	2	2	2	3	9
Insurance	1	1	1	1	4
Other Services	1	1	1	2	5
Total Expenses	158	170	138	149	615
Projected Income					
Parent Fees	40	61	89	123	313
Title XX	16 *	25 *	29 *	35 *	105
Food Program	14 *	24 *	18 *	24 *	80
United Way	40 *	0	0	0	40
Employer Contracts	20 *	20 *	10 *	0	50
Donations	0	10	5 *	0	15
Miscellaneous Fundraising	15	0	0	0	15
Total Income	145	140	151	182	618
Balance	-13	-30	+13	+33	+3

*Restricted funds

considerable demands on the director. As a result, she either ends up working many extra hours for the center without pay or hiring additional staff to handle the administrative workload.

There are two ways an organization can deal with administrative costs. One is simply to create a major category called *central administration* and lump all salaries, rent, and other administrative expenses in this general category. Another approach is to engage in *cost allocation*. Here the idea is to charge to each activity or program a reasonable percentage of central administrative costs.

The budget for the Hippety Hop Child Care Center displayed in Table 1 is an example of the cost allocation approach to budgeting. Administrative and other overhead costs (such as rent, utilities, and insurance) are allocated to the various components of the center. For instance, it was determined that 50% of the director's time is devoted to activities that concern or benefit all center components equally. One half of the director's salary, therefore, was spread equally among the four components.

The balance of the director's time is spent working directly with the specific components. However, the percentage devoted to each activity varies. For that reason, the second half of the director's salary was allocated among the four components on the basis of how much attention each would require. By combining these two figures, 18% of the *Administrative Salaries* line item was allocated to the infant component, 27% to the toddler component, 23% to the middle component, and 32% to the preschool component.

Even though cost allocation requires time and careful analysis on the part of budget preparers, it does enable members of the organization to get a fairly accurate reading on how much each component of the program costs. In the budget in Table 1, it can be seen that the toddler component is costing far more than it is generating in income. By knowing each component's true costs, center leaders are able to make better informed decisions about whether or not each one should be continued as is, restructured, or discontinued.

Step 3:
Allocate Income

Using the same list of activities developed in Step 1 and costed out in Step 2, it is now time to consider how much income can be expected from each activity. Again, last year's budget and the current year's financial statements can be helpful. This step is a bit tricky because there are certain funds specifically earmarked for a particular activity as well as income that has no such restrictions and can be put anywhere.

Here it is important to understand the difference between *restricted* and *unrestricted* funds. Unrestricted funds are monies received with no particular instructions or limitations as to how or when they are to be used. Parent fees, general donations, and income from fundraising efforts are all examples of unrestricted funds. Restricted funds, on the other hand, are those received with special limitations as to the time period or the purpose of their use. Child care subsidies from a state or federal agency often arrive with very specific strings attached which dictate how and when the funds may be used.

The budget in Table 1 shows that the Hippety Hop Child Care Center received a restricted grant from the local United Way agency for the operation of its infant care component. It also has signed a contract with a local employer for providing child care for its employees; monies received under this agreement are restricted to use in those components where the employees' children are enrolled.

Once restricted funds and unrestricted funds have been sepa-

rated, the process of allocating income is as follows (see Table 1):

• Put all restricted income into the proper program activity or component. That is, any income clearly attributable to a specific component should be put into that component and marked with an asterisk. Later on, as you are going through the process of balancing the budget, it is important to remember that these funds cannot be transferred from one component to another.

• Cover all the most basic administrative costs with unrestricted income.

• Allocate the balance of unrestricted income across all the components and activities listed. You may want to allocate it on a percentage basis. Calculate the fraction that each program expense total is of the total budget and use this fraction to calculate how much money should go to each component. Or you may want to use a simpler method and divide the money on a roughly equal basis among components. The first method, while more work, does help you assess the relative cost effectiveness of programs when you get to Step 4 below. However, the second method is much less work. Ultimately, it does not matter how you allocate the unrestricted funds to programs and projects *at this point* because you must make adjustments later on to put everything in balance.

• Understate all income estimates by at least 10%. Just as you left some margin for error on expenses, so you must be equally conservative on income forecasting. For example, in projecting the amount of income that will be derived from parent fees, you should never assume that your center will operate at 100% capacity all year. Most directors factor in an under-enrollment of 10-15%.

Step 4:
Compare

This is often called the *read it and weep* step. It should be clear by this time that some activities must be given up if the budget is going to balance. There is simply too much expense and not enough income. In fact, if you discover that income is adequate to cover expenditures *at this point* in the budgeting process, there should be great concern that the organization is not reaching far enough or being ambitious enough. Put another way, if you can pay for all of your wishes, you are not wishing hard enough. Your reach should exceed your grasp so that your center can continue to grow in its ability to provide services and programs to the public.

However, center decisionmakers are not acting responsibly when they decide to undertake more than the center can pay for. Many activities should be considered even though only some will be undertaken immediately. The examination of a potential activity one year is valuable in planning for that activity another year.

In comparing one component or activity to another, decisionmakers can use the criterion of cost effectiveness. Which activities come closest to paying for themselves? Which have the highest cost relative to the income they bring in? These kinds of questions are clearly of prime concern in a

center operated on a for profit basis. A for profit center will not survive for long if many of its components are operating in the red.

In the budget in Table 1, for example, the infant component is projected to operate at a loss for the year. If this center were operated on a for profit basis, it would not make good business sense to continue to operate this component unless (a) some means were found to generate increased revenues or (b) it was decided that infant care was such a critical need in the community that by offering it the center introduces a large number of new families to the center and thus benefits all other components.

Cost effectiveness should also be of more than passing interest to a non profit center. Such a center will not be able to serve the public well if one money-losing component severely drains the resources from all other components. There is also a danger here. Remember that non profit organizations are not in business primarily to make money. Their missions may dictate that they carry on certain activities that are *not* cost effective.

How would we feel, for example, if the only activities engaged in by a certain church were its profitable rummage sales and Bingo games. We (and most likely the Internal Revenue Service) would be concerned that a more fundamental mission of the church was not being fulfilled. Similarly, for a non profit center, cost effectiveness, while an important criterion, is not the only one. The primary criterion should relate to the mission of the organization, its purposes, goals, and objectives.

Step 5:
Set Priorities

Anyone who has sat through a budget session in which programs and activities are debated for inclusion in the next year's budget knows what a difficult session it can be. Some people, who may have been silent for a time, suddenly emerge with a pet project that simply must be included. Others, wishing to be more fiscally restrained, may urge the rejection of any new activities.

In the end, a priority setting session must relate not solely to dollars and cents but to a fundamental assessment of the organization's reason for being. It is too easy in the heat of the moment to argue for or against an activity on its own merits or on cost effectiveness. But it is important to ask: "Is this activity really central to what we are about? Does it help us get where we want to be in a year? in two years? in five years? Is it more important to build up a reserve to protect the organization over the long term?" These are difficult questions, but in asking them the decisionmakers are fulfilling a fundamental role in deciding what course is best for the organization and, in the case of non profit centers, most clearly in the public interest.

Step 6:
Adjust and Balance

Once activities have been put in some semblance of priority order, a little negotiation is still possible as the budget is adjusted and put into balance. In the case of the Hippety Hop Child Care Center, if the infant care component is a high priority but there is simply not quite enough to cover it, perhaps some money can come out of the preschool component budget which is projected to generate excess income. If the infant care component is dropped instead, monies that were allocated to it can be moved to other areas if those monies are unrestricted. One must be careful, obviously, not to move monies that can only be used for the infant care component itself. For example, the United Way grant as well as the parent fee income generated by the component would be lost to the organization.

Until now, our budget has been skewed conservatively. We have understated income and overstated expenses. Even though the budget is balanced on paper, it would appear that there is far more money coming in than going out. Careful budgeting, however, requires this approach. It is almost always the case that certain expenses have been forgotten and certain anticipated income comes in short. In the event that the actual financial picture results in income far exceeding expenses, center decisionmakers have the enviable task of deciding what to do with the additional money.

Step 7:
Approve

Once all the initial groundwork is completed on the budget, there should be some formal closure to the process. If the center is a small sole proprietorship, this approval step may involve no more than having the owner pull all the budgetary computations together in the form of a final budget and

reviewing the assumptions behind this budget one last time. In a larger for profit corporation, the approval step may involve a center director submitting a budget proposal to an executive director or a corporate office. In a non profit center, the budget will need to be submitted to a board of directors or to a parent organization for official approval.

Because so much hard work and careful consideration happens in the earlier steps, centers often tend to treat the approval step as a mere formality. This is especially common in non profit centers. Board members may assume that since the staff spent so much time developing the budget, they are in no position to question it. However, in voting to approve a budget, the board is exercising its fiduciary responsibility in setting financial limits and boundaries for the staff. The board is also implicitly agreeing to make sure that the projected revenues will be forthcoming, particularly those funds that have to be raised.

A board of directors should never approve a budget based on a *wish and a prayer* that projects unrealistic fundraising goals. If such a project is approved, and the funds are not raised, it is the trustees who must take responsibility. Thus, a good question to ask during the *approval* process is: "Do we really know how every projected revenue dollar will be earned or raised, who will be responsible, and whether the targets are realistic?"

On the expense side, a responsible board member should ask how estimates were determined. For example, if the line item for postage is $2,500 and the board

member is told by staff that the number was arrived at by taking last year's figure, a good question might be: "Is that a realistic figure given the fact that postal rates have increased by 20% and we have added 300 people to our mailing list?"

Indeed, because the previous year's budget is so often the primary document upon which so many estimates are made, it is easy for the budget preparers to forget to take obvious changes into consideration. Trustees should challenge the budget document, not because they doubt the ability of the staff, but because it is they, not the staff, who are ultimately responsible for the fiscal health of the organization.

A center owner, an executive director, or a chief fiscal officer in a corporate headquarters all have equivalent responsibility to a board of directors in considering the approval of a center's budget. As such, they should take this responsibility seriously and be certain the budget is sound before granting their approval.

Step 8:
Monitor and Amend

One common mistake in the budget process is to assume it has come to an end once the final document is approved. Indeed, the very word *final* is a misnomer when talking about a budget. Few budgets can hold up over time without being amended and modified to accommodate new information and new conditions as the year wears on. For this reason, a center should have in place a process by which the budget can be reviewed and, when necessary, changed.

Two extremes should be avoided. Whoever has approved the budget should not insist that the document *is it* and force the staff to stick to it without modification throughout the fiscal year. On the other hand, they should also not be willing to say that the budget document is only a *rough approximation* and give staff instructions to "come as close as possible." Rather, a formal documented procedure should be set up that allows staff some flexibility but gives those ultimately responsible the final say on any significant changes in the budget figures.

For example, in a $100,000 budget, a board of directors may tell the executive director the following (which would be documented in the minutes of the board meeting at which it was approved): "So long as you feel you can balance the budget, you may shift up to 15% or $2,000 (whichever is less) out of or into any account. However, if more significant changes are to be made, you must present a revised budget to the board for approval."

By way of example, let us say that the line item *Equipment* has a budgeted amount of $20,000. Using the guidelines previously listed, the director may, at her discretion and without board approval, move up to $2,000 to some other expenditure category or may choose to spend $2,000 more in that category. The director should not do the extra spending, however, unless she is relatively confident that the budget can still be balanced by additional income or by shifting the $2,000 from some other category where it is not needed. If the director anticipates that an additional $4,000 is necessary for equipment, then the full board must be consulted and an amended budget must be submitted and approved.

Post Script

Mary Phillips is no longer the director of the Hippety Hop Child Care Center. Her failure to keep costs under control ultimately cost her her job. But the organization's board of directors also learned an important lesson. Members of the board had always assumed that the budget was the director's problem. They were surprised and dismayed to find themselves facing a severe deficit when the director resigned.

Ultimately, budgeting and monitoring of the budget should be a shared responsibility. Sound budgeting procedures, shared among key decisionmakers, will not only help a child care center control costs but can serve as an important planning tool for any organization.

Dr. Thomas Wolf is president of the Wolf Organization, Inc., a consulting firm in Cambridge, Massachusetts. This article was adapted from his book, **The Nonprofit Organization: An Operating Manual** *(Englewood Cliffs, NJ: Prentice-Hall, 1984).*

Preparing and Using Monthly Financial Status Reports

by Roger Neugebauer

*T*he budgets of most child care programs are precarious, with little margin for error. A drop in fee income of only 2-4%, or an unnoticed escalation in utility costs, can have a disastrous impact on a center's financial stability. Child care directors do not have the luxury of being able to wait until the end of the year to deal with balancing the budget. They need to be monitoring the center's financial position continually to catch monetary tremors before they swell into economic earthquakes.

One effective monitoring tool is the *monthly financial status report*. This report gives the director a stop-action view of how closely the center is adhering to the annual budget. It helps pinpoint areas where expenses are exceeding projections or where income is falling behind.

Developing the Report Format

There are two main components of the monthly financial status report — the annual budget as projected on a month-by-month basis and an up-to-date record of actual revenues and expenditures. These two pieces of information are summarized and analyzed on a one-page chart (see page 21).

On the lefthand side of this chart are listed categories of income and expenses. In listing these, break out categories that are meaningful to you — don't automatically use the categories from a standard budget form. Don't clutter the chart with minor items such as *Postage Stamps* or *Photocopying*. Rather, consolidate these into more meaningful categories such as *Office Supplies and Services*. On the other hand, you may want to subdivide major categories such as salaries into subcategories which vary independently, such as *Administrative Salaries* and *Program Salaries*. Ideally, the annual budget, the accounting system, and the status report should all be organized with the same categories so that data can be transferred and

compared easily. The financial information can then be presented in four columns. In the first column, Column A, is recorded the actual financial activity of the center for the year to date. For example, Column A in the chart below shows that the Honey Dew Nursery had received $18,800 in *Parent Fees* and expended $23,800 in *Salaries* as of June 30. This information should be readily available from the center's accounting records.

Setting Monthly Targets

In Column B is recorded the financial activity for the year to date as it was projected in the annual budget. Column B shows that the Honey Dew Nursery had projected, or anticipated, having received $18,400 in *Parent Fees* and having expended $23,400 in *Salaries* as of June 30.

There are two methods for developing the information for Column B — one simple and one complicated. The simple method involves dividing the amount for each category in the annual budget by 12. This yields a monthly budget. (For a nursery school operating ten months during the year, the annual budget is divided by 10.) When the monthly financial status report is prepared, this monthly budget is simply multiplied times the number of school months which have elapsed in the current year. If, for instance, a center projects collecting $60,000 in parent fees in the annual budget, the monthly budget amount for parent fees would be $5,000 ($60,000 ÷ 12). The projected activity in this category as of June 30 would then be $30,000 ($5,000 x 6). This amount is the target the center will strive to achieve.

This simple method is probably accurate enough for small programs and for programs where enrollment, staff schedules, and major expenses do not vary significantly from month to month. For many centers, however, income and expenses do not flow in and out evenly from month to month. Fuel costs may be much higher in the winter, enrollment may be lower in the summer, CETA workers may need to be replaced by paid staff six month into the year, etc.

To set realistic targets in these centers, income and expenses need to be methodically projected on a month-by-month basis. To do this, enter the center's annual budget on the lefthand side of a wide sheet of paper. Under *Salaries* list each position separately. To the right make a column for each month. Now go through each income item and determine how much of each type of income will be received each month. For example, if enrollment typically declines during the late spring and summer, the *Parent Fees* income should be lower in these months. If the only major fundraiser is scheduled for September, most *Fundraising* income should be recorded under this month.

Then do the same for all expense items. For administrative and teaching staff who work stable schedules, their salaries should be divided equally over the 12 months. For personnel working part of the year or with variable schedules, their likely salaries for each month should be predicted as carefully as possible. Substitute expenses should be concentrated in months where absenteeism is typically high in your center. If supplies and equipment are purchased in big orders several times a year, these expense items should be attributed properly to these months. If insurance is paid for in quarterly payments, it should be charged to the months when payments will be made.

When the entire budget is analyzed in this manner, the resulting monthly budgets are to be used for the status report. For the June 30 report, for example, the cumulative amounts for each category in the January through June budgets will be entered in Column B.

Computing Variations

In Column C is entered the difference between Column A and Column B. If the actual amount (Column A) is larger than the projected amount (Column B), the variation is recorded as a positive amount. In the chart below, the actual amount collected in *Parent Fees* income ($18,800) was larger than the amount projected ($18,400), so that the variation is a positive amount (+$400), meaning that actual income exceeded that which was projected. When the actual amount is less than the projected amount, the variation is expressed as a negative amount (see *Title XX* and *Food Program* below).

While Column C shows the amount of the variation, Column D indicates its magnitude. In this column is recorded the percentage by which the actual amounts vary from the projected amounts. It is computed by dividing the amount in Column C by the amount in Column B and multiplying the dividend by 100 (C/B x 100 = D). Thus when this formula is applied to parent fee income in the chart below ($400 ÷ $18,400 x 100), the actual income is found to be 2% above the projected amount. When the amount of variation in Column C is a negative amount, the percentage of variation in Column D will be a negative value as well (see *Title XX* and *Food Program* below).

Interpreting the Report

First check the bottom line. On this chart the bottom line is the *Balance*, the difference between total income and total expenses. In the case of the Honey Dew Nursery, income exceeded expenses by $1,000 for the first six months, so the balance under Column A is +$1,000. This would appear to be cause for celebration. However, moving over to Column B, the balance projected for this date was +$3,000. This means that the school fell $2,000 short of its target for the first six months — a cause for serious concern.

When a significant variation is found in the balance, the next step is to pinpoint the cause. Look at the *Total Income* and the *Total Expenses* categories to see if large variations are apparent. In the Honey Dew case, the actual income ($38,000) only fell short of the projected income ($38,200) by $200 — or by -1%. On the other hand, actual expenses ($37,000) exceeded projected expenses ($35,200) by

Honey Dew Nursery Monthly Status Report

	A Actual Activity as of June 30	B Projected Activity as of June 30	C Amount of Variation	D Percentage of Variation
Income				
Parent Fees	$18,800	$18,400	+$400	+2%
Title XX	13,500	13,600	-100	-1
Food Program	5,600	5,700	-100	-2
Fundraising	100	500	-400	-80
Total Income	$38,000	$38,200	-$200	-1
Expenses				
Salaries	$23,800	$23,400	+$400	+2%
Substitutes	1,500	1,100	+400	+36
Food	6,300	5,700	+600	+11
Curriculum Supplies	700	400	+300	+75
Curriculum Equipment	600	600	0	0
Office Supplies	350	300	+50	+17
Occupancy	3,750	3,700	+50	+1
Total Expenses	$37,000	$35,200	+$1,800	+5%
Balance	+$1,000	+$3,000	-$2,000	-67%

$1,800 — or by +5%. Clearly the bulk of Honey Dew's problem has to do with higher than anticipated expenses.

To pinpoint the problem more precisely, next examine Columns C and D. Look for income categories with high negative amounts or percentages and for expense categories with high positive amounts or percentages. In the Honey Dew case the most serious problem is with *Food* expenses which were running 11% over the budget for a total of $600 by June 30. Spending under the *Curriculum Supplies* and *Substitutes* categories will also have to be radically altered as these categories are running 75% and 36% over the budget. The amount of deficit incurred in the *Salaries* category is also high

($400), although the changes needed to bring salaries back into line are less serious since salaries are only running 2% over the budget.

Even when a center has more money left over than it anticipated, it is still instructive to look for the cause of the surplus. If the surplus is the result of the fact that a large piece of equipment has not yet been purchased, this is only a temporary surplus. This money needs to be set aside for when the equipment is actually purchased. If, on the other hand, the surplus is the result of higher than expected income from parent fees or fundraising, or of lower than projected expenses for substitutes or supplies, this surplus is real. It is money in the bank. It is available for buying new supplies, giving

raises, or setting aside in an emergency fund.

Tailoring the Report

This chart should be modified to meet the specific needs of each center. A center with a small budget could probably do without Column D, for instance. A center with a large budget may want to break down the categories, especially the *Salaries* category, into more specific line items, in order to pinpoint variations more narrowly. Centers can also consider adding two more columns to record the actual and projected amounts for the most recent month. If there is a problem category, a review of this category on a month-by-month basis can indicate whether the situation is getting better or worse.

How to Perform Cash Flow Analysis

by Roger Neugebauer

Did you ever have trouble meeting your payroll even though your center was operating in the black on paper? Chances are you have a cash flow problem. In child care centers, where income is seldom far in excess of expenses, irregularities in the flow of cash in and out of the center can easily result in a temporary financial pinch. To avoid such crises, a center needs to monitor the flow of money closely. Cash flow analysis is a tool for doing this.

The cash flow analysis method described below can be used by for profit as well as non profit centers. The charts used as examples apply to non profit centers but can be modified for for profit centers by substituting appropriate budget line items.

Why Analyze Cash Flow?

Cash flow analysis enables you to predict when your center won't have enough cash in the bank to pay its bills — and helps you decide what to do about it.

Cash flow analysis also enables you to realize short term investment opportunities by pinpointing periods when excess resources will be available. Cash does not always flow into a center at the same rate it flows out. Many factors may cause a center to be unable to meet its payroll even though its budget for the year is in the black — equipment and insurance may have to be paid in large one-shot payments, enrollment may dip for certain months, the welfare department may be late with its payments. By carefully analyzing the expected flow of cash in and out of the center in future months, a director will be better able to manage expenditures and income so as to insure that the center can always pay its bills. In addition, when a center is just opening or adding a new component, a cash flow analysis will tell the director how many months the program will operate in the red before it reaches the breakeven point, as well as how much start-up money will be needed to cover debts in this period.

How to Do It

A cash flow analysis is commonly, but not necessarily, performed on a month by month basis for the upcoming 12 months. The idea is to start with the annual budget for your center and to project when the income in this budget will be received and when the expenses will occur. In the analysis, the center's predicted receipts and disbursements in each month are listed on a flow chart such as the example illustrated in part on page 24 for the Hippy Dippy Child Care Center (HDCC). On this chart those receipt and disbursement items which are not obvious or routine should be clearly identified, as in the example.

List expected receipts. All of the center's potential sources of income should be listed. Then, for each month, the expected receipts from each source should be recorded. Receipts for each month should then be totaled. It is critical here to list as receipts for a month only cash which you expect actually to receive in that month — not income which has been earned or even income which is due. For example, if welfare pays its bill for July in August, it should be recorded as a receipt in August.

List expected disbursements. All expense categories should be listed, and for each month the expected outlays in each category should be recorded and totaled. Once again, disbursements should be recorded when the case is *disbursed*, not when the expense is incurred. For example, if equipment purchased on credit in April is paid for in May, it should be recorded as a disbursement in May.

Compute cash balance. For each month, subtract total disbursements from total receipts. This will tell you if you will have enough

cash on hand to cover cash disbursements in each month. In the example on page 24, HDCC had a cash surplus of $345 in July and a cash deficit of $856 in August.

Next, the cash balance in the month should be added to the amount of cash the center had available at the beginning of the month. When HDCC entered July, it had $200 in the checkbook. When this $200 is added to the $345 July cash surplus, it shows that the center will have a cumulative cash balance of $545, i.e., it will have $545 in the checkbook at the end of July. When this $545 is added to August's deficit of $856, it reveals that the center will be $311 in the red at the end of August.

Analyze cash flow. In analyzing the cash flow chart, the key item to focus on is the cumulative cash balance at the end of each month. Months where this is a negative amount, or an extremely low positive amount (such as August, below), will be your crisis months.

Next, you need to analyze the chart to find a solution for each crisis. One solution this analysis commonly reveals is to defer major purchases in the crisis month or in

the preceding months. HDCC could eliminate its cash deficit in August by deferring a $350 purchase of outdoor equipment. Other potential solutions include: (1) trimming ongoing disbursements through the crisis month; (2) scheduling staff vacations during months when enrollment is expected to dip so as to lessen the need for substitutes; (3) speeding up the flow-in of income (for example, offering parents a 5% discount for paying fees two months in advance, negotiating with United Way to make an advance on some of its regular monthly funding, or rescheduling fundraising projects to an earlier date); (4) seeking to extend credit terms on purchases; (5) applying for short term loans; or, if all else fails, (6) scheduling a new fundraising project prior to the crisis month.

Cash Flow Analysis Tips

Fee income computation. For centers with sliding fee scales or multiple sources of funds, computing expected fee income can be a complex process. To simplify this process, a center could use a projection format such as the example illustrated below. The center first lists all sources of funds which are based upon rate per child. The var-

Projected Fees Earned

Source	Fee/Child	July Units/Month	July Receipts	August Units/Month	August Receipts
Parent Fees	$150/month	10 children	$1,500	7 children	$1,050
Parent Fees	120/month	5 children	600	3 children	360
Parent Fees	80/month	5 children	400	5 children	400
Title XX	7.80/day	270 child-days	2,106	297 child-days	2,317
School Lunch	1.40/day	630 child-days	882	594 child-days	832

ious rates for these sources should be listed. In the example, parents pay different fees per month based on the center's sliding fee scale. The income expected to be *earned* under each rate for each month should then be computed.

Note: These computations tell you when fees are earned, not necessarily when they are paid. The $882 earned under *Child Care Food Program* funds in July is listed on the Cash Flow chart under August because the reimbursement for this item is generally received three weeks after it is earned.

Degree of accuracy. It is neither possible nor necessary to project all disbursements to the penny for months far in the future. For items which cannot be calculated exactly, estimates need only be made to the nearest $50 or $100. Also, to allow for unpredictable changes and unexpected slippages, a center might increase the monthly disbursements total by 5% and decrease the monthly receipts total by 5%.

Refined analyses. For months when cumulative cash balances are projected to be very low or in the red, a center may find it beneficial to perform a cash flow analysis on a weekly basis. This may pinpoint the week or weeks when the center will have no cash to pay its bills, so there will be a clearer idea of how long purchases will need to be deferred or when and for how long a loan should be taken.

Ongoing and historical uses. Instead of redoing an analysis whenever a crisis approaches, centers should perform an analysis prior to entering a new year and regularly update this chart throughout the year. When changes occur in any

---

Hippy Dippy Child Care Cash Flow

Expected Receipts	July	August
Parent Fees	$2,500	$1,810
Title XX	2,211	2,106
Child Care Food Program	926	882
United Way	875	875
Fundraising	300 *	0
Total Receipts	$6,812	$5,673

Expected Disbursements		
Staff Salaries	$3,468	$3,468
Substitutes	280	350
Fringe	544	556
Legal and Audit Fees	100	100
Program Development/Training	50	0
Rent/Mortgage	425	425
Utilities	50	40
Food	950	890
Equipment, Supplies, Services	200	550 **
Insurance	250	0
Loan Repayment	150	150
Total Disbursements	$6,467	$6,529
Monthly Cash Balance	$345	$(856)
Opening Cash Balance	200	545
Cumulative Cash Balance	545	(311)

 * 4th of July fundraising profits
 ** Includes $350 purchase of outdoor equipment

---

receipts or disbursements items, they should be entered for all future months, and new balance totals should be computed. Not only does this make forecasts more accurate, but it also helps you monitor the effects of any corrective actions you have taken.

Once a month has passed, you should correct the entries for the month to reflect what actually hap-

pened. This will provide an exact historical record of your center's cash flow pattern which will be extremely helpful in developing cash flow analyses for future years.

Marlene Scavo, director of Child Support Services at Ft. Lewis, Washington, and David Delman, director of Fiscal Services in Greensboro, North Carolina, provided editorial assistance in preparing this article.

Step-by-Step Guide to Break Even Analysis

by Keith Stephens

- *How many children must I serve each day to break even?*

- *How many children can I afford to lose if I raise my rates by 10%?*

- *How many more children will I have to serve to break even if I reduce my rates by 10%?*

- *How much discount can I offer?*

- *What is my maximum profitability?*

Break even analysis can provide answers to these critical questions. This analysis identifies for you the point at which you will generate enough revenues to cover your expenses.

Break even analysis is a managerial tool that can help you answer these questions and manage your organization more effectively. It is based on the characteristics of your organization. Whenever the basic characteristics change, your break even must also change. Therefore,

break even analysis is not static but is dynamic in nature. You must continually review your expense mix and the other assumptions about your operations.

In this article, I will walk you through the steps of performing a break even analysis. All the examples are drawn from the results of our cost study of over 2,000 for profit centers.

The numbers used in Tables 1, 2, and 3 for "ABC Child Care"

represent the actual 1990 average figures for all of these centers. Break even analysis is a valid tool for non profit and for profit centers alike — all the steps are exactly the same. The only difference is that when I refer to *profit*, a non profit performing this analysis would be measuring *surplus* or *fund balance*.

Step 1:
Understand Fixed Versus Variable Costs

Break even analysis requires an understanding of the relationships between revenues, fixed cost, and variable cost.

Fixed costs are those that tend to stay constant at least in the short term. Fixed costs are incurred without consideration for the number of children you serve — rent, property taxes, a vehicle lease, your director's salary are likely examples of fixed costs. These costs are the same in a given facility whether you are serving one, ten, or 100 children.

Variable costs are those that increase as the number of children you serve increases. Teachers' salaries are by far the largest variable cost in a child care center. The more children you serve, the more teachers you hire. Other variable expenses include teaching supplies, maintenance, and food. These expenses all increase and decrease as the number of children in your center changes.

Mixed. Some costs have both fixed and variable components. Telephone service and liability insurance are examples. Sometimes your lease may have a fixed base with additional rental due as a percentage of sales.

Step 2:
Analyze Your Costs

Now you must divide all your operating costs into fixed and variable categories. In Table 2, you can see the break down of costs for ABC Child Care. You need to prepare a breakdown such as this for your center.

Start by identifying all your fixed costs. In Table 2, you can see which

---

Table 1
ABC Child Care Profile

Licensed Capacity	107
Weekly Fee	$70
Revenue Capacity	$389,480
Actual Revenue	$262,563
Operating Expenses	$246,382
Operating Income	$16,182

---

costs were identified as fixed. Some expense line items are mixed, including both fixed and variable costs. In ABC Child Care, for example, portions of the insurance and utilities costs were fixed, and portions of these costs varied depending upon the number of children enrolled.

Now calculate your variable costs. To do this, simply subtract the fixed costs in each expense item from the total costs.

Step 3:
Calculate Your Variable Cost Percentage

Next you want to determine your variable cost percentage. You do this by dividing your variable costs by your sales revenues.

For the ABC Child Care Center, this means dividing $175,514 in variable costs by $262,563 in total revenues. The result is .668 or 66.8%. For every dollar of revenue this center earns, 67¢ is spent for the variable costs of providing child care services.

Step 4:
Compute Your Break Even Point

To compute the break even point, divide your fixed cost by 1 minus the variable cost percentage. In our example, $70,868 in fixed costs is divided by 1 minus .668, resulting in a break even point of $213,458. This means that the ABC Child Care Center will need to generate $213,458 in revenues in order to break even.

Since ABC's tuition rate is $70 per week, or $3,640 per year, dividing

---

the break even point by the annual fee per child of $3,640 tells us that the ABC Center needs 59 children per day to break even.

If you want to have a visual display of your break even analysis, you can set it up in graph form as in Table 3.

Putting Break Even to Work

Having completed your break even analysis, you can put this analysis to work to evaluate the impact of various changes to your operations.

Raising tuition. Say we are considering raising our tuition rate from $70 to $80 per week. We want to know how many children we could lose and be in the same financial position as before the rate increase.

First we must recalculate our revenues — as to what they would have been at our existing level of operation. This is done as follows:

$80 / 70 \times \$262,563 = \$300,072$ —

This is the revenue we would earn at the higher tuition rate serving the same children currently in our center.

Next we recalculate our variable cost percentage:

$\$175,514 / \$300,072 = 58.5\%$

Now calculate the new break even point:

$\$70,868 / 1 - 58.5 = \$170,284$

Because we are earning more profit on each child served, the number of children needed to break even is reduced. At our new revenue rate, this equals 41 children instead of 59. By increasing our rate $10 a week, we have reduced our break even point by 18, from 59 to 41 children.

Since our center was earning an operating profit of $16,182, let's calculate the number of children needed to earn the same amount of profit at our new rate. To do this, simply add profit in as a fixed cost.

Fixed cost	$70,868
Profit	$16,182
	$87,050

Then divide, as before, by 1 — variable cost rate.

$$\frac{\$87,050}{1 - .585} = \$209,759$$

By raising our rate $10 a week, we will make the same amount of profit at $209,759 in revenues as we earned with $262,563 in revenues at $70 a week. Again, converting this to children, $209,759 / $4,160 = 50 children. We were serving 72 children. Consequently, by raising our rate $10 a week, we can afford to lose 22 children and be in the same profit position as before the price increase. Of course, management must make the changes in variable cost come about before this profit will be realized.

Determining the feasibility of discounts. Understanding your variable cost and knowing your variable cost percentage helps determine the maximum discount you can offer and still be better off than if a space were left unfilled. For ABC Child Care Center, we know the variable cost rate is .668. For every dollar of child care revenue, ABC spends 67¢ to provide

Table 2
ABC Child Care Cost Analysis

	Total Cost	Fixed Costs	Variable Costs
Staffing			
Salaries:			
Owners/Officers/Managers	$16,363	$16,363	0
Salaries: Staff	119,005	10,000	$109,005
Payroll Taxes and Insurance	14,049	2,736	11,313
Special Instruction, Training, and Education	1,799	0	1,799
Program			
Activities Expense	2,197	0	2,197
Teacher Supplies and Materials	8,363	0	8,363
Food and Kitchen	11,085	0	11,085
Facility			
Building Rent	25,335	25,335	0
Utilities	4,900	2,400	2,500
Janitor Maintenance and Repair	8,376	1,200	7,176
Property Taxes and Insurance	1,610	1,610	0
Depreciation	5,821	5,821	0
Vehicle			
Lease/Rental or Mileage	483	483	0
Gas, Oil, and Repair	2,368	0	2,368
Insurance — Vehicle	420	420	0
Administration			
Accounting and Legal Fees	4,119	500	3,619
Office and Computer Supplies	2,417	0	2,417
Telephone	2,056	1,000	1,056
Equipment Rental or Lease	201	0	201
Contributions	347	0	347
Insurance — General and Liability	6,800	1,000	5,800
Dues/Subscriptions	391	0	391
Taxes/Licenses	810	0	810
Travel/Entertainment	840	0	840
Bad Debt Expense	403	0	403
Miscellaneous	2,775	0	2,775
Advertising and Public Relations	3,048	2,000	1,048
TOTAL OPERATING EXPENSES	**$246,382**	**$ 70,868**	**$175,514**

services. Consequently, ABC could discount their tuition rate up to 33% (1 – .67) and still be better off than if the space were empty.

Of course, a center cannot discount all of its space or it will never show a profit. However, as a special inducement, introductory offer, or multiple child discount, if there are spaces available, it is wise for ABC Child Care Center to accept as little as two-thirds their regular fee for those spaces.

Computing maximum profitability. To find out the maximum profitability for your center at a given tuition rate, make these calculations:

First, determine your maximum potential revenue by multiplying your licensed capacity times the weekly fee times 52 weeks. (For ABC Child Care Center, these calculations would be: 107 x $70 x 52 = $389,480.)

Second, determine your maximum annual variable costs by multiplying your variable cost percentage times the maximum annual revenues (.668 x $389,480 = $260,173).

Third, calculate your maximum annual costs by adding your maximum annual variable costs to your annual fixed costs ($260,173 + $70,868 = $331,041).

Finally, determine your maximum annual profit by subtracting your maximum annual costs from your maximum potential revenues ($389,480 – $331,041 = $58,439).

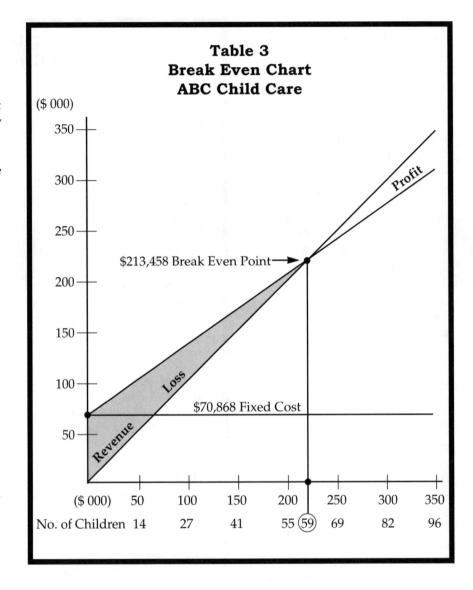

**Table 3
Break Even Chart
ABC Child Care**

These are three examples of the power of break even analysis. Once you have developed an understanding of your fixed and variable cost relationships, you can use break even analysis to evaluate many business alternatives.

Keith Stephens, a CPA, is the former president of Palo Alto Preschools, once the country's largest privately owned child care chain, and past president of the National Association for Child Care Management.

Child Care Center Management Software Buying Guide:

Eight Key Questions

by Roger Neugebauer

Every year more child care centers take the plunge and buy computers to assist with administrative tasks. If you are on the verge of committing to computers, this can be a point of high anxiety. This guide is designed to ease your anxiety. It suggests eight important questions you need to answer in selecting software that will meet your needs and your budget. These questions were developed based on the insights offered by Exchange Panel of 200 members currently using center management software.

1. Does it meet MY needs?

Your needs come first! Take time to establish your priorities. Review all the management tasks involved in keeping your organization afloat longer. Identify those that can no longer be performed effectively manually — monthly billings? payroll? classroom schedules? USDA reports? Your completed list of borderline unmanageable tasks should become the heart of your software shopping list. Don't be distracted by all the peripheral bells and whistles a program offers — if a program doesn't address your prime needs, pass it by.

An important consideration here is whether a program allows you to maintain records and print reports in keeping with your information needs. Does it allow you to store all the information you now record? Can it record and bill families at the unit you deliver services — hourly, daily, weekly? Does it organize files by children's names or family names? Can it handle parents with different last names? If your center receives grants, can the software maintain fund accounting? Can it account for third party payments?

If you provide services in more than one location, you will want to be sure that the program handles multi-site operations in a way that works for you. Many Panel of 200 members expressed frustrations with finding software that was truly an effective tool for manag-ing multi-site operations. Even software packages advertised as having multi-site capabilities sometimes fell short of delivery on this promise.

You will want to find out if reports can be generated that break out income and expenses and other data on a center-by-center basis. Can data be entered on a computer at each location and transferred by disk or modem to the central office? Can individual centers print out form letters and reports to meet their needs?

2. Is the software easy to use?

Most likely, you are not a computer hacker — you do not go to sleep at night pondering bits and bytes and baud rates. You need software designed for computer novices. You want it to be easy to use. Of course every software vendor will tell you that his or her product is easy to use. So how do you evaluate ease of use?

First, you should find out about installation. Take a careful look at what is provided to help you install the software. This may be in the form of written instructions, a program that comes on disk with your new software that walks you through the installation process, or an audio or video tape with installation instructions. If these instructions are not clear to you now, chances are they won't make any more sense when you are sitting in front of your new computer.

Second, you should find out how difficult it is to learn how to use the software. Find out if training is included in the purchase price, if training is available at an extra charge, if the software includes a tutorial program on disk, or if training materials are provided on video tape or in manuals. Does this training appear appropriate for your needs and the needs of any staff members who will use the software?

Third, the software should be easy to use on a daily basis. If the recording of basic information requires going through many steps, swapping disks in and out of your computer, or constantly looking up codes and commands, whoever has

the job of maintaining the software will soon revolt. As one vendor pointed out, "Ease of use directly translates into a positive attitude by the operator. A person's attitude towards a program is essential in deriving maximum productivity from the software."

The flip side of ease of use is speed. Sometimes a program is "easy to use" because at every step of the way the program asks questions and gives choices. This is great at first; but after you are familiar with the program, you may have the choices memorized and want to enter the information more quickly. If the program requires you to go through all these extra steps for-ever, its ease of use may become a handicap.

3. Is it flexible?

When you first use your center management software, you will be thrilled to print out billings for all parents without hitches. But as you acclimate to what your program can do, you will begin to expect more and more of it. You may want to add new information to reports, you may want to redesign how the bills are printed. In short, you want your program to be flexible.

The most common shortcoming identified with center manage-ment software by Panel of 200 members was lack of flexibility. They expressed frustration with not being able to add or expand fields on data screens and with reports that couldn't be adjusted to provide information in the form it was needed.

To find out if a program offers flexibility, ask the vendor to show

you how you can modify a report, how you can create a new report, or how you can modify or add information fields. Find out if you can do this easily yourself or if it must be done by the vendor for an extra charge.

You also want a program to be flexible in the way it interfaces with other software products. For example, if you plan to send out form letters to your parents, you may want to create the letter on your word processing program and then pull in the names and addresses from the center manage-ment software.

4. What if I need help?

As one panel member reported, "Most child care people are not comfortable with computers. We need to know that if we have a problem we can get on the phone and someone will save us."

When you buy a software program, you buy a company. Before making your final decision, check out the seller as much as the software. You want a reliable vendor who will be there to serve you for the long haul. It may be as important for you to run a credibility check on your vendor as it is for the vendor to check your credit.

In this market, checking on vendor stability is especially important. In the nine years we have been publishing these buying guides, we have listed over 50 companies offering center management soft-ware. The average life span for these companies has been just over two years — several companies have served this market for many years and some have come and gone in a matter of months.

Longevity is certainly one measure of vendor stability. Vendors who have had a product on the market for a long time have a track record that is open to examination. In addition, the longer a product is on the market, the more improvements a vendor may have made. However, longevity alone is not an absolute guarantee of quality. New companies may not have much of a track record, but they have had the opportunity to incorporate the latest technological advances into their programs. And every old company with a solid reputation started out as a new untested venture.

Nevertheless, if you are thinking about purchasing a new product where you will be one of the first customers, you should make sure the product is 100% complete before paying any money and insist on a high level of support.

Whether a vendor is an old standby or a new kid on the block, carefully evaluate the support they will provide to you after the sale.

• Does the software come complete with a manual that will answer most of your questions — in plain English, not computerese?

• Does the software include on-line help which you can turn to if you have a question or a problem?

• Does the vendor offer a toll free hotline? What hours is it staffed?

• Does the hotline have adequate staffing so you can quickly be connected with someone who can help you?

• If you encounter a problem, can they provide remote help whereby they connect via modem and work

on your software as if they were sitting in your office?

• Do they offer regular upgrades at low or no cost?

• Also find out what happens if you upgrade your computer. Can you transfer the program and all your data to your new computer on your own or will you need their help in making the transfer?

5. Is it guaranteed?

Find out if the vendor stands behind his product. Don't accept verbal statements that satisfaction is guaranteed. Insist on seeing a written warranty that spells out under what conditions a full refund will be given.

But don't allow a solid warranty, or no risk trial period, to lull you into making a hasty decision. Once you purchase a program, it is a major undertaking to enter in all your center's information. This effort will be wasted if you later decide the program doesn't meet your needs. Insist on a warranty, but don't rely on it as an excuse for not doing careful research before you make a purchase.

6. Who can I call?

One of the best means of checking out a software product is to talk to other center directors already using the product. Ask each vendor whose software you are considering for the names of users of their product in your area. The perfect reference, of course, would be another director you know personally and whose opinions you trust. At a minimum, it would be helpful to have the names of directors who

operate centers similar to yours. Call these directors and ask them about ease of start-up, ease of use, flexibility, and — most importantly — support. Has the product delivered on all the promises made by the vendor and does the vendor provide support on a timely basis?

Talking to other directors is a much more reliable means of checking out software than having vendors evaluate each other's products. Even a well-intentioned vendor will have a difficult time being totally objective about the merits of a competitor's product. In fact, beware of vendors who spend more time criticizing their competitors' products than talking about their own.

7. Can I try it out first?

Before signing on the dotted line, try to test the program in real life. Nearly all the vendors offer a demonstration disk you can use to try the program out on your own computer. It is best if this demonstration disk gives you the opportunity to work with the real system you will be buying — not just a self-running demo that simply highlights the features of a program.

8. Can I afford it?

Price should be one of the last factors you consider. Once you understand all the benefits a program offers, or fails to offer, you are in the position to assess whether the price is fair. Certainly a high price does not guarantee a quality product. On the other hand, you would be better off not computerizing at all than buying a low cost program that doesn't do the job.

Financial Evaluation Tools

*"An effective director is a cynic,
always asking questions,
never relaxing
when things
seem to be going well,
ever alert to signs of trouble."*

Financial Management Assessment Guide

by Roger Neugebauer

The soundness of a center's financial management system is determined by the extent to which it meets these criteria:

Security — The system should provide safeguards against accidental or fraudulent loss of assets as well as insure that all financial obligations are met.

Efficiency — The system should minimize time spent on paperwork and procedures.

Effectiveness — The system should provide accurate information to decisionmakers on a timely basis.

The following questions are designed to be used as guides, by both non profit and for profit centers, for assessing whether the major components of a center's financial management system meet these criteria.

Establishing the Budget

____ Does your center annually develop a formal budget which balances projected income and expenditures?

____ Does your center annually establish program goals and strive to allocate sufficient funds in the budget for achieving these goals?

____ Are income projections in the budget realistic — i.e., are estimates of fundraising, grants, and in-kind income achievable; and are losses of potential income due to typical under-enrollments taken into account?

____ Have all potential sources of income been explored, such as parent fees, employer contributions, United Way, public subsidies, tax credits?

____ Are expense projections in the budget realistic — i.e., are likely price increases for supplies and services factored in, and is provision made for unexpected costs such as repairs and replacements of equipment?

____ Does the budget provide for staff development, staff benefits, payroll taxes, leave time, salary increases, evaluation, and future planning?

____ Are funds set aside each year for long-range capital improvements?

Receiving and Spending Money

____ Are all monies received documented with duplicate copies of prenumbered receipts?

35

_____ Are all monies received promptly deposited into the center's bank account?

_____ Have procedures been established for avoiding overdue payments and for collecting those that do occur?

_____ Are all disbursements made by prenumbered checks and supported by valid invoices, receipts, or other documentation?

_____ Do procedures for signing checks and withdrawing funds from savings accounts incorporate safeguards to avoid the improper expenditure of funds?

_____ Can signed checks always be obtained on time so as not to delay purchases or paydays?

_____ Is the petty cash system secure — i.e., is money kept in a safe place, is documentation maintained for all purchases, and are periodic checks made to verify the balance in the fund?

Recordkeeping and Monitoring

_____ Has your accounting system been designed to meet the specific information needs of the center — i.e., can financial data needed for decisionmaking and reporting be readily obtained?

_____ Is data on income and expenses recorded in such a form that it can be applied directly in preparing tax reports, grant claim vouchers, monitoring reports, and annual budgets?

_____ Whenever possible, is bookkeeping and checkbook reconciliation performed by someone other than the person(s) who receive money, write checks, and handle petty cash?

_____ Are records maintained of the center's assets and liabilities, such as major equipment and appliances, savings accounts, insurance policies, outstanding loans, and tax liabilities?

_____ Does the center maintain a written schedule of reports and tax payments due to public and private agencies, and is this schedule adhered to?

_____ Are checking account balances reconciled monthly?

_____ Is a trial balance prepared monthly?

_____ Is a cash flow report periodically prepared and analyzed?

_____ Is a financial status report comparing current income and expenditures against the projected budget prepared and analyzed on a monthly basis?

_____ When financial problems or opportunities are identified in cash flow and financial status reports, are these situations reacted to quickly?

Credits

Assistance in preparing this guide was provided by:

• Annice Probst from the Preschool Association of the West Side in New York City;

• Marlene Scavo, director of child support services at Fort Lewis, Washington; and

• Carl Staley and David Delman of United Day Care Services in Greensboro, North Carolina.

Number Crunching: Monitoring Your True Enrollment

by L. Steven Sternberg

Anyone who has directed an early childhood program for at least a week recognizes that strong enrollment is vital to the success of a center. A small change in a center's enrollment can make the difference between financial stability and disaster.

But keeping tabs on your enrollment is not always a simple procedure. If your center enrolls some children part time and some full time, a simple head count of enrolled children will not give you a meaningful enrollment number.

To monitor enrollment accurately, you need to be able to add up all the hours of service your center is providing and convert this total into units of full-time care. You need to be able to calculate your full-time equivalent (FTE) enrollment.

This article will lead you through a three step process for calculating and analyzing FTEs.

There is no commonly held definition of full-time care (it's really not just a math but also a political problem) — how much time must a child spend in a program to be called full time? Politics are far beyond the scope of this paper; I'll stick to the math.

The number you select will depend upon the nature of the program you offer as well as the needs of the population you serve. If you operate a preschool offering a four-hour morning and a four-hour afternoon session, your full time enrollment would be 8 hours a day. If you serve working parents, and your center is open from early in the morning to well into the evening, you could define full time as 9, 10, 11, or 12 hours a day.

Defining your center's total capacity is also a political statement of sorts. One definition of capacity is *licensed capacity*; you may choose to use this as your maximum potential enrollment. However, many centers are not comfortable providing care for as many children as

Step 1:
Set Basic Assumptions

Before you even start crunching numbers, you need to define what your center considers *full-time enrollment* and *total capacity*. These numbers will be used as the baseline for all the calculations that follow.

the licensed capacity allows and set a limit below this number. In any case, you need to determine a number that represents your definition of total capacity.

Step 2: Calculating FTEs

To calculate your FTE enrollment, you first need to total the number of hours of enrolled care your center is providing on a weekly basis. (Note: While I have chosen to do the calculations in this article on a weekly basis, you can, of course, calculate FTEs on a daily, monthly, or annual basis.) Let's take the examples of ABC Kids' Place and XYZ Child Care, both of which:

- define full-time care as 10 hours per day;

- define total capacity as 60 children; and

- serve 50 children.

The weekly hours of care provided by both centers are detailed in the following table.

By adding all the enrolled hours of care in these two centers, we find that ABC Kids' Place provides a total of 1,550 hours a week and XYZ Child Care provides 1,950. To determine the FTEs for these centers, we use the following formula:

Child FTE = Total Enrolled Child Hours/Definition of Full Time

Plugging in the numbers, we find that ABC has a weekly FTE enrollment of 31:

1,550 hours/50 hours per week = 31 FTE

And XYZ has a weekly FTE enrollment of 39:

1,950 hours/50 hours per week = 39 FTE

Enrollment at ABC Kids' Place

Full time, five days a week	= 20 children =	1,000 hours per week
Full time, three days a week	= 10 children =	300 hours per week
Half time, three days a week	= 10 children =	150 hours per week
Half time, two days a week	= <u>10</u> children =	<u>100</u> hours per week
	50 children	1,550 hours per week

Enrollment at XYZ Child Care

Full time, five days a week	= 30 children=	1,500 hours per week
Full time, three days a week	= 10 children=	300 hours per week
Half time, three days a week	= <u>10</u> children=	<u>150</u> hours per week
	50 children	1,950 hours per week

This means that even though ABC has enrolled 50 children, it is only delivering the equivalent of full-time care for 31 children. XYZ also has enrolled 50 children, and is delivering the equivalent of full-time care for 39 children. XYZ Child Care is providing 26% more weekly enrolled care than ABC Kids' Place.

Note on school-age care: If your program serves school-age children as well as preschool children, you should consider school-age children as part-time enrollees for purposes of calculating FTEs.

Add the total number of hours that school-age children are enrolled in your program to the total enrolled hours for all children before dividing by your definition of full-time care per week.

If your program serves *only* school-age children, you may want to define full-time care as the maximum length of time a school-age child can attend your program. Thus *full time* may mean 15 to 25 hours a week in your program.

This will give you a more meaningful number for internal monitoring. However, you must be aware that in comparing your FTEs to those of a garden variety of preschool programs you will not be comparing the same number of hours of enrolled care.

Step 3: Putting Your FTE to Work

FTE is the key that unlocks a wealth of evaluative data. It provides an accurate gauge for monitoring and analyzing the performance of your center. By calculating and recording FTEs every week, you can spot enrollment trends that may not be obvious by looking strictly at the number of enrolled children.

For example, let's assume that ABC Kids' Place adds ten children to its half-time, two days a week program and loses five full-time, five days a week children. This would mean that the number of children enrolled would increase to 55. However, when you calculate the new FTE, you would find that the center has actually lost ground in that its FTE is now 28.

Another way of analyzing enrollment trends is to track the center's occupancy rate on a weekly basis. Use the following formula to calculate your occupancy rate:

Occupancy Rate = FTE/Total Capacity

Running the original numbers for ABC Kids' Place, we find that it had a 52% occupancy rate:

31/60 = 52%

After the enrollment changes, its occupancy rate dipped to 47%:

28/60 = 47%

FTE can also provide you with a standard basis for comparing your center's enrollment with that of other centers. Commonly used points of comparison, children enrolled and licensed capacity, have little comparative value. As we have seen in the comparison between ABC and XYZ, the number of children enrolled is not an accurate indicator of hours of service provided. Likewise, licensed capacity tells you little more than

the size of the building, not how much it is being used.

By using FTEs as your yardstick, you have a reliable measure of your center's performance. Your FTE should be as familiar to you as the balance in your checkbook.

Steve Sternberg has been the director of the University of Michigan Children's Centers for 11 years. This article is a result of his work on the recently published **Child Care Decision Support System***, a software modeling program for child care professionals.*

Financial Reports Every Director Needs

by Teresa P. Gordon

To do a good job running a child care operation, you need prompt, accurate, and appropriate financial reports. It's really frustrating to find out, on November 10, that food costs were 50% higher than normal in September — too late to take corrective action to avoid an October repetition. Accuracy and promptness depend on the quality of the accounting or bookkeeping personnel you have working for you. Getting appropriate reports often depends on your knowing what to ask for. This article will discuss some major types of financial information that most directors need.

Keeping the Cash Flowing

The essential ingredient for successful financial management of a child care center is keeping the enrollment at the maximum possible level and collecting parent fees promptly. While it may not be in written form, you need to have daily information regarding enrollment, attendance, waiting list, and similar statistics. For example, many larger centers have found that they have a pattern of daily absences that allows them to enroll slightly more than licensed capacity. This, of course, requires very close attention so that a *contingency plan* can be used the day every child shows up!

• **Aging of accounts receivable.** The director of a center needs to stay on top of accounts receivable on at least a weekly basis. You need to know who isn't paying and why. There will always be a few bad debts — those people who withdraw their children without warning, owing you for several days. But prompt attention to the slow payers can hold down bad debt expense. If you are the director of a multi-center operation, your center directors would probably be responsible for the daily and weekly fee collections. You would want a monthly report usually referred to as an aging of accounts receivable. This report lists your clients by name and the amounts that they owe. Several columns are used to classify the *age* of the unpaid fees. This report can be prepared manually by going through the cards or ledgers for each client. It should be an automatic report from a computerized accounts receivable system.

• **Cash reports.** A director needs to be aware of the cash situation on a daily basis. A daily cash report might be as simple as a list of the bank balances for the previous day, the deposits to be made for the day, and the bills that must be paid in the near future. However, more sophisticated cash flow projections are often needed.

Child care fee collections are generally easy to predict or forecast — you can probably count on a fairly equal weekly amount. Unfortunately, the bills you have to pay tend to come in chunks. Rent is due at the first of the month. Payroll has to be met perhaps twice a month. Insurance, on the other hand, is often paid once a year.

A computerized accounts payable system usually produces a report or schedule of unpaid bills by due dates. This can be very helpful in analyzing cash needs and preparing a cash forecast.

• **Cash forecast.** A formal cash forecast might be a report prepared several times a month. This report will list the amount currently in the bank account, projected receipts for the next few days or weeks, projected expenditures, and how much will be left after the bills are paid. If the cash in the bank account is negative, you can take steps to borrow money short term or make arrangements to delay certain payments.

• **Annual budget.** One of the best ways to stay in tight control over operations is to have an accurate budget. A budget is a plan of operation stated in dollars. Generally, you prepare an annual budget at the beginning of the year. When you do a good job on the budget, it becomes an excellent basis of comparison to be sure that you are operating in accordance with the original plan.

However, no budget is ever perfect — unexpected things always happen. When major changes are needed, a budget can be revised during the course of the year. However, many managers prefer to leave the budget alone and

simply explain the large variances caused by unplanned events or situations.

• **Budget comparison report.** To get the greatest benefit from a budget, it should be incorporated into the accounting system or at least presented with actual results on a monthly basis. The exact format of a budget comparison report usually depends on your software package if your accounting system is computerized.

If your books are kept manually, you can design the report any way you like — as long as it stays fairly simple. Most budget comparison reports list actual revenues and expenses for the month and year to date. A dollar or percentage variance is also shown. Many directors find that it is also nice to have a column for the original total annual budget. Some software packages have a column that gives a percentage of sales or revenue for each item on the income statement. This is probably not very helpful for a child care center; if you have an option, it would be better to have the percentage over or under budget.

The budget comparison report should be on your desk no later than the fifteenth of the following month. (This is a realistic target — of course, the earlier the better.) The first thing you look for is the profit or loss for the month and for year to date. Next, look at the variances from budget. Pick out the major differences. You may already know why the expenses are over budget in buildings and grounds maintenance — you remember the plumbing problem you had last month. Other items may not be so easily explained. Never hesitate to

ask your bookkeeping or accounting staff for help — there could be a bookkeeping error rather than a real problem.

Based on your analysis of any problem areas highlighted by the budget variances, you may decide to take corrective action by changing policies, procedures, etc. Sometimes nothing can be done other than trying to hold down other expenses or increase revenues. Of course, you could also decide that the budget is wrong and needs to be revised.

An alternative to budget comparisons might be a report showing this month's actuals as compared to actuals from the same month one year ago. If you have no budget, this might be another way of getting a handle on *out-of-control* situations.

These comparison reports can be as summarized or as detailed as you desire. A multi-center operation, for example, might have a budget comparison report for each separate center. A non profit might want separate reports for separate funding sources. In any case, the executive director should have a combined report for the total organization that would include child care, management, general, and all other program activities.

Regular Financial Statements

Almost any bookkeeper or computer package will present you with regular monthly balance sheets and income statements. The income statement is usually part of the budget comparison report discussed above. While you've been anxiously awaiting the income statement, you may not be quite sure what to do with the balance sheet when it appears on your desk.

• **The balance sheet** is a listing of the assets (what you own), the liabilities (what you owe), and the difference (owner's equity, or fund balance for non profits). Assets and liabilities are often segregated between *current* and *non-current*. Current assets, such as short-term investments, accounts receivable, and inventory, will generate or become cash within one year or less. Current liabilities, including most of your accounts payable and accrued expenses (like payroll taxes) and any short-term borrowings, will use up cash within the coming year.

Current assets less current liabilities is called *working capital*. Obviously, current assets need to be greater than current liabilities. Bankers like to analyze financial well-being by computing liquidity ratios. The *current ratio* is current assets divided by current liabilities and the *acid test ratio* is current assets without inventory divided by current liabilities.

Accrual Accounting

For meaningful income statements and balance sheets, be sure that you are getting reports prepared on the *accrual basis* rather than the *cash basis*. This means that revenues are recorded when earned (whether or not you've been paid) and expenses are recorded when incurred (whether or not you've paid the bills).

It is often convenient to keep the books on a cash basis — recording revenue when you make deposits and expenses when you write the checks. However, this cash basis bookkeeping can be easily adjusted to accrual accounting at the end of the month. The bookkeeper prepares a schedule of unpaid bills and outstanding receivables and makes a journal entry to accrue the additional expense and revenue. This journal entry is reversed or backed out at the first of the following month.

With accrual accounting, your balance sheet is much more useful. I know of a non profit center which got into deep financial difficulty because of inadequate financial statements. The board of directors was unaware that there was a large pile of unpaid bills stashed away in the bookkeeper's desk drawer that didn't show up anywhere in the regular monthly reports.

• **Statement of changes in financial position**. If you operate a for profit center, your annual report probably includes something called a *Statement of Changes in Financial Position*. Since many bookkeepers do not know how to prepare this particular report, you might not be able to get it on a monthly basis. However, it can be a very useful report for both for profit and non profit organizations. To be useful, ask your accountant to prepare the report on a cash basis (rather than the typical working capital basis).

This report will tell you where all the money went. Certain types of expenditures do not show up on an income statement — purchases of major equipment items with a useful life longer than one year, note or mortgage payments, etc.

Some types of cash receipts are not revenue and therefore do not appear on the income statement — loans from the bank, sales of capital stock, etc. The statement of changes in financial position will explain the major sources and uses of cash and tell you how you got from the beginning cash balance to the ending cash balance. This could be very helpful if you ever get into the unfortunate situation of wondering why you have to borrow more money from the bank when the reports show a large profit.

Special Purpose Reports

• **Unit cost analysis**. If you are operating under special contract provisions, you may need to keep track of additional special information. In Texas, for example, many non profit centers have contracts with the state to provide child care at a flat unit rate. These centers need to keep a close eye on their unit costs. In addition to the budget comparison report, they generally need a monthly report showing the number of units of service provided, the average daily enrollment, and the unit cost.

Even if you don't operate under a unit rate reimbursement system, you may find it helpful to periodically evaluate your daily or weekly cost per child. This information will help you decide on the proper fees to charge (competition permitting) or may serve as a warning that operating costs are getting out of hand. To prepare such a report, your bookkeeping staff will need to keep track of enrollment or attendance days or weeks — something not normally maintained in an accounting system.

• **Special analysis.** When you get ready to prepare budgets or when you spot a major problem on the budget comparison report, you may want to know the details of specific accounts. For example, if your reports list a total for *utilities expense*, you might want a schedule prepared that separates gas, electricity, and water by month for the previous year or two. This might make it clear where the problem lies, since it should reveal the seasonal nature of this item. When the item *supplies* is too high, you may want a special report on exactly what types of things have been included.

This kind of special analysis should not be necessary every month. If you regularly need more detail, have your accountant modify your chart of accounts to fit your needs. It is a lot easier to record electricity, gas, and water in three separate accounts when the original bills are paid than it is to go back and reconstruct the information after the fact. On the other hand, if you can't foresee any need for this much detail normally — this was a once in five year problem — it is cheaper to prepare the books using fewer account titles.

Conclusion

The varieties of management reports discussed in this article can be in any style that is useful and meaningful to you. Financial reports for external users have to follow particular formats, but internal management reports do not have to conform to generally accepted accounting principles and can be designed for your particular needs. Some reports can be very informal and prepared only when requested. Other reports should be regularly prepared and presented to you in a standard format.

Getting too many reports that you don't need or use is almost (but not quite) as bad as not getting enough. Those of you with computerized systems may see more printouts than you know what to do with! If a report is appearing on your desk, be sure you know what it is supposed to mean. Ask for an explanation of why you are getting it and what you are supposed to do with it.

Bookkeepers and accountants prepare many schedules and work papers that you don't usually need or want to review. For example, depreciation schedules list build-ings and equipment and amortization schedules may indicate monthly accruals of interest or insurance expense. This information is always available to you on request but is not something you need to study every month.

What about information you are not getting? I may have mentioned some reports that you have never seen but that sound useful. Explain to your accounting staff what information you need and any ideas you have on what the report should look like. When the report is presented, be sure you understand what it says. If it is unclear, ask for a different presentation next time. After a few tries, you and your staff will find a format that meets everyone's needs, and it can become a standard or regular report.

Teresa P. Gordon, a certified public accountant, has been working with Texas child care providers since 1977. She also teaches accounting at Houston Baptist University and is a doctoral candidate at the University of Houston.

When You Think You Need an Audit — Points to Consider

by Teresa P. Gordon

• *"Mrs. Jones, the bank will not be able to process your loan application for the expansion of your child care center without audited financial statements."*

• *"All agencies receiving United Way funding will be required to have an annual audit conducted by certified public accountants based on a newly adopted policy of the Board of Trustees."*

• *"Since your center has received governmental funding from the county, you will have to present audited financial statements to the county commissioner's office by September 30."*

Confronting situations like these can produce a good bit of anxiety for any director — especially if it is going to be your first experience with an audit. You don't quite know what to expect or how to select an audit firm. You may be concerned about the expense involved. And what sorts of things will the auditors be looking for? Or maybe you've never had an audit but are thinking that maybe it would be a good idea on general principle.

When Do You Need an Audit?

An audit can be a sort of *annual physical* for your organization. It is especially beneficial to assure the board members of a non profit that charitable and public funds have been properly handled. In the for profit sector, it is also beneficial when the management and the ownership are separated, as may be the case with a corporation. On the other hand, a sole proprietor or

small partnership may be so intimately involved in day-to-day operations that they will not feel a need for an audit. The purpose of the audit is to assure *external* users that the financial statements fairly represent the activities and financial position of the organization. Having *audited financial statements* may play an important role in your dealings with funding sources, creditors, bankers, and boards of trustees.

Alternatives to an Audit

In our society, the credibility of financial reporting is increased when an independent third party is involved in the preparation of external financial reports. Certified public accounting firms are licensed in each state to provide this type of service. In years past, there was only one choice — audited financial statements. Since 1979, accountants have added two other services which provide less assurance to the users of the financial statements. *Compilations* and *reviews* are available to organizations that are *non-public* — your stock is not sold on a stock exchange. Since less work is involved, these services are less expensive than an audit.

A *compilation* provides no assurance to the user. The accountants take information you provide and present it in the appropriate format for your type of organization. This type of report would probably be satisfactory for purposes of opening an account with a vendor or sending to the credit bureau.

A *review* provides limited assurance to the external user. The accountant will obtain knowledge of your business, make inquiries about your accounting procedures and operations, and analyze the reports in various ways, such as comparing results with the previous year or budget or computing financial ratios. She will want to be sure that the financial statements conform to the requirements of generally accepted accounting principles. This intermediate level of assurance is often sufficient for a bank loan application and may also satisfy some of your donors or funding sources.

However, many times only an audit will do. The work involved is much more extensive. The accountants will study the internal controls in your organization to see how much reliance they can place on your accounting system. They will examine documents —including minutes of board meetings, leases, insurance policies, and contracts. They may send *confirmation requests* to clients, vendors, and banks. In addition to satisfying external users, a good *clean* audit will provide you peace of mind knowing that the people you've hired to handle the accounting and bookkeeping are doing a good job.

Finding an Accounting Firm

When you decide you need general purpose financial statements for outside parties, how should you go about finding an accounting firm? If your organization is a corporation (profit or non profit), selecting an accounting firm is usually a task for the board of directors. It is a good policy to have a separate audit committee which will select the firm and receive progress reports from the accountants as well as the final report. Regardless of who winds up with the responsibility, here are some points to consider:

• Shop around for an accounting firm just as you would for a major purchase of playground equipment. Get a proposal from at least three different firms. Other centers, the United Way, banking institutions, and board members are sources of referrals. The accounting firm must be independent if you want an audit or a review — a CPA on your board cannot accept the engagement.

• Expect to invest several hours with representatives from each firm. They will need to meet with you to obtain an understanding of how your center operates, what sort of records you maintain, and so forth. Based on this information, they will estimate how long it will take to perform the requested service.

• Request a *written* proposal. It should cover such points as a description of the scope and objectives of the examination or review, target days for beginning and ending, the number and experience levels of the staff that will be assigned, the reports that will be provided, and an estimate of the cost. Accountants are usually reluctant to set a single price since it is not possible to foresee all the complexities that may be encountered during the engagement. But they should be able to give you a range and perhaps a ceiling.

• Ideally, the firm selected should be familiar with the child care business. They should know about any special peculiarities such as government contracts and non profit accounting.

• You should also make inquiries about their policy of rotating staff. Nothing is more frustrating than explaining the same things over and over again each year to the new auditor that shows up! Continuity of staff will save time and aggravation.

• Some non profits have made arrangements with accounting firms for *discount rates*. Sometimes this means that you get the newest, least experienced auditors and that your work is given low priority by the firm. Be careful about such arrangements — you usually get what you pay for in accounting as in anything else!

• In selecting a firm, consider what other type of services you might be needing. Can the firm handle your tax returns and other reports to the Internal Revenue Service? Can they provide management advisory services? Some firms provide *write-up* services with their in-house computer system that would provide monthly statements as well as a year-end report.

Keeping the Cost Down

There are a number of things you can do to save money on an audit engagement. The most important prerequisite for a smooth audit is a good accounting system with proper checks and balances. The smaller your organization, the more difficult it is to have a good system of *internal controls*. But any size center should be able to provide the basics. For example, someone other than the bookkeeper should reconcile the bank statement promptly each month. In a very small center, that person could be YOU!

Since accountants' rates are based on the time it takes to perform the audit, anything you or your staff can do to help speed up the process can save you money. For example, be sure you have everything organized before the auditors arrive. The books should be closed through a trial balance. Bank statements should be reconciled. Have the records gathered together conveniently in one place. Minute books, leases, contracts, insurance policies, and letters from donors restricting the use of funds are some of the non-accounting items that will be needed.

It also helps if the bookkeeper or a clerk is available to pull the invoices and other records that the auditors ask to see. They may also be able to prepare certain schedules that the auditors will need, such as a schedule of fixed assets or an analysis of what's in the *miscellaneous* account.

What Do You Get for Your Money?

When the accountants finish the engagement, you will receive a set of financial statements with a cover letter. Many times the accountants have prepared the statements, written the notes, typed, and bound them. But technically, the financial statements are yours. The only thing you bought from the accountant was that cover letter! It may be one of the most expensive pieces of paper you've purchased so you should be sure to read it carefully.

Accountants almost always use the standard wording suggested by the American Institute of Certified Public Accountants. The terms *compilation*, *review*, and *audit* have precise technical meanings to accountants, and this can be confusing to the uninitiated. A board member seeing a compilation letter for the first time will probably feel uneasy!

The review letter generally has three paragraphs. The compilation and audit letters generally have two paragraphs. The joke among investors is to watch out for any letter with more than two paragraphs. A middle paragraph of an audit letter is sometimes added to describe a problem area or reservation. This is called a *qualified opinion*. What you want is an *unqualified opinion*. This means that your financial statements meet the minimum standards and provide the user a fair representation of the financial condition of your organization.

Other Kinds of Audits

One of the most anxiety producing events in anyone's life is a letter from the Internal Revenue Service notifying them of an audit. Even non profits are audited to be sure they still qualify as tax exempt. Auditors from a government funding source have also been some-

thing many of us have had to endure. These audits are often far more detailed than the type of audits conducted by a public accounting firm. Legislation may require very detailed examinations of surprising items. For example, some audits have involved confirmation letters to universities to be sure an employee really did get a degree they claimed on an employment application!

An IRS audit focuses on whether you are in compliance with various tax laws and regulations. The contract audit is concerned only with revenues and expenses of a particular program or activity. The independent audit is the only one which looks at overall operations.

Let's face it — no one likes to see the auditors coming. They have to be provided a place to work. Records may have to be brought out of storage. Other activities get behind as the bookkeeper spends time with the auditors. Your time is also involved in explaining the operations or answering *internal control questionnaires*. Nevertheless, you'll probably find it much easier to work with the public accountants you hire than to deal with auditors from other sources. After all, if you don't like them, you can fire them. And they know it.

Teresa P. Gordon, a certified public accountant, has been working with Texas child care providers since 1977. She has conducted several workshops for child care providers in conjunction with the Title XX Day Care Providers Association and other organizations. She also teaches accounting at Houston Baptist University and is a doctoral candidate at the University of Houston.

Financial Policies

*"A smart director acts quickly
to solve a problem,
an effective director anticipates
and avoids problems by
establishing policies and procedures
to deal with the myriad situations
that arise along the way."*

Is Your Salary Schedule Up to Speed?

by Roger Neugebauer

Low pay has been a hot topic for many years in the early childhood arena — and deservedly so. There is no question that people employed in our profession are seriously underpaid. If more resources were available for salaries, this would relieve a great deal of stress from employees and centers, and environments for children would improve.

But even within a strictly limited budget, there is much a center can do to improve center performance by the way it structures its salary schedule. In this article, I will offer some ideas on how to evaluate the impact of your salary schedule. In a second article, I will present several model salary schedules.

Both of these articles are the result of an analysis of more than 100 salary schedules submitted by Exchange Panel of 200 members. Based on this review, here are four basic questions to consider in evaluating your current salary schedule:

1.

What are we paying for?

Sometimes it's important to step back and ask some really basic questions: *Why are we paying people? What are we expecting to get in return?*

In child care centers, when you hire someone, you could be . . .
• paying for time;
• paying for skills; or
• paying for results.

You need to decide which of these factors you are paying for, because your choice dramatically impacts how you pay people.

If you are paying for time, your assumption is that you are paying for a warm body to fulfill ratio requirements over a period of time. In order to maintain adequate coverage, you would simply need to pay enough to attract and retain staff who meet minimum legal requirements.

If you are paying for skills, your assumption is that people knowledgeable and practiced in early childhood education will perform significantly better than persons without training and experience. Therefore, you would tailor your salary schedule to attract well prepared individuals and to reward their continuing acquisition of knowledge and skills.

If you are paying for results, your assumption is that all that really matters is who performs well on the job. You would design your salary schedule to reward those who are effective performers.

It is my observation that large numbers of centers behave as if they are simply paying for time. By not attaching any monetary value to skills or performance, these centers get what they pay for — mediocre to poor performance.

On the other hand, the overwhelming majority of salary schedules I reviewed for these articles reflect a strong bias toward paying for knowledge and skills. There is considerable research support for this bias. The landmark 1976 National Day

---

"Automatic increases assure staff that their value is noted and will be acknowledged in predictable increments at predictable times. In a historically underpaid field such as child care, automatic increases validate the necessity to upgrade salaries for all who work in the field."
— **Working for Quality Child Care**

Care Study concluded that "... caregivers with education/training relevant to young children deliver better care with somewhat superior developmental effects for children (Ruopp)." More current research, the 1988 National Child Care Staffing Study, found that teachers with either a bachelor's degree or specialized training in early childhood education at the college level exhibited higher quality caregiving (Whitebook).

Less than 5% of the salary schedules reviewed gave significant weight to on-the-job performance in setting salary levels. Many centers require that employees receive a satisfactory rating before receiv-

ing a step increase, but very few awarded significant upgrades for above average performance.

2.

Is our pay equitable?

The premise behind the equity issue is that people should receive equal pay for equal work. There are several ways to evaluate equality of pay — you can compare the pay of a teacher in your center with the pay of people doing comparable work in other professions, teachers in other centers, or other teachers within your own center.

Clearly the pay of child care teachers compares poorly to the pay of kindergarten teachers, for example. Many centers are struggling creatively to take small steps toward narrowing this gap. Only a concerted effort by a broad spectrum of players in the child care arena will make a serious impact.

Equity from center to center is another matter altogether. A center committed to providing quality services certainly wants to attract and retain the best teachers available. One way to do this is to offer

salaries above the community average. At least once every two years, you should do a market survey on teacher salaries in your community to make sure you are not falling behind. In addition, you should keep an eye on salaries offered by new centers when they open.

It is also important to be alert to equity issues within your own center. Sometimes when you have a mix of new and long-term teachers, inequities will develop. You may pay two teachers performing the same job with the same level of performance at significantly different levels. This can potentially be discouraging to the lower paid teacher.

3.

Should we offer annual increases?

Centers grant salary increases based on the following factors:
• responsibility;
• longevity;
• cost of living; and
• performance.

It is possible that there still exist a few staff cooperatives where all staff members are paid the same regardless of the job they perform. With these possible exceptions, all centers today offer increased salaries as staff assume new jobs with increasing responsibility within the center. In the next article, we will examine some of the issues involved in granting promotions.

Most centers also make some provision for granting annual increases based on longevity and/or cost of living. While such increases are viewed as important and expected, the way in which they are administered does raise some interesting questions and consequences.

Longevity salary increases are based on the assumption that the longer persons work in a job, the better they will perform. While this may be true in some professions, there is little evidence to support it in child care. The National Day Care Study found little relationship between years of child care experience and caregiver or child behaviors (Ruopp). The National Child Care Staffing Study found "child care experience is a poor predictor of teacher behavior toward children" (Whitebook).

From these findings we draw several conclusions. If we want teachers' performance to improve, we can't abandon them in their classrooms. We need to provide continuous feedback, regular training, and ready support to help them improve. Using longevity as a reason for raising salaries without any reference to improved performance does not appear to be justified.

Cost of living adjustments are made to compensate for the impact of inflation. If an employee's salary stays the same but the cost of living increases, her salary has in effect decreased.

Not all employees are equally impacted by inflation. Someone earning $30,000 per year is not nearly as impacted by a 5% increase in the cost of bread as someone earning $10,000. However, since the average child care teacher earns just below the poverty level (Whitebook), there is

little question that annual adjustments are of vital importance for most employees in this profession. For a center to guarantee annual cost of living adjustments could be a hollow promise. Every salary increase must be paid for with a commensurate rise in income. If your center gives an across the board cost of living increase of 5% and your income declines 5%, you could be courting disaster. Many centers inject this reality into their personnel policies with statements such as "Every effort will be made to provide annual cost of living raises subject to the availability of funds."

Such cautious promises offer scant assurance to staff members living on the edge of poverty. If the center can't give an annual increase, they will have to wait 12 months for a much needed raise. Certainly being sincere about exploring every avenue to increase salaries is

essential. Another small way to ease anxiety is to review financial projections quarterly or semi-annually with the idea of offering smaller, more frequent adjustments. (Of course, then you will have to figure out a way to alleviate the stress on your bookkeeper.)

Determining the amount of an annual cost of living adjustment is not an exact science. Many companies peg their increases to the Consumer Price Index (CPI). The CPI is calculated by the price of goods and services purchased by a family of four with an annual income of $12,000. This index, therefore, has little relevance for families of different sizes or in higher income brackets. But because the majority of child care teachers do earn under $12,000, the CPI is a fairly reliable measure for centers to use as a benchmark.

4.

Should we offer merit raises?

There is much to be said for paying for performance instead of longevity. You want staff who

---

"Few companies can afford the kind of financial incentive that makes any real difference in the lives of their employees. Most financial rewards are quickly adjusted to. Although management seldom hears, workers make fun of minor increases, cynically tallying the depreciating effect of inflation and taxes."
— David Viscott, MD

---

work hard and continue to improve to believe that their contributions are valued. You can show appreciation by frequently observing and acknowledging their good deeds, by providing all the materials and moral support they need, and by publicly praising their performance. However, it is hard to give a clearer, more welcome signal than cash.

Clearly people don't gravitate to child care for its financial benefits. Over and over again, teacher surveys have shown that the true rewards of teaching relate to making a difference in the lives of children. However, at some point, even the most committed teacher will become discouraged if year after year they do a great job for the center but are paid no more than anyone else, or less than teachers in other centers.

If your center is considering granting merit raises, here are some points to consider:

• Merit raises should not be given in place of cost of living increases, but in addition to them. If raises are only given to exceptional performers, you run the risk of alienating the majority of your teachers who may be performing adequately but not spectacularly. Some centers employ systems whereby teachers with unsatisfactory performance are not given raises, those with satisfactory performance are given small raises, and those with superior performance are given larger raises.

• Small merit raises may be more harmful than no raises at all. Giving an employee a token raise for meritorious performance is more likely to induce cynicism than pride. If you are going to award merit raises, they must be perceived as worthy of the effort.

• A merit raise system is only as effective as the evaluation system upon which it is based. If you are going to base pay on performance, you need to be sure you are measuring performance objectively and fairly. You need to have in place an evaluation instrument that all staff view as valid. (Having their input in its development will go a long way toward establishing its validity.) Those performing the evaluations must be skilled at observing and giving feedback.

• Annual evaluations for salary determination should not be viewed as a substitute for ongoing employee appraisals. If an employee is to use supervisory feedback to improve her performance, this feedback needs to be frequent, nonjudgmental, and non-threatening. An annual salary evaluation goes against all of these guidelines. Even with a merit raise evaluation system in place, you need to regularly engage in giving specific, objective feedback to employees to give them the information they need to improve their own performance.

As a center director, you need to invest your limited resources wisely in order to maintain a stable, high quality organization.

We recommend, wherever possible, giving a combination of cost of living and merit raises. You need to bring out the best in your staff by rewarding their great efforts as individuals as well as by doing everything in your power to raise the salaries of all teachers. In the next article, we will present specific examples of systems to use to accomplish both goals.

References and Resources

Ruopp, Richard et al. *Children at the Center*. Cambridge, MA: Abt Associates, 1979.

Sibson, Robert E. Compensation (*Fifth Edition*). New York: AMACOM, 1990.

Townsend, Robert. *Further Up the Organization*. New York: Alfred A. Knopf, 1984.

Viscott, David, MD. *Taking Care of Business*. New York: William Morrow and Company, Inc., 1985.

Whitebook, Marcy. *Who Cares? Child Care Teachers and the Quality of Care in America*. Oakland, CA: Child Care Employee Project, 1989.

Working for Quality Child Care. National Center for the Early Childhood Work Force, 6536 Telegraph Avenue, Suite A-201, Oakland, CA 94609.

Guidelines for Fine Tuning Your Salary Schedule

by Roger Neugebauer

I n one of my first forays into the child care world, some 20 years ago, I applied, unsuccessfully, for a job at a staff cooperative. All employees at New Morning Children's Center were paid the same hourly wage and shared equally in responsibilities and decision making. The team spirit of the place is what attracted me to it.

Even in my brief encounter with the center, it was clear that this team spirit was developing a few chinks. The founders of the center shared a strong commitment to equality of pay and power. However, state licensers looked upon the staff structure with horror and were aggressively fighting it. In addition, as new staff members came on board whose ideologies and priorities did not match the founders, internal enthusiasm for equal pay declined.

Eventually, New Morning gave in to the pressures of capitalism and began paying the cook, the administrative coordinators, and the teachers differing amounts. Eventually, too, it changed its name to something like Preschool Prep Learning Center. Eventually, too, it went out of business.

The moral of this story is never turn down a future publisher who can give you bad press. It also demonstrates that the administration of salaries is not a simple mechanical procedure. Rather, it is direct expression of the values of the organization. How differences in pay are distributed, and the size of these differences, intentionally or unintentionally, communicate what the organization values.

Pay differentials are typically spelled out in a center's salary schedule. In research for this article, we analyzed over 100 salary schedules submitted by Exchange Panel of 200 members. In these schedules, four factors were used to measure the monetary value of employees: responsibility, training, experience, and performance. In this article, I will share with you how centers weigh these factors in developing their salary schedules.

Pay for Responsibility

None of the centers whose schedules were reviewed were staff cooperatives — all centers paid differing amounts for persons carrying out different responsibilities. Pay differences by position are in fact quite dramatic, as can be seen in Table A. A lead teacher typically earns 50% more than a teacher aide, and directors earn 50% more than a lead teacher.

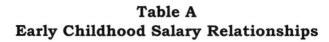
The 1988 National Child Care Staffing Study (Whitebook) also found significant differences in the average hourly wages of center employees:

Director	=	$9.85
Teacher/Director	=	6.38
Teacher	=	5.58
Assistant Teacher	=	4.86
Teacher Aide	=	4.48

In the staffing study results, the pay differentials among teachers is not as dramatic and the differential between teachers and directors is more dramatic than in the *Exchange* survey. The differences may be accounted for by the samples — the staffing study examined 227 randomly selected centers in five cities, and *Exchange* examined 100+ hand-picked centers from throughout the country. The five year time difference may also be a key factor. During these five years, the supply of qualified teachers has decreased, causing an escalation in the wages offered to attract and retain experienced teachers.

In any event, we are not recommending that your center adapt either of these pay patterns. We are simply reporting what is standard practice in the early childhood arena.

What we are strongly recommending is that you take a close look at your own pay patterns. Do the differences in your pay for different positions truly reflect the value you place on these positions? The way you invest your resources in personnel should support your understanding about what it takes to deliver quality child care.

In the salary schedules we reviewed, for example, it was clear

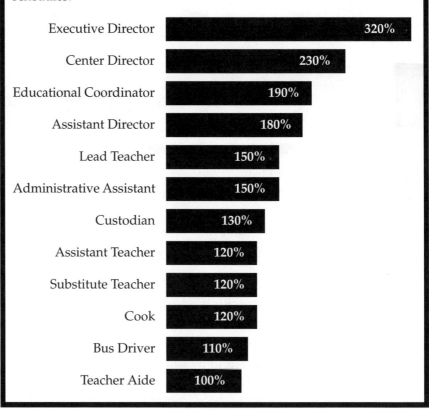

Table A
Early Childhood Salary Relationships

This chart demonstrates the relationship of average salaries for different positions in early childhood centers, using Teacher Aide salaries as the base. For example, the average Lead Teacher salary is 150% of the average Teacher Aide salary. Based on a review of over 200 salary schedules.

Position	%
Executive Director	320%
Center Director	230%
Educational Coordinator	190%
Assistant Director	180%
Lead Teacher	150%
Administrative Assistant	150%
Custodian	130%
Assistant Teacher	120%
Substitute Teacher	120%
Cook	120%
Bus Driver	110%
Teacher Aide	100%

that a growing number of centers have identified the lead teacher as a key to quality. In these centers, lead teachers are paid anywhere from 65% to 85% more than teacher aides.

Pay for Training

Centers clearly place a value on training. The more training a teacher has, the more she is likely to be paid. However, how training is factored into salary schedules varies considerably.

About one in four centers build training into job requirements, but offers no financial incentives. For example, a center might require that a teacher aide have a high school diploma, an assistant teacher have at least two years of college, and a lead teacher have a college degree. In these centers, an assistant teacher with a college degree would earn no more than one with two years of college, and a candidate with only a high school degree would not be considered for an assistant teacher position.

The majority of centers, however, recognize the value of training in establishing job requirements as well as in setting salaries within job categories. In these centers, an assistant teacher with a college degree would earn more than an assistant teacher with two years of college. As can be seen in Table B, typically a teacher with an AA degree will earn 15% more, and one with a BA degree 25% more, than a teacher with only a high school degree. A master's degree only adds another 5% to one's pay.

Some centers place additional value on education that is specifically related to early childhood education. In these centers, for example, a teacher with an AA degree in early childhood education is valued just as highly as a teacher with a bachelor's degree in an unrelated field (Table B).

While the 1976 National Day Care Study (Ruopp) found training relevant to young children was a better predictor of teacher performance than years of education overall, the 1988 National Child Care Staffing Study (Whitebook) yielded more mixed results. In the latter study, it was found that teachers with either a bachelor's degree *or* specialized training at the college level performed equally well in the classroom. In addition, it found that "specialized training at the post-secondary level is more effective in preparing good teachers than is specialized training at the high school or vocational education level."

In the days when the supply of teaching candidates seemed inexhaustible, there wasn't great pressure on centers to pay more to hire teachers with college training.

Directors would rationalize their fiscal conservatism by observing that in their experience college trained teachers often weren't well prepared for the real world of child care.

Research findings now make it clear that teachers with college degrees or college level ECE training will typically do a better job. With the returning shortage of qualified teachers, it would be a mistake for centers not to place high value on college education in establishing or refining their salary schedules.

Pay for Experience

Three out of every four center salary schedules we reviewed offered some form of annual pay increases. Increases ranged from 1.5% to 5% annually, with the average falling in the 3% range.

These increases tend to be described more as cost of living adjustments than as rewards for improved performance. As was observed in the first article in this series, experience tends to be a poor predictor of teacher performance (*Exchange*, March 1994). Teachers with more years on the job are not necessarily better performers than less experienced teachers. Therefore, centers are probably exercising good judgment in not investing heavily in longevity.

Cost of living increases, on the other hand, are very important to teachers. With salaries as low as they are, teachers have little cushion against the impact of inflation. Slightly less than half of the salary schedules we reviewed stated that there were no automatic cost of living increases.

Table B
Typical Educational Differentials

Child care centers typically pay more to employees with higher levels of educational attainment. Using the average pay for high school graduates as the base (100%), the following are the average increases provided for education:

Education	Percentage
MA degree in ECE-related field	135%
MA degree in unrelated field	130%
BA degree in ECE-related field	130%
BA degree in unrelated field	125%
AA degree in ECE-related field	125%
AA degree in unrelated field	115%
High school diploma or equivalent	100%

When funds permitted, these centers typically give across the board increases in the range of 2% to 4% to all employees.

Most of the other salary schedules we reviewed treated annual increases regressively, i.e. the higher your salary the lower your annual increase. In some cases, this is done intentionally. Recognizing how low their entry level salaries are, some centers deliberately gave employees at the bottom third of the salary schedule a higher percentage annual increase than employees at the top third.

In many centers, the regressive nature of their salary schedules appeared to be unintentional. In some, annual increases varied unpredictably from year to year and from position to position. In others, where the center elected to increase all employees' hourly wages by a flat amount every year (typically 10¢ or 15¢), the result is the higher your hourly wage, the lower the percentage your increase will be.

From reviewing salary schedules, we conclude that all centers need to take a close look at their provisions regarding annual increases. First, consider whether you want to lock your center into automatic annual increases for all employees. Especially for your low income employees, automatic increases offer some degree of security. However, if your center is struggling to achieve financial stability, annual increases may not always be affordable.

Second, in granting cost of living increases, you should deliberately decide what your priorities are.

Do you want to give an equal percentage increase to all employees, or do you want to give a higher increase to low income employees, or do you want to invest the greatest share of the increases in your top employees?

Pay for Performance

In the first article, we made a case for paying for performance rather than longevity. We suggested granting raises based on how well teachers perform, not on how long they have been at the center.

While a strong case can be made for merit raises, in fact, the concept is not a popular one in this field. Less than one in 15 of the salary schedules we reviewed offer any form of merit pay. Tying pay to performance is often viewed as running counter to the nurturing team spirit we promote in our centers. This case was strongly put by one of our Panel of 200 members (see "No to Merit Pay" box). In addition, many directors are reluctant to attach dollars to performance since measures of performance are so subjective in this field.

Those few centers that do tie pay to performance do so in a variety of ways. The most common approach is a two to four category rating system. One center rates each employee annually as either *unsatisfactory*, *satisfactory*, or *highly satisfactory*. Employees rated unsatisfactory are given no annual increase and are scheduled for close monitoring. Those rated satisfactory are granted a 3% increase, and those rated highly satisfactory earn a 6% raise.

Several of the more ambitious plans we reviewed calibrated their

reward systems more finely. For example, employees might be awarded points for attendance, training attended, teaching skills, staff relations skills, and parent relations skills. Employees' annual increases would then be calculated based upon how many points they earned — if they earned 50% of all possible points, they would earn 50% of the maximum possible raise.

One after-school program offered a unique approach. They start all teachers at a low entry level wage. Then, over the course of two years, they rapidly move up those teachers who demonstrate good skills into teaching positions paid above the going rate.

Putting Together the Pieces

Now the hard part. Once you've decided what your center intends to value monetarily in its salaries, you need to translate these values into a usable salary schedule. Here are some factors to weigh in developing or refining your schedule:

Simplicity. Heed *Accounting Law #1* — "Salary schedules inevitably expand to fill every square on the spreadsheet." Resist the urge to make your salary schedule more elaborate than it needs to be. Many small and some not-so-small child care organizations get by with no more than a list of starting salaries for each job category. Every year the director then either decides on giving an across-the-board raise or makes decisions on a one-to-one basis.

Security. The main disadvantage with very simple salary plans is that they fail to provide employees with a long range view. Employees who plan to make a career of child care want to know what they can aspire to — What is the maximum salary they can earn? How can they advance within the center? A good salary schedule informs employees about their career options and opportunities.

Clarity. Some of the salary schedules we reviewed could just as well have been written in Chinese — maybe they were. They were incomprehensible. Give your new salary schedule the man-on-the-

street test. Have several of your friends not involved in child care review it. When they can understand it, it's ready to be unveiled at your center.

Flexibility. Some of the salary schedules we reviewed left no room for maneuvering. The steps and levels for all positions were set in stone. Make your plan flexible enough so that you can add positions, upgrade or downgrade positions, or change step sizes without redoing the entire plan.

Liability. Before committing to any salary schedule, you should evaluate the long range worst/best case scenario. What if your salary plan works and you totally avoid turnover? What would your total salary costs be three years from now? Five years from now? Can you afford this?

Relevancy. At the beginning of this article, I observed that your salary schedule should be a direct expression of your organization's values. Sometimes, however, in develop-

One View: No to Merit Pay

It is our policy NOT to give merit increases or bonuses. We are aware that this is somewhat of an unusual policy, but our reasoning is tied to our respect for teachers and our philosophy, which understands that quality education comes from a community of professionals working together to serve the needs of the children and families in its care.

Teachers need to be paid the highest salaries possible for the challenging work they do. Our board of directors makes significant efforts to provide maximum funding for salaries and benefits. Teachers get "rewarded" with knowing the salary increase is maximal (ours has ranged from 6% to 8% per year) and that the board and administration are continually working to provide a place where teachers can practice their profession.

We have no teacher aides in the school, only teachers and head teachers, who have supervisory and administrative responsibilities. We have hired them to do the same job (within job classifications), not to do a "better" job than others. Moreover, we believe that a primary obligation of the professional early childhood administrator is to develop team building skills. ECE teachers need to have the skills to be able to work with peers sometimes under stressful conditions.

If we were to try to reward some teachers at a differential rate, it would be very difficult to make a decision that would accurately reflect the precise truth about who deserved what. Merit pay is by nature exclusionary and we believe counterproductive to building a stable, quality environment in which to teach. No matter what criteria "merit" is measured by, if monetary value is assigned individually, team boundaries are crossed, possibly damaged, and probably discouraged. The hierarchical relationship between the administration and the individual teacher is promoted to the exclusion of the teacher's development of complex, sophisticated, and subtle communication with his/her peers. This is the very communication necessary for meeting the complex, sophisticated, and subtle educational needs of young children and their families. This, in our view, is counterproductive to our goal of respecting our teachers as professionals and contrary to our view of what quality education is all about.

— *Susan Britson, Step One School, Berkeley, California*

ing a schedule you get so wrapped up in the mathematics and logistics that values and goals fade into the background. You should analyze your new or your current salary schedule to see if it truly supports your values. Are the positions that are most valuable to your organization properly rewarded? Are the factors you value the most (training, experience, or performance) rewarded the most?

Three Types of Salary Schedules

In developing your salary schedule, you have some choices to make. The salary schedules we reviewed fell into three general categories. One in three of these were very simple or basic plans; most of the rest were traditional salary schedules; and less than one in ten fell into the innovative category.

The basic plans were not much more than lists of positions with starting salaries. In some cases, these spelled out the starting, mid-range, and top of the line salary for each position. While these plans are seldom inspiring, they are probably perfectly adequate for small, stable centers.

What we call the traditional salary schedules are grids with multiple levels and steps. Typically, the columns across the page represent different levels of education (high school diploma, AA degree, etc.), and the rows down the page represent years of employment. In some centers, there is a separate grid for each position, while in others all the positions are covered in one mega-grid.

The advantage of these traditional schedules is that they can be easily

understood. People are accustomed to seeing salaries presented in grids and can easily figure out where they currently fit in, where they can progress, and what they need to do to get there (complete that AA degree, survive ten years, etc.).

A possible disadvantage is that the beauty of these plans is often only skin deep. The traditional schedule looks very impressive — it looks organized and standardized, and it fills the page with numbers that appear to have been calculated with great precision. Yet some of the most impressive looking grids

we reviewed were seriously flawed. Some had steps that increased in erratic non-patterns; some had step increases that were so tiny as to be insulting; and one contained math errors that resulted in the assistant teacher making more than the lead teacher after six years.

A few of the schedules we reviewed were innovative. There were some creative attempts to factor in performance, ongoing training, and participation above and beyond the call of duty. Unfortunately, a few of the most creative plans were also some of

Table C
Traditional Salary Schedule

	I	II	III	IV	V	VI	VII	VIII	IX	X
1	1.00	1.04	1.08	1.12	1.16	1.20	1.24	1.28	1.32	1.36
2	1.02	1.06	1.10	1.14	1.18	1.22	1.26	1.30	1.34	1.38
3	1.04	1.08	1.12	1.16	1.20	1.24	1.28	1.32	1.36	1.40
4	1.06	1.10	1.14	1.18	1.22	1.26	1.30	1.34	1.38	1.42
5	1.08	1.12	1.16	1.20	1.24	1.28	1.32	1.36	1.40	1.44
6	1.10	1.14	1.18	1.22	1.26	1.30	1.34	1.38	1.42	1.46
11	1.20	1.24	1.28	1.32	1.36	1.40	1.44	1.48	1.52	1.56
21	1.40	1.44	1.48	1.52	1.56	1.60	1.64	1.68	1.72	1.76
31	1.60	1.64	1.68	1.72	1.76	1.80	1.84	1.92	1.96	2.00
41	1.80	1.84	1.92	1.96	2.00	2.04	2.08	2.12	2.16	2.20
51	2.00	2.04	2.08	2.12	2.16	2.20	2.24	2.26	2.30	2.34
61	2.20	2.24	2.26	2.30	2.34	2.38	2.42	2.46	2.50	2.54

NOTE: This is an abbreviated model. To save space we have left out Steps 7–10, 12–20, etc.

the most complicated ones — it would take a computer whiz to calculate all the points and percentages. Overall, however, we appreciated the courage centers demonstrated in blazing new ground with these plans and only wish that we could convince some foundation to fund a study of their impact.

We attempted to capture the best thinking we observed in the 100+ salary schedules we analyzed and present it in two models. These models are presented in Table C, "Traditional Salary Schedule," and Table D, "Performance Based Salary Schedule."

Before we present these models, a major note of caution is in order: Do not adapt these models in your center! These are presented as starting points only. You need to modify these to incorporate your own values, priorities, and fiscal realities.

Model 1: The Traditional Approach

This model is in the form of the standard grid with levels going across the page and steps going down the page. Here is how to modify it to your needs:

Decision 1. What increments do you want to build into your grid? In Model 1, we set the increases for the levels in 4% increments. These increments typically account for levels of education. We set the increases for the steps, which typically account for annual increases, in 2% increments.

We purposely made the steps smaller than the typical 3% incre-

ments to provide more flexibility. When increments are large, the center has an all or nothing choice — you either move an employee up to the next step or you don't. With smaller increments, you can decide to move each employee up one, two, or even three steps a year, or you can move them up one step every six months.

One disadvantage with these small steps is that it adds to the size of your grid. If you want to include all staff members on the same grid, you may need to include as many as 70 to 100 steps.

We also chose, for simplicity's sake only, to make the increments for the steps uniform throughout the grid. Thus the salaries of employees at the bottom and top of the grid would increase at 2% for every step. What this means is that employees at the bottom end would receive smaller increases in actual dollars and cents than those at the top. You may elect to reverse this by starting the increments at 3% or 4% at the bottom and gradually reducing them to 1% at the top end.

(Note: Throughout this article we refer to salaries and salary schedules in reference to all employees. Many centers actually pay hourly wages for some employees and annual salaries for others. We are not arguing for or against this classification of employees. We use the term salaries as a generic term for all monies paid to staff.)

Decision 2. What is your base salary, i.e., what is the starting salary for your lowest paid employee? Once you set this entry level amount, you can translate all the increments on your grid to actual monetary amounts. For

example, using our grid in Table C, if your base salary is $5.00 per hour, the succeeding amounts in row 1 would be $5.20, $5.40, $5.60, etc. Step 2 amounts would be $5.10, $5.30, $5.50, etc.

Decision 3. How much are you going to reward various levels of education? For example, if we were to take the typical educational differentials from Table B, here is how they would fit into our salary schedule:

High school diploma starts at
  Level I
AA degree would start at Level V
BA degree would start at Level VII
MA degree would start at Level IX

You may elect to value these levels differently or to define the levels differently. Some centers, for example, set levels based on credit hours of college completed. Others factor in CDA status or workshop attendance.

Decision 4. Where do you want to set the entry point for each position at your center? If we were to use the typical position differentials from Table A, here is how they would fit into our model:

Teacher Aide	=	Step 1
Bus Driver	=	Step 6
Assistant Teacher	=	Step 11
Lead Teacher	=	Step 26
Center Director	=	Step 66

As with educational levels, you will need to take the job categories used at your center and place them on the grid based on how you value them.

Decision 5. When will center employees qualify for moving up a step or to another level? Do

Table D
Performance Based Salary Schedule

How to Use This Instrument: For Step 1, insert the points assigned for the employee's position. For Step 2, insert the points earned for the employee's highest level of education completed. For Step 3, insert the number of points earned first for years of satisfactory performance at your center, second for the years of above average performance, and third for the years of superior performance. Now determine the employee's new hourly rate by completing Step 4.

Step 1 — Responsibility _____

Teacher Aide	1.00
Cook	1.20
Assistant Teacher	1.20
Custodian	1.30
Lead Teacher	1.50
Assistant Director	1.80
Director	2.30

Step 2 — Training _____

AA Degree	.05
ECE-Related AA Degree	.10
BA/BS Degree	.10
ECE-Related BA/BS Degree	.20
Master's Degree	.15
ECE-Related Master's Degree	.30

Step 3 — Experience/Performance

Years of satisfactory performance
  (add .02 points/year) _____
Years of above average performance
  (add .04 points/year) _____
Years of superior performance
  (add .06 points/year) _____

Step 4 — New Hourly Rate Determination

Multiply total points earned in Steps 1 through 3 times base rate for center.

_____ points x $_____ per hour = $_____ per hour

employees move up one step every year automatically, or only if they receive a positive evaluation, or only if monies are available? Do employees progress to a higher level every time they complete a higher level of education?

Model 2: Performance Based Approach

This model is a variation of some of the innovative schedules we reviewed. It assigns significant weight to a staff member's performance in setting annual increases. Here is how to modify it to your needs, keeping in mind that every point awarded in Steps 1, 2, and 3 is worth 100% of your base rate:

Decision 1. What is your base salary, i.e., what is the starting salary for your lowest paid employee? You will use the hourly rate for the base salary in Step 4.

Decision 2. What value do you want to assign to each job category in your center? In Model 2, we have used the differentials from Table A. You will want to modify these to reflect your center's values.

Decision 3. What value do you want to assign to each level of education? In Model 2, we have used the differentials from Table B. You will want to modify these to reflect to your center's values.

Decision 4. How many points do you want to award for different levels of performance? Keep in mind that if you go this route you must find or develop a tool for measuring performance that is viewed by all concerned as fair.

Once you have completed these adjustments, you should test it out. Based on your recent experience, use this format to determine, hypothetically, the salaries of several employees at different levels in your organization. Does this result in salaries that are fair? Does it result in any radical increases or decreases in current pay levels? Can you afford it?

If your test is unsuccessful, keep tinkering with the points or come up with a similar set of steps that fit your needs better.

A Final Caution

Your organization may well have a salary plan in place, so you may not be interested in going through a big production to establish a new one. That is probably a wise decision. However, I would encourage you to at least take the time to review your current schedule against the key points raised in the two articles in this series. Make sure that you are getting the maximum positive impact out of the resources you devote to salaries.

Credits

We reviewed over 100 salary schedules from Exchange Panel of 200 members in preparing the two articles in this series. The following centers' plans were especially helpful :

Central Learning Center, Memphis, TN; Children's Learning Center, Yardley, PA; Children's Programs Inc., Brookfield, WI; Community Children's Project, Jackson, WY; Gertrude B. Nielsen Child Care and Learning Center, Northbrook, IL; Graham Memorial Preschool, Coronado, CA; Gretchen's House, Ann Arbor, MI; Janet Rich Day Care, Rochester, NY; Learning Tree Montessori, Seattle, WA; Moffett Road Baptist Child Development Center, Mobile, AL; The Nursery Foundation of St. Louis, St. Louis, MO; St. Elizabeth's Day Home, San Jose, CA; Wausau Child Care, Inc., Wausau, WI; World Bank Children's Center, Washington, DC.

References

Ruopp, Richard et al. *Children at the Center*. Cambridge, MA: Abt Associates, 1979.

Whitebook, Marcy. *Who Cares? Child Care Teachers and the Quality of Care in America*. Oakland, CA: Child Care Employee Project, 1989.

State-of-the-Art Thinking on Parent Fee Policies

by Roger Neugebauer

There are two fools in every market; one who asks too little, one who asks too much.
— Russian proverb

No one wants to make foolish mistakes when it comes to the tricky business of setting parent fees. It's a difficult balancing act, setting fees high enough to adequately reward staff and low enough to be affordable to families. It's no less difficult setting fee policies that are flexible enough to meet the needs of parents under stress yet tough enough to protect the center from financial hardship.

To give centers guidance on setting fees and fee policies, we analyzed over 150 fee policies submitted to us by members of the **Exchange Panel of 200.** *In this article, we will share some of the best thinking we discovered in these documents.*

A Bargain at Twice the Price: Fee Schedules

There is a tremendous variation in the rates early childhood programs charge. In the fee schedules we reviewed, for example, the daily rate for full day care of a four year old ranged from $7.80 to $31.05. These variations reflect regional cost of living factors, staffing levels, competition, family incomes, and outside support.

In the "Fee Relationships in Centers" box (see page 63), you can see the relationship between what centers charge per day for different services. For example, if Your Average Children's Center charges $20.00 per day for full day care for preschoolers, it would charge $25.60 per day for infants, $23.00 for toddlers, and $9.00 for school-agers (after school only). If Your Average Children's Center charges $20.00 per day for full day care, five days a week, they would charge $13.00 per day for half day care and $23.80 for three days a week care.

The relationship among fees for preschoolers, toddlers, and infants is fairly consistent. However, the differential in fees for preschoolers and school-age children attending in the afternoon only varies dramatically.

In some centers, the after-school fees are as little as 15% to 20% less than preschool fees, while in others they are as much as 75% to 80% lower. Part of this enormous differential depends upon whether or not transportation is included in the fees and whether or not the space is being provided at low or no cost. But even when these variables are factored out, fees for after-school care still vary widely. This would seem to indicate that there is not a common agreement regarding the structure and staffing of school-age programs.

Cheaper by the Dozen: Multi-Child Discounts

There is also wide variation in the discounts centers provide for the second and third children from the same family enrolled in a center at the same time. Slightly under half of the policies we reviewed made no provision at all for multi-child discounts. In those that did, the amount of discount varied from 5% to 50% for a second child, and from 10% to 66% for the third child.

Some of the typical policies:

If you have more than one child enrolling in the center, you will receive a family discount. The fee for the second child will be two thirds tuition, and the third child will be one third tuition. — **Colorado Springs Child Nursery Center**, Colorado Springs, Colorado

Parents enrolling more than one child will pay full fee for the youngest child and be given a 10% discount for each other child. — **Ebenezer Child Care Centers**, Milwaukee, Wisconsin

There is a discount for the second child in the family of 20%. A third child could attend at a 30% discount. — **Euclid Avenue Preschool**, Cleveland, Ohio

Most policies are a little fuzzy as to which children get the discount. Some imply that the discount applies to the most recent enrolling child, while a few indicate that the discount is applied to the child(ren) paying the lowest fees.

Fee Relationships in Centers

In analyzing fee variations, we used the daily fees charged for preschool children (three and four year olds) attending full day, five days a week as the baseline. We found that fees charged for different types of services varied on average as follows:

Infants (full day, five days a week)	+28%
Toddlers (full day, five days a week)	+15%
Preschoolers (full day, three days a week)	+19%
Preschoolers (half day, five days a week)	-35%
School-Agers (before and after school, five days a week)	-26%
School-Agers (after school only, five days a week)	-55%

To Be or Not to Be: Charges for Absences

The greatest amount of ink in the policies we reviewed was consumed explaining to parents how and why fees are charged even when the children are absent. Clearly, this is an area where centers have experienced a hard sell. Therefore, it is important that the policy statement on absences be clear and persuasive. Here are some of our favorite examples:

We are prepared for each child each day whether the child attends or not. There will be no refunds for days absent. Each family will be allowed two weeks of absenteeism with no charge. — **Hester's Creative Schools, Inc.**, Greensboro, North Carolina

Tuition is the same every payment regardless of days missed due to illness or holidays. Think of this as a yearly commitment for your child, not in terms of days of attendance. — **Breezy Point Day School**, Langhorne, Pennsylvania

To assure that we can provide the highest quality of services, it is essential that the financial status of the center remain stable. Expenses cannot be sufficiently reduced to overcome losses due to absenteeism. Therefore, we must require that each family financially support space guaranteed for your child(ren) even if the child is absent. — **Pow Wow Child Development Centers**, Johnson City, Tennessee

Please note that tuition must be paid in full without deduction for absences. This is because our staffing and other operational expenses are arranged on the basis of fixed enrollment levels and must be met on a continuing basis. Few of the operating costs of the facility are eliminated when a particular child is absent. — **HeartsHome Early Learning Center**, Houston, Texas

Centers struggle to develop absence policies that meet the centers' needs for financial stability, yet are sensitive to the needs of families. About half the centers provide discounts or credits for family vacations and/or extended periods of illness. Here are some of the clearer, more creative policies on "approved absences":

Families enrolled in our 12 month program prior to June 1st of that year are entitled to one free week of vacation. This vacation week is not transferable from year to year. . . . This vacation week is offered on a Monday through Friday service week only. — **Rainbow Express Preschool**, Lansdale, Pennsylvania

There will be no credit for absences of one week or less. A $45 non-attendance fee will be charged for the second consecutive week of absence and up to four weeks. Your child's place will not be held after the fourth week. — **Another Generation Preschool**, Sunrise, Florida

The vacation allotment has already been figured into your child's contract at the time of enrollment. Your child's regular rate remains the same every month, regardless of when he/she goes on vacation. — **Gretchen's House**, Ann Arbor, Michigan

If your child is absent from the center three or more days in one week due to sickness, conditions beyond your control, or preapproved vacation time, your tuition charge will be reduced by 40%. — **Children's World Learning Center**, Euless, Texas

Some centers waive fees for absences due to a variety of other causes: "in-patient hospitalization," "death in the immediate family," "court-appointed visitation," "center closings due to inclement weather" (only two centers out of the 150+ waive fees for this reason), "parents on mater-nity leave," and absences "at the request of your doctor."

Pay Me Now or Pay Me Later: Payment Terms

With the exception of drop-in programs which charge after the fact for actual hours attended, centers today require payment in advance. Not too many years ago, collecting after the delivery of services was common, and commonly this resulted in major cash flow stresses as expenses were incurred ahead of income.

A slight majority of centers require payments on a monthly basis. This clearly is the low-hassle route as it minimizes the number of collections that must be made. It also gives a center considerable flexibility in managing cash flow. Most centers divide the annual fee into 12 equal payments, although a few invoice each month based on days of service to be delivered. In some communities, however, parents cannot afford to pay 30 days in advance. Therefore, a significant minority of centers collect on a weekly basis.

Some centers give parents a choice of paying on a weekly, bi-weekly, monthly, or semester basis. In these cases, discounts are given to those paying on the longer term basis.

Most centers prefer to receive payments by check — some even have policies against receiving payments in cash. Surprisingly, only a small minority allow payments by credit cards.

What's Up Front?: Registration Fees and Deposits

At enrollment time, nearly all centers collect from parents a registration fee and a deposit. The primary purpose of these charges is to provide security for the center — to assure that parents are serious about enrolling their children and to cover unpaid fees if a child is withdrawn abruptly.

Registration fees, variously referred to as "application fees," "enrollment fees," and "reservation deposits," range from $15 to $75. We found little correlation between registration fees and service fees — i.e., centers charging the highest fees for child care don't necessarily impose the highest registration fees. For most centers, registration fees are a one-time charge. However, many centers, particularly centers operating on a ten month schedule, impose a smaller "reenrollment fee" every year.

Registration fees are typically non-refundable. One center offers a refund if a child or family encounters an "unavoidable crisis" which forces them to withdraw in the first 30 days. Several centers observed that the registration fee was refundable in special instances "at the discretion of the director."

Security deposits (which are seldom referred to as "security" deposits) range from one week's to one month's fees. Most centers ask a two week deposit and many ask for one month. These deposits are refundable if parents comply with center fee policies. For example, typical statements on deposits read:

At time of registration, a refundable deposit is required. The deposit is refunded if the family gives the director of the center a written notice two weeks prior to withdrawing from the center. If this notice is not received. the family will forfeit the deposit. — **Early Childhood Options in University Circle**, Cleveland, Ohio

A two-week deposit is required prior to a child starting the center program, preferably at registration; however, an alternate payment schedule can be arranged if the entire deposit cannot be paid at time of registration. If a child is withdrawn at the end of the program year, the two-week deposit can be refunded. If a child is withdrawing prior to the end of the program year, the two week notice must be given; but deposit can only be refunded if a replacement can be found within that two week period. — **The Children's Center**, New Milford, Connecticut

From a center's point of view, registration fees and deposits are necessary for financial stability. However, from a family's perspective, they can add up to a serious hurdle. If a family must pay up front for a registration fee, a one-month deposit, and the first month's tuition, this could run anywhere from $500 to as much as $2,000 per child.

Realizing the cash flow strain this can cause, some centers try to soften the blow. For example, **The Children's Center** (as noted above) offers to work with families to collect the deposit over time. Another alternative, which is used by other services but not by any of the centers whose policies we

reviewed, is to ask parents to guarantee their fees with a credit card. In that way, no money would be collected unless the family defaulted on their fees.

With concern, we noted that none of the fee policies we reviewed included a provision for refunding interest accrued on deposits. If your policy does not address this, you may want to check to see if your policies are in compliance with your state's usury laws.

This Is the End, My Friend: Withdrawals

Most centers spell out fairly specific policies for procedures for withdrawing a child from the program. These policies are designed to give the center adequate notice so it can collect what is due from the outgoing family and find a child to fill the vacancy.

A typical policy:

Thirty days written notice is required to withdraw a child from the program. This enables the center to process an application from the waiting list. Payment is required for 30 days following the withdrawal notice, whether or not the child continues to attend the center during that period. — **Play and Learn Centers**, Fort Washington, Pennsylvania

Many centers also spell out specific policies for temporary withdrawals due to family vacations or illnesses. Often a center will place a child on extended absence on a priority wait list so that he has the opportunity to fill the first vacancy when he is ready to return.

This issue most frequently arises during summer vacation months. Here is a typical way centers deal with such withdrawals:

Persons signing a 12 month agreement and wishing to withdraw for the summer months of July and August may do so by informing the center director in writing by April 1 and paying the September tuition by June 1. If the child does not return in September, the tuition is forfeited. — **The Children's Learning Center**, Yardley, Pennsylvania

All Dressed Up with Nowhere to Go: Late Pick-Ups

This obviously is another hot issue. Clearly, it is a major imposition on teachers when they must wait until a late parent shows up. And it can be anxiety-producing to young children. Most centers have learned that they must be firm about late pick-ups or it quickly mushrooms. Here are some typical policies designed to discourage lateness:

Since the center closes at 6 pm, a late pick-up charge of $5 will be assessed for each quarter hour or fraction thereof that a child is left beyond 6 pm. This fee is payable immediately to the employee who has remained with your child. — **Early Explorations**, Encinitas, California

Once the center closes, the teacher who remains with children is paid directly by the parent. Charges are $3 for the first five minutes and then $1 per minute. All payments are to be made by the end of the week. If payment has not been made, First Care will pay the staff member and will add twice the amount to our state-

ment. — **First Care, Inc.**, Glen Ellyn, Illinois

Most centers also recognize that being totally inflexible regarding lateness places even more stress on families already operating on the edge. Here are examples of policies designed to be less burdensome:

You are allowed three late pick-ups with a maximum tardiness of up to 30 minutes. — **Pulama Keiki Preschool and Daycare**, Lihue, Hawaii

If you know you are going to be late, call the center. If is difficult for both your child and staff if a child is left at school without knowing why. — **Child Care Center**, Evanston, Illinois

No fees for late tuition or late pick-ups. We trust families will cooperate. Families who are habitually late in paying or picking up their children will be asked to find another early childhood program. — **St. Elizabeth's Day Home**, San Jose, California

On average, centers charge 75¢ per hour for late pick-ups, and most policies provide that payments be made on the spot to the teacher staying with the child. **The Reston Children's Center** in Reston, Virginia, imposes progressively stiffer penalties, with the first lateness being charged at $1 per minute, the second at $2 per minute, and the third at $4 per minute. **The World Bank Children's Center** in Washington, DC, even spells out that it is the "center's front office clock" that will be used to define lateness.

The Check Is In the Mail: Late Payments

Another chronic problem for child care centers is collections. People in early childhood education usually are not hard-nosed collectors, so late payments can easily get out of hand if not dealt with decisively.

The better fee policies clearly define when fees are due and when payments become late. Typically, monthly fees are due by the first of the month and become overdue by the fifth of the month. Weekly fees are typically due by Monday and are late by Wednesday.

When fees are late, most centers impose late fees ranging from $5 to $20. One center imposes a late penalty of 10%. If parents are late with their fees several months in a row, or fall more than a month behind (two weeks behind in some centers), directors typically reserve the right to disenroll the child (with any deposit being forfeited).

There are two problems with flat charges for late payments. First, once a payment is late and the late penalty has been incurred, there is no incentive for parents to quickly make amends — whether they are one day late or two weeks late, the charge is the same. Charging interest that accrues on a daily basis makes delays progressively more painful.

Second, late charges may violate state usury laws. States limit the amount of interest you can charge for overdue payments. Typically, the limit is in the range of 1.5% per month. Thus, if your monthly fee is $350, the maximum late pay-

ment you could charge would be $5. Review your late payment policies in light of applicable state laws!

Here is an example of a late payment policy that clearly has been developed with legal requirements in mind:

It is further agreed that any payment which is in default shall bear interest at the maximum legal rate and from the due date until paid. The promiser hereby waives demand notice of presentation. In the event it is necessary to refer this matter to an attorney for collection, it is mutually agreed that the prevailing party shall be entitled to reasonable attorney's fees and that the venue of any action shall be King County, Washington. — **Learning Tree Montessori**, Seattle, Washington

Another way to avoid bad debts is to confront problems early and work out solutions that meet the center's needs as well as a family's. By encouraging families experiencing financial difficulties to let you know in advance about problems they may have with fee payments, you can often work out a schedule of payments that will help the family, but will also assure the center that payments will eventually be made. Here is one center's approach:

If your family should have an unusual or emergency type financial problem that may effect the prompt paying of tuition, please call or stop by the office and talk with the administrator or bookkeeper. Often we can work something out until the crisis or emergency subsides. — **Kirkmont Presbyterian Preschool**, Beavercreek, Ohio

Roger's Rules for Effective Fee Policies

1. Don't sell yourself short. The fees you charge should be based on what it costs to provide a level of quality you can believe in. If you set your fees to be in line with what other centers in your community charge, you may or may not be setting them high enough to cover your costs. If you keep your fees low because you fear that parents may not be able to afford higher fees, you are resigning your center to a mediocre level of quality. Rather, you should set your fees based on what quality care costs and then work hard to find ways to offer scholarships and discounts for families who truly can't afford your program.

2. Don't set policies you won't enforce. It is easy to write tough policies to deal with all your problems. However, policies accomplish their purpose only if they are enforced by real people in real life. The cleverest late pick-up policy is worthless if you lack the commitment to enforce it, or if you only enforce it intermittently. And if you have one policy you don't consistently enforce, it takes the teeth out of the rest of your policies.

3. No small print, no surprises. Parents won't be influenced by policies they aren't aware of. At intake, carefully review in person your key policies on withdrawals, absences, late pick-ups, and late payments so parents clearly know in advance what the rules are. Many centers require that parents sign a statement or contract agreeing to these policies and, in some cases, agreeing that they were briefed in advance about these policies.

4. Watch the tone. In writing policies it is natural to slip into a negative, legalistic tone. This often leads to policies that are far from family friendly. One manual, for example, stated that it was including a strict late pick-up penalty because "inconsiderate behavior by parents forced us to do this." Don't lecture or moralize. Show respect for parents, assume their intentions are good, and take their perspective into account. State your policies in straight-forward, non-judgmental fashion.

5. Write policies well. Some of the policies we reviewed were so garbled that we couldn't understand them. Many were littered with misspellings and grammatical errors. Some of the policies were far too complex — one center's policies on vacation credits took four pages to explain and a degree in mathematics to calculate. After you have written your policies, have them reviewed by people outside your staff — center parents, your neighbors, your grandmother. Then quiz them to see if they understand your policies.

6. Attend to presentation. Just as a delicious dinner can be diminished with lousy presentation, the best policies can be undermined if poorly presented. If no one on staff has an eye for graphic design, see if you can find a volunteer among your parents to give you some layout and design advice, or lean on your printer for a little free consultation.

7. Help parents find help. Some of our favorite fee policies included advice to parents on how to qualify for public subsidies. We were truly amazed by how few centers' policies informed parents of how they could save money with the federal child care tax credit. Make your policies useful tools for parents as well as your center.

Implementing a Sliding Fee Scale System for Your Center

by Roger Neugebauer

I n many communities, the phenomenon is the same. Growing numbers of families who need child care services find they don't earn enough to afford child care fees, but they earn too much to qualify for public subsidies. One means centers have found to assist families caught in this financial crunch is the sliding fee scale. Such fee systems are designed to adjust fees according to families' abilities to pay — fees are set low for low income families and are gradually increased as families' incomes increase.

There are several philosophies on the design of sliding fee scales. One approach calls for sliding fees to be based on the actual costs of care at the midpoint in the scale. Scales developed on this premise subsidize families at the low end of the scale by charging families at the higher end more than the actual cost of care.

A second approach calls for the top fee in the fee scale to be set at the actual cost of care. Under this system, no family pays more than the actual cost of care. Reduced fees are subsidized strictly by outside funds raised and in-kind contribu-

tions received. This second approach is the one described in this article. Many of the suggestions, however, apply to either approach; those that do not can be readily modified.

The ideas in this article on how to develop and administer a sliding fee scale have been provided by 27 child care centers in 23 states. These centers freely shared information in an *Exchange* survey about their fee scale policies, experiences, and problems. Since the survey was initially completed in 1979 when an earlier version of this article appeared, some of the

centers may have subsequently changed their fee scales. In addition, inflation will have bumped most income figures quoted up at least 20%. However, the steps described below for developing a sliding fee scale are as valid today as they were in 1979.

Evaluating Your Resources

Before you actually set up a sliding fee scale, you need to determine if you have enough money available to support the scale. For every parent's fee that is reduced, you must secure outside funding equal to the amount of the reduction. Calculating how much money you will need to raise is fairly easy — actually raising the money may be a problem.

• **Calculate your actual-cost budget.** Your first step is to establish what your program would cost to operate if you received no income, whether in-kind or in-cash, other than parent fees. Be sure to add to this budget an estimated cost for *regular in-kind contributions* such as free rent or volunteer staff. The fee level required to support this actual-cost budget will be your center's full fee.

• **Total outside contributions.** Now add up all contributions other than parents' fees that you project your program will receive in the next year to fund this budget. Include in this total all cash contributions from grants, donations, and fundraising efforts as well as the costs saved through in-kind contributions. Thus, if your center expects to receive a United Way grant of $5,000, free rent worth $5,000, and the equivalent of one volunteer teacher worth $10,000, your outside contributions would total $20,000.

It is at this stage that the most damaging errors are committed. Striving to help as many parents as possible, fee scale planners often make unrealistically high projections of the amount of money they can raise. Then six months down the line when it becomes apparent that they will not raise that much money, they are faced with the agonizing choice of either raising parents' fees or lowering teachers' pay to make up for the deficit. To avoid this dilemma, a center's fundraising projections should be on the conservative side.

• **Assess impact of contributions.** To determine whether these contributions are sufficient to support a sliding fee scale, you must calculate what percentage of the actual-cost budget they cover. For example, if your actual-cost budget is $80,000 and your contributions total $20,000, they will cover 25% of the program's actual cost.

To estimate how extensive a fee scale your contributions will support, multiply this percentage

by 2. The resulting percentage will equal the largest fee reduction you will be able to offer to parents, given your available contributions. For example, if your contributions cover 20% of your budget, the lowest fee on your fee scale can only be a 40% reduction of your *full fee*. If contributions cover 25% of the budget, your lowest fee can be 50% of your full fee. (See Table 1.)

The above guideline assumes that parents' fees under a sliding fee scale will be evenly distributed at all fee levels. If you expect, given the distribution of incomes among your consumers, that the distribution of fees will differ, you need to adjust this estimate accordingly.

Assume, for instance, that by using the formula you calculate your lowest fee to be a 40% reduction. Yet, because the vast majority of your potential consumers have very low incomes, you expect that most will qualify for the lowest fee level. Therefore, the lowest fee you will be able to offer may only be a 30% or 25% reduction.

Among the surveyed centers, maximum fee reductions ranged from as little as 27% to as much as 81%. Most centers were able to reduce fees down to about 50% of their full fee.

Developing the Fee Scale

The following steps outline one approach for developing a scale

which fairly reflects families' abilities to pay, yet which is easy to administer. It is not presented as the correct or best approach. Centers should freely modify the steps to suit their own purposes.

To demonstrate how to apply this approach, a hypothetical "Center XYZ" will be followed through the steps. This center, which is open 50 weeks a year, computed its *full fee* to be $50/week and decided it could afford a fee scale with reductions down to 50% of this full fee.

• **Define "ability to pay."** There are no established guidelines as to how much families can afford to pay for child care. As a result, every center must decide for itself how to express families' abilities to pay in terms of fees. One means to assure that all families are treated fairly is to set fees in the fee scale at a specific percentage of family income.

Surprisingly, while struggling with this issue independently, the surveyed centers were remarkably consistent in their conclusions. Nearly all set their fees within the fee scales between 9% and 12% of gross family income. (In the steps below, we will assume that Center XYZ set its guideline percentage at 10%.)

• **Assess impact of tax credits.** Nearly all parents will have their child care costs offset to some degree by federal and state child

---

Table 1. Estimating Maximum Fee Reductions

$$\frac{\text{Annual contributions}}{\text{Annual actual-cost budget}} \times 100\% \times 2 = \text{Maximum fee reduction in a sliding fee scale when fees are evenly distributed}$$

care tax credits. Thus, in striving to determine how much parents can afford to pay, fee scale planners should take into account the extent parents are being assisted by various tax credit provisions.

• **Determine cut-off point.** The cut-off point for the fee scale is the income level at which families begin paying the full fee. Families with incomes below the cut-off point will pay reduced fees. The cut-off point varied widely among surveyed centers—from $14,000 to $35,000/year, with an average of about $24,000/year.

Ideally, the cut-off point is set at the income level at which the full fee equals the guidelines percentage of family income. This point can be determined by applying the formula in Table 2. In applying this formula, Center XYZ found the cut-off point to be $25,000 — i.e., the full fee ($50) was 10% of the income of a family earning $25,000/year:

$$\frac{\$50 \times 50 \text{ weeks}}{10\% \times .01} = \$25,000/\text{year}$$

• **Determine the bottom step.** The bottom step in the fee scale is the income level at which fee reductions stop — all families with incomes below this level pay the center's lowest fee. In the survey, the bottom step ranged from $4,800 to $15,000/year, with an average of $8,600. Many centers set the bottom step on their in-house fee scales at the income level families become eligible for public subsidies.

As with the cut-off point, the bottom step should be set by applying the percentage guideline. In Center XYZ, therefore, the lowest fee, $25

(50% of $50), should represent 10% of a family's income at the bottom step. This step can be calculated simply by multiplying the cut-off point by the maximum percentage the fee will be reduced under the fee scale. In Center XYZ, this computes as follows:

Cut-Off Point   Bottom Step

$25,000 x 50% = $12,500

• **Set steps of fee scale.** To set the steps between the cut-off point and the bottom step:

1. Subtract the bottom step income value from the cut-off point income value and divide the remainder by 9. This resulting amount constitutes the income increment for the scale.

2. Subtract the lowest fee from the full fee and divide the remainder by 10. This figure constitutes the fee increment for the scale.

3. Add 1 income increment to the bottom step and 1 fee increment to the lowest fee. This pair constitutes the second step of the scale.

4. Add 8 more income increments and fee increments in pairs. The eighth income and fee increments make up the last step in the scale. The top of this step should be at the cut-off point.

Following this procedure, Center XYZ computed income increments of $1,389 and fee increments of

$2.50. The *Straight Percentage Fee Scale* (Columns A and B) in Table 3 results from adding these increments.

• **Evaluate the scale's suitability.** Once the scale is set, it should be evaluated against three criteria.

Does it fairly reflect families' ability to pay?

In a scale developed using the above steps, the midpoint of every step will be very close to the guideline percentage. The only disparity will arise if the steps are too large. If the individual steps are in increments of $2,000 or more, families at the beginning of a step will pay a significantly higher percentage of their income than families at the end of the same step. To reduce the size of steps which are too large, simply add additional steps to the scale.

How many families' fees will be affected?

It is a useful exercise to perform a trial run of a new scale on paper. In an ongoing center developing a fee scale, current families could be polled (in unsigned questionnaires) as to their incomes to see where families would be distributed on the scale. If it is found that very few fees will be reduced by the fee scale, a center needs to decide whether to drop the fee scale altogether since too few families will benefit or to raise the cut-off point on the scale so that higher income families get a reduction.

Table 2. Computing the Cut-Off Point

$$\frac{\text{Weekly full fee} \times \text{Number of weeks center open}}{\text{Guidelines percentage} \times .01} = \$ \text{ X/Year}$$

Table 3. Center XYZ Sliding Fee Scale Options

A. Straight Percentage (10%) Scale — Gross Family Income	B. Weekly Fee	C. Modified Scale — Gross Family Income	D. Weekly Fee (B) as Percentage of Family Income (C)
Above $25,000	$50.00	Above $25,000	—
23,613—25,000	47.50	23,501—25,000	9.8 %
22,224—23,612	45.00	22,001—23,500	9.9
20,835—22,223	42.50	20,501—22,000	10.0
19,446—20,834	40.00	19,001—20,500	10.1
18,057—19,445	37.50	17,501—19,000	10.3
16,668—18,056	35.00	16,001—17,500	10.5
15,279—16,667	32.50	14,501—16,000	10.7
13,890—15,278	30.00	13,001—14,500	10.9
12,501—13,889	27.50	11,501—13,000	11.2
Below $12,500	25.00	Below $11,500	—

In the more likely event that too many families qualify for large reductions, the center may not be able to subsidize all the reductions. In that case, the guideline percentage can be increased so that the entire scale applies to a lower income range. An alternative solution is to adjust the bottom step to a lower income level while leaving the cut-off point as it is.

The second alternative would have the effect of increasing the size of all steps and requiring families at the lower end of the scale to pay a higher percentage of their income. The *Modified Scale* in Table 3 shows the effect (Column D) of lowering the bottom step in the XYZ scale. In this case, the resulting disparity (9.8% to 11.2%) is not great. In fact, nearly all of the surveyed centers required lower income families to pay a higher percentage than higher income families, with the average difference between the top and bottom steps being about 2.5 percentage points. Differences of this magnitude probably have little effect on comparative abilities to pay.

Is the scale easy to understand and administer?

Scales developed by the above steps will normally have steps with odd dollar amounts. Most centers find parents can more easily understand steps expressed in even $500 or $1,000 steps. A scale with uneven steps can easily be modified to one with even steps by rounding the increments to the nearest $500 or $1,000 level. For example, the XYZ scale was modified by rounding the increments from $1,389 to $1,500, resulting in the *Modified Scale*, which not only made it easier to understand but also lowered the bottom step. The only potential problem with adjusting increments is if they are changed so much that a large disparity in percentage of incomes paid by families results.

Some centers also find scales are easier to understand when income levels are expressed in monthly amounts. This can be accomplished by following the above process and then dividing all income amounts by 12.

A center may also find that fees expressed in odd amounts are cumbersome to collect and account for. Fee increments can be rounded also. However, much more care needs to be taken here as small changes in weekly fees have a large effect on percentage of family income. Another means of adjusting fees to even amounts is to change the number of steps to a number that results in even fee increments.

Measuring Ability to Pay

The most complicated ongoing aspect of administering a sliding fee scale is measuring families' incomes. This is not surprising when you consider that state welfare manuals devote hundreds of pages to outlining their income computation policies. Numerous policy guidelines must be set outlining the types of income and expenses to be considered.

• **Identify sources of countable income.** The first consideration is whose income will be counted. All centers surveyed considered the income of both parents. Most did not count the income of children, although a few included income of children over age 18. A minority also considered the income of other adult relatives and friends residing in the household.

Center policies also vary as to the types of income that are counted. Nearly all centers count earned income and cash benefits (veterans, unemployment, social security, workmen's compensation, etc.). A majority include child support payments in income computations. A lesser number consider rental income, stock dividends, and interest income.

• **Develop a computation method.** Income is received in a wide variety of units — weekly, biweekly, semimonthly, monthly, quarterly, seasonally, retroactively, and unpredictably. A center must develop a computation method that results in all families' income being treated uniformly.

Regular income is dealt with most uniformly by converting it all to a single unit. Most often, monthly income is the unit selected. Income is converted to a monthly unit by multiplying weekly income by $4\frac{1}{3}$, multiplying biweekly income by $2\frac{1}{6}$, multiplying semimonthly income by 2, dividing bimonthly income by 2, and dividing quarterly income by 3.

Computing irregular income on a uniform basis is nearly impossible.

The suggestions listed below highlight the types of problem areas encountered with irregular income:

— Seasonal income (when income is received only certain months of the year — such as teachers' incomes). Spread income out on 12 month basis, then convert to monthly. To do this, multiply monthly income (when fully employed) by the number of months employed per year, then divide by 12.

— Fluctuating income (when income varies significantly from week to week — such as piece work or on-call, part-time work). Average income over a set period of time. For example, add up all income over previous 5 weeks, divide by 5, then multiply by $4\frac{1}{3}$ to arrive at an average monthly income.

— Self-employed income (when persons run their own businesses — proprietors, consultants, artists, etc.). Extremely difficult to compute without going over the person's books item by item. The simplest approach is to ask for the income shown on their previous year's income tax statement or the income estimated for the current year on their Declaration of Estimated Tax.

Some centers avoid all the problems of income computation by asking families to estimate their current annual income and simply accepting their statements.

• **Identify income deductions.** A majority of surveyed centers similarly avoid the entire difficult issue of what deductions to allow by not allowing any — considering only gross family income. Those centers that do allow deductions most often deduct taxes and child support payments. A number of centers allow deductions for medical bills, debts, and housing costs.

These last deductions are more difficult to treat simply and fairly. A center is put in the position of deciding when liabilities are excessive, irresponsible, out of date, or unavoidable. **The Friendship House Child Development Center**, Washington, DC, has resolved this issue by deducting only medical bills in excess of 10% of family income and housing payments in excess of 30%.

Some centers make provisions for special income adjustments. A few allow parents to apply for temporary income adjustments due to emergency circumstances. Others simply treat outstanding liabilities on a case by case basis, while one permits parents to appeal income determinations to the board for adjustment.

• **Consider family size.** Most centers try to make some allowance for the size of the family that must be supported by family income. Frequently centers deal with this issue on the fee scale itself by lowering fees as family size increases. For example, fees might be lowered by $3, $4, or $5 for each additional family member. The problem with this approach is that it is difficult to establish any rationale for determining how much fees should be adjusted.

A few centers have developed interesting alternative approaches. **The Day Care Center, Inc.**, in Norwich, Vermont, for example, deducts $1,000 from annual income for each child in the family.

Grace Child Center, New Orleans, Louisiana, on the other hand, divides monthly family income by the number of family members, weighted as follows: a single parent counts as 2, all other adults count as 1, children under 10 count as ½ except for single children who are counted as 1. This recognizes the special financial strains with single parents or single children.

• **Consider additional children in care.** Most centers try to provide some relief for families which must pay for child care for more than one child at the same time. One-half of the surveyed centers charge the second child 50% of the first child's rate. Some centers reduce fees on a case by case basis for the second child, while others charge a second child a flat rate of $4-$5/week. About one-fourth of the centers charge the same rate for the second child as the first.

• **Monitor fee reductions.** The major danger with a fee scale is that a center will award more fee reductions than it can afford. If fee reductions exceed the available contributions, this means that the center may not be able to meet its payroll by the end of the year.

One center calculates the average fee that the center needs to collect in order to break even and then monitors the average fee granted on a week by week basis. A similar approach is to calculate the amount of fee reduction for each step on an annual basis. As fee reductions are granted, a running total of annual reductions is maintained. When this total equals the amount in the contributions fund, no more fee reductions are offered

— all remaining slots are filled at the full fee.

Weighing the Alternatives

The sliding fee scale described above is the most popular approach to relating fees to ability to pay. However, there are a number of viable alternatives to accomplishing the same objective.

• **Straight percentage system.** YWCA Child Care, in El Paso, Texas, has implemented one of the simplest and fairest approaches. All non-Title XX parents whose incomes fall within certain limits have their weekly fee set at 2% of their gross monthly income. These fees work out to be 8.7% of a family's gross income.

• **Fee reduction formula.** The Camden-Kershaw County Child Care Center, in Camden, South Carolina, uses a simple formula to compute a reduced fee for all families falling below a set income level. The weekly fee is computed by dividing the gross family weekly income by the number in the family times 5. For example, a family of 4 would pay a weekly fee of $12 ($240 ÷ 4 x 5 = $12).

• **Negotiated fee.** An after-school program in Brookline, Massachusetts, negotiated fee reductions on an individual basis. Parents seeking a reduction met in private with a representative of the board. She simply asked the parents to state what fee they believed they could afford to pay. The exact amount was generally discussed for about five minutes, and both

parties agreed to a final fee. When available subsidies were exhausted, no more reductions were offered. As it turned out, few parents asked for large fee reductions.

• **Sliding fee scholarships.** The Government Center Child Care Center, in Boston, Massachusetts, has combined a sliding fee scale system with a scholarship approach. The center developed a fee scale similar to the "Straight Percentage Scale" in Table 3. However, this scale is not automatically applied in computing all families' fees. Instead, any family enrolling in the center can apply for a scholarship. When a family applies, its income is determined and then (using the fee scale system) the amount of their fee reduction, if any, is established. This fee reduction is their scholarship.

One advantage of the sliding fee scholarship approach is that it does not commit the center to reduced fee levels. Under the standard fee scale approach, a center establishes a fee scale and publishes this as the center's fee plan. If this center overcommits to too many low fees and exhausts its available funds, it is in a bind. It either must recompute all families' fees or temporarily suspend the fee scale.

Under the scholarship approach, on the other hand, the fee scale is only a tool for computing scholarships. When the scholarship fund is exhausted, no more scholarships are awarded. The center's published fees are the full fees and these need not be changed.

Tried and True Techniques for Collecting Fees

Ideas from center directors

Collecting overdue fees is one of those ugly jobs that no center director enjoys. But directors who are lax in collecting fees often are confronted with even uglier tasks — raising fees or cutting salaries to make up for lost revenues due to unpaid fees. Happily, such dire measures can be avoided by adopting and consistently enforcing the following fee collection procedures. These procedures have been employed with great success by the directors listed at the end of this article.

• Spell out fee policies at enrollment

When parents are enrolling their children, they should be informed that the center cannot operate with stability unless all fees are paid on time. Fee payment schedules and procedures should be clearly outlined verbally and then presented to the parents in writing. This discussion should cover not only when and how to pay fees, but also what actions the center will take when fees are late, and what steps parents can take when they are caught in a crisis and know they will have difficulty paying fees in a timely manner. To avoid future misunderstandings and disputes, some centers have parents sign a copy of a fee policies statement (which includes the actual fee for their child) at enrollment.

• Keep in close touch with all parents

Parents who are most likely to fall behind in paying fees are either those who are unhappy with the program and feel little motivation to pay their fees on time or those parents who are experiencing personal difficulties and feel uncomfortable about asking for special consideration. Therefore, one of the most effective steps you can take to avoid fee delinquencies is to maintain good relationships with parents.

If the director keeps in close contact with the parents, she will be able to detect signs of disgruntlement early and deal with them before they get out of hand. Likewise, if a director is on good terms with parents, they will feel more comfortable approaching her if they are in difficult straits and need to make some special arrangements on deferring fee payments.

• Be alert for freeloaders

Directors in several communities have reported instances where a parent will enroll a child in a center for several months without paying the fee and then transfer the child to another center and then to another. Directors try to screen out such parents by checking up on parents who seem overly eager to enroll their children without even seeing the program. In some communities, directors have curtailed this practice by exchanging names of parents who leave without paying fees.

• Make it easy to pay

The more trouble parents have to go to in order to pay fees, the more likely they are to delay doing so. If fees are to be paid to the director, for example, and the director is frequently on the phone or not to be found, this will frustrate parents and result in payment lapses.

Many centers have locked metal boxes with slots so that parents can drop their checks off effortlessly when they come to pick up their children. One center has a desk in its reception area so that parents can sit down and write out their checks. Other centers send out invoices with stamped return address envelopes so that all parents have to do is to slip the check in the envelope and drop it in a mail box.

Still other centers have found that parents appreciate the option of paying fees with a commercial credit card. Such a system gives parents the option of deferring their payments on the credit card. Meanwhile, the center is paid in cash for charge slips it turns in (less a typical 5% service charge) to the bank.

• Collect fees in advance

To encourage the timely payment of fees, most centers have adopted a policy of requiring fees to be paid before service is provided. Some centers require fees for an upcoming month to be paid in full by the first of the month, while others collect fees for the up-coming week on Monday of that week.

From an administrative point of view, collecting fees for a month in advance is clearly advantageous. With monthly fees, the center's income for the month is known and on hand early in the month. Also there are one-fourth the checks to process. In many communities, however, parents find it difficult to pay for a full month in advance and prefer the weekly fees. Some centers have dealt with this dilemma by establishing a monthly fee policy and then working out biweekly or weekly fees for parents for whom the monthly fees are a hardship.

For those centers that currently collect fees after the fact, we have some good news. Centers that have converted from post-payment to pre-payment policies have experienced little resistance from parents when the reasons for the change were clearly explained.

• Collect a deposit

It is now common practice for centers to collect at enrollment the first month's fee plus a deposit of one additional month's fee. This deposit is held and applied toward the fee for the last month. This policy helps avoid the common practice of not paying the last month's fee when a child is removed from a program.

Be sure to check into applicable state laws regarding the collection of deposits. These laws may require that interest be paid to parents for the deposit while it is in the hands of the organization.

• Enforce late payment penalties.

Many centers have successfully discouraged late payments by charging penalties. A center collecting fees on a weekly basis, for example, will typically charge a penalty of $5 for fees received later than Tuesday.

Once again, it is important to review your penalty in light of applicable state laws. Some centers have had the legality of their penalties challenged as being interest charged in excess of permitted limits. To avoid this complication, some centers raise their fees by a small amount and offer reduced fees for parents paying on time.

• Offer to deal with problems in advance

All the centers surveyed for this article go out of their way to assist families experiencing temporary financial difficulties. As one director observed, "We don't believe that getting rid of problems is the answer. We try to stick with families having difficulties — we do not want to compound their problems. In ten years we have rarely lost any money in operating this way."

Some centers have a small scholarship fund set aside so that fees for families in crisis can be partially subsidized for short time periods. Some centers lower fees temporarily with the understanding (agreed to in writing) that the amount of the reduction will be made up over a set period of time when the crisis is over. Other centers assist families in securing assistance from public agencies, church groups, or other charitable organizations.

All centers stress from the day parents enroll their children that they will only be able to be flexible in times of family crisis if the center is notified about a problem immediately. If a parent is reluctant to discuss a problem and starts falling way behind in fees, the center may have few options to offer.

• Act quickly on delinquencies

Directors must be vigilant to keep overdue fees from turning into bad debts. By acting immediately when an account becomes overdue, you can often nip a problem in the bud. If you wait too long, the amount of money overdue may become so large that it is almost impossible for a family to pay it off.

If you are reluctant to press parents when fees are overdue, this can also set a dangerous precedent. When people don't have enough money to pay all of their bills, they tend to defer paying whatever bills they can without resistance. If they know they can pay their fee to your center a week late without any consequence, they are more likely to do so.

It is especially important to be vigilant as summer approaches. This is often the point at which delinquencies occur. Parents planning to move or withdraw their child for any other reason may be tempted to avoid paying their final bills knowing that they soon will have no need of your services.

For a parent who is late only rarely, a written notice of delinquency will probably suffice. However, for chronic late payers, immediate personal contact may be required.

Those who make a practice of not paying bills on time are not likely to be influenced by form letters, no matter how threatening.

When contacting a delinquent parent, it is important not to show anger or disrespect. Work at maintaining the dignity of the parent, and your dignity will remain intact.

• Offer repayment options

If a parent falls behind, it may not be the best strategy to insist that the overdue amount be paid in one lump sum. Centers should negotiate a realistic repayment plan with parents of limited means. If a parent is experiencing financial difficulty, he may be unable to pay off a large debt all at once; but he may be able to pay it off gradually by paying a little extra with every fee payment. Or parents may agree to take out a loan in order to pay off the debt.

• Have parents sign a promissory note

When parents agree to pay delinquent fees of a substantial nature, you should follow up on their expressed willingness by asking them to sign a promissory note. A typical promissory note establishes interest amounts for late payments and specifies that all collection costs are the responsibility of the debtor. (Standard forms for promissory notes can be purchased at most office supply stores.) A key advantage to having a signed promissory note is that it fixes the amount owed, thus strengthening your case if legal action is required.

• Minimize bad check losses

Bounced checks are not a serious problem for small businesses that know their customers well. However, from time to time all centers have customers' checks returned by the bank. Several procedures can be implemented to minimize losses from bad checks. First, before depositing checks, make sure that they are signed, that the date is correct, and that the printed and written amounts are correct. Second, try to deposit checks on the same day that they are received — this reduces the possibility that checks will be returned due to insufficient funds or because an account was closed. Third, when checks are returned, notify parents immediately to give them the opportunity to pay in cash or to deposit additional funds into their account.

• Sue in small claims court

In extreme cases, some centers have found it necessary to sue parents in small claims court to collect delinquent fees. The advantage of suing in small claims court is that they operate informally — lawyers aren't required; both parties simply discuss the case with a judge. There are some disadvantages, however. First, when a case is scheduled, the center may be required to have a representative in court, possibly for a full day, waiting for the case to be heard. Second, winning a judgment by no means guarantees that you will collect the debt, as the court itself has no means of enforcing its decisions. One center has found it necessary to go to the local sheriff to have judgments enforced.

The act of going to small claims court may have more impact than the collection of a single debt. If parents know that you are willing to go to court, they may be less likely to push you to that extreme.

• Stop providing care

The ultimate penalty, when all remedies have been exhausted, is to stop providing child care for families who fail to pay their fees. Most centers have seldom, if ever, found it necessary to exercise this option, as its mere threat is often sufficient to produce action. Other centers, in extreme cases, have refused to accept children for care until parents paid overdue fees and have achieved positive results with such steps.

While this laundry list of fee collection procedures may seem a bit extreme, having them in place does make a difference. Centers that consistently enforce the early steps in the process seldom need to use the sterner measures. Centers that demonstrate a willingness to go all the way seldom experience losses.

To conclude with a positive example, one large center that implemented fee collection procedures such as these has not lost a single penny in delinquent fees in five years.

Credits

The following center directors provided ideas for this article: Tracy Altzeni, Apple Tree Children's Centers, Urbandale, Iowa; Phil Roberson, Swan Lake Children's Center, Bartlesville, Oklahoma; Charles Wilson, Magic Years Learning Center, Webster, Texas; Elizabeth Schilling, Creative Child Care, Columbus, Ohio; Jeanne Sasaran, Loma Alta Preschool, San Diego, California; Carl Staley, United Day Care Services, Greensboro, North Carolina; Charlene Richardson, Child Development Center, Chula Vista, California; and Margaret Bridgers, Margaret Ann Nursery School, Lexington, Kentucky.

How Centers Spend Money on Quality

by John Morris and Suzanne Helburn

*I s there a difference in the budgets of centers providing better quality care? What do their budgets look like compared to centers providing lower quality care? Data from a recent study — **Cost, Quality, and Child Outcomes in Child Care Centers** (CQO) — allowed us to construct budgets comparing center cost breakdowns (see Table 1 on page 79) by quality of service provided.*

Briefly, we found that better quality centers spend more per child on staff wages, staff benefits, and administrative salaries and benefits than centers providing lower quality. There is little overall difference in costs per child on other expenses such as for facilities, materials, and food.

Furthermore, the higher labor and management costs per child carry through to proportionately higher total cost rather than to a different distribution of costs. The higher total cost per child was also reflected in proportionately higher total revenue, so that good quality centers offset higher total cost per child with higher total revenue. However, on average, surplus or profit per child did not differ significantly between lower and higher quality centers, indicating that there is little financial reward for providing higher quality. We did find differences in finances by level of quality among the three sectors of for profit, independent non profit, and church-affiliated centers that raise questions about the prevalence of mediocre care in general in the industry.

About the Study

The CQO study involved an in-depth study of 401 child care centers in four states: Los Angeles in California, Colorado, Connecticut, and North Carolina. Extensive financial and quality data were collected in the spring of 1993 on a random sample of 50 for profit and 50 non profit centers in each state through on-site interviews with center directors or owners and day-long observations by trained observers of two randomly selected classrooms where possible — one infant/toddler and one preschool room.

Process quality — emphasizing health and safety characteristics, caregiving, developmentally appropriate activities, and children's interactions with each other and with adults — was measured through three widely used observation instruments: the Early Childhood Environment Rating Scale (ECERS, Harms and Clifford, 1980) or the Infant/ Toddler Environment Rating Scale (ITERS, Harms, Cryer, and Clifford, 1990); the Caregiver

Table 1
Budgets for Higher and Lower Quality Centers
(Values Per Child Hour and Annual Figures)

Expense Category	Per Child Hour		Annual Values	
	Higher Quality	Lower Quality	Higher Quality	Lower Quality
Classroom staff wages*	$1.18	$0.93	$157,999	$118,423
Classroom staff benefits*	0.22	0.15	29,381	18,590
Administration salary and benefits	0.37	0.29	36,791	27,823
Staff training	0.01	0.01	1,526	1,060
Contract labor	0.03	0.03	3,618	3,160
Occupancy	0.28	0.23	38,352	30,645
Food cost	0.09	0.09	12,395	12,417
Insurance	0.03	0.03	3,685	3,753
Other operating cost	0.18	0.16	22,490	20,152
Overhead	0.01	0.03	2,291	3,266
TOTAL COST*	$2.38	$1.94	$306,874	$237,726
TOTAL REVENUE*	2.44	2.00	315,626	253,132
Surplus or deficit**	$0.06	$0.06	$8,752	$15,406
Total donations	$0.23	$0.20	$26,560	$19,988
FTE children			70	66

*Significant difference at 5% level.

**Annual mean surplus is affected by extreme values in size of center.

Interaction Scale (CIS, Arnett, 1989); and the Teacher Involvement Scale (TIS, Howes and Stewart, 1987).

ECERS and ITERS observations are scored from 1 to 7 based on about 35 aspects of quality. We used an average of these individual scores to score each room. An overall index of quality was constructed for each center combining scores for both observed rooms as well as for the CIS and TIS scores. Like ECERS and ITERS, the overall index was scaled from 1 to 7.

The scale is interpreted as follows:

1 — Inadequate: Health and safety needs not met; no warmth or support from adults observed; no learning encouraged.

3 — Minimal: Basic health and safety needs met; a little warmth and support provided by adults; few learning experiences.

5 — Good: Health and safety needs fully met; warmth and support for all children; learning in many ways through interesting activities.

7 — Excellent: Everything in "good" plus children encouraged to become independent; teacher plans for children's individual learning needs; adults have close relations with each child.

To study differences in center costs among lower and higher quality centers, we divided centers into two groups. Centers were categorized as providing higher quality if either their average ITERS and ECERS score *or* their overall quality index score was 4.5 or higher. Other centers were classified in the lower quality category.

By this criterion, 148 centers provided higher quality and 253 provided lower quality.

Budgets for Higher and Lower Quality Centers

Table 1 shows budgets for higher and lower quality centers in two ways. Columns 1 and 2 give costs, revenue, surplus (profit), and value of donations per child hour, and columns 3 and 4 give annual budget estimates for the average center.

In order to provide a more accurate estimate of the effect of quality, it is necessary to eliminate the effects of other cost factors — in particular, regional differences, the impact of profit status, and of differing age compositions of children served.

The figures in Table 1 represent mean values, holding constant region and profit status (for profit, independent non profit, and church-affiliated). Although the percentage of center FTE composed of preschool children affects cost per child, it does not have much effect on average cost comparisons between lower and higher quality centers. Asterisks identify figures that show statistically significant differences in the two quality groups.

Higher quality centers served slightly more children (70 FTE compared to 66). The budgets reflect the study's findings that higher quality teaching staff, better adult-child ratios, and lower staff turnover (implying higher wages) lead to higher quality care. Both staff wages and staff benefits were significantly higher in higher quality centers. They totaled $1.40 per child hour in the higher quality centers but only $1.08 in the lower quality centers.

The study also showed that administrator tenure at the center and prior experience, as well as their effective involvement in curriculum planning, lead to higher

quality. Table 1 shows that administrator salaries and benefits totaled 37¢ per child hour in higher quality centers and 29¢ per child hour in lower quality centers. (This figure includes an imputed salary for owner-operators who reported no salary and salaries and benefits for all owners, directors, and curriculum coordinators.)

The study also showed that indoor square footage per child was positively related to quality and the budget shows a similar difference, although this difference is not statistically significant. Other than occupancy, other non-labor costs were almost identical in the two groups and combine for less than 20% of the total cost.

Total cost and total revenue were both significantly higher in higher quality centers, both by 44¢ per child hour — that is, on average, the higher quality cost about 20% more than the lower quality centers. Interestingly, there was no difference in surplus per child hour of 6¢ per child hour. The two columns showing annual surplus do appear to show a higher average surplus in lower quality centers despite their slightly smaller size.

This appears to be the effect of a small number of very large and profitable mediocre centers. It does not appear to be indicative of the situation for most centers. In general, these results seem to indicate that higher quality centers can recover their higher costs through higher revenues, but, on average, there were no financial gains from higher quality.

Sector Differences

We also investigated possible differences in the cost of providing quality by centers with different ownership and found such differences among church-related centers, secular non profit centers, and for profit centers.

Not too surprisingly, for profit centers showed the lowest labor costs ($1.42 for higher quality and $1.15 for lower quality) and secular non profits the highest ($1.96 and $1.75). Perhaps more interestingly, higher quality church-related centers had almost the highest labor costs of all ($1.94), while labor cost per child hour for lower quality church-related centers were among the lowest ($1.23).

A similar difference between higher and lower quality centers was apparent for non-labor costs. Higher quality church centers spent 18¢ more per child hour on non-labor costs than lower quality church-related centers. By contrast, higher quality for profit centers spent only 9¢ extra and higher quality secular non profit centers actually spent 14¢ per child hour less on non-labor costs than lower quality secular non profits. Nearly all of these differences were in occupancy costs, not program. Regardless of quality, for profit centers had higher non-labor costs than either group of non profits.

These differences may reflect differences in subsidies. Higher quality secular non profits received 16¢ per child hour more than lower quality secular non profits, almost the difference in costs. Even among for profits, the higher quality centers averaged 5¢ per child hour more subsidies than lower quality non profits, adding to the difference in costs. Among church-related centers, however, the lower quality centers received 12¢ per child hour more subsidies.

The bottom line was that lower quality church-related centers, with a total cost of $1.54 per child hour, were the cheapest source of child care in the study, and they generated a surplus averaging 10¢ per child hour. For profit centers averaged about $2.00 per child hour ($2.20 for higher quality and $1.86 for lower) and provided the lowest cost (not necessarily the lowest fee) high quality care. The secular non profits and the higher quality church-related centers averaged over $2.40 per child hour.

What may be happening in the church-related center sector is that some churches are subsidizing parents' affordability at the expense of quality, while others promote quality and are very similar, financially, to other non profit centers. In the secular non profit sector, better quality centers seem to have higher donations than lower quality secular centers, but otherwise there is not much difference in finances within this sector.

Conclusions

1. There is a cost to improving quality in child care, but it is small except in church-related centers.

2. Higher quality centers put their extra dollars into labor and management primarily — not facilities, supplies, or program.

3. The higher cost of providing quality was offset by higher revenue — that is, one can provide higher quality without a financial penalty, but there is little financial reward.

4. Higher quality centers were no smaller than lower quality centers.

5. For profit centers provided the cheapest higher quality care and churches provided the cheapest lower quality care.

6. Lower quality church centers received higher subsidies than higher quality church centers, and may be focusing on affordability for parents more than quality.

7. Compared to lower quality secular non profit centers, higher quality secular non profits received more subsidies, but their costs (including subsidies) were similar, suggesting an efficient allocation of subsidies to provide quality — that is, the subsidies seem to have gone to the right centers within this group.

8. The quality within sectors is not related to cost in secular non profit centers. Higher quality increases cost only modestly in for profit centers. There is a large difference in cost for quality in the church sector. These extra costs are covered by extra revenues, except in the church sector. If this is the case, why don't centers in the secular non profit and for profit sectors provide better quality on average? Perhaps there is a shortage of highly skilled directors.

References

Arnett, J. "Caregivers in Day Care Centers: Does Training Matter?" *Journal of Applied Developmental Psychology*, 10, 1989, 541-552.

Harms, T. and R. M. Clifford. *Early Childhood Environment Rating Scale.* New York: Teachers College Press, 1980.

Harms, T., D. Cryer, and R. M. Clifford. *Infant/Toddler Environment Rating Scale.* New York: Teachers College Press, 1990.

Howes, C. and P. Stewart. "Child's Play with Adults, Toys and Peers: An Examination of Family and Child Care Influences." *Developmental Psychology*, 23, 1987, 423-430.

John Morris is professor of economics at the University of Colorado at Denver. He served as economist on the **Cost, Quality, and Child Outcomes Study** *as principal investigator of numerous projects examining the economics of various social services, in particular, of child care.*

Suzanne Helburn is professor emeritus of economics at the University of Colorado at Denver and was the coordinator and one of the principal investigators for the **Cost, Quality, and Child Outcomes in Child Care Centers Study** *on which results of this article are based.*

Fundraising Strategies

*"The components of a successful
fundraising effort are a
program effectively addressing a
recognized need,
an audience of donors sympathetic
to the cause, and a strategy
that brings the donors
and the program together."*

Where the Bucks Are: Sources for Funds to Grow Your Child Care Business

by Keith Stephens

Starting a child care business and building it up into a profitable operation requires entrepreneurial skills, hard work, determination to provide a quality service, respect for the consumer, and good luck. And, in most cases, it requires an infusion of money from the outside.

Finding the money you need to finance the process of growth can be a frustrating, fruitless experience unless you do your homework. Prior to hitting the streets looking for money, you need to put together a solid business plan which spells out where your business is headed, how you will do it, benchmarks for judging your progress, and why you will be successful. No one will give you money unless you can assure them of what you expect to accomplish — and can demonstrate a reasonable expectation for a solid, profitable return.

Then you need to identify likely sources of money. There are a wide range of financing alternatives to consider, but each is best suited to businesses at different growth stages. People get in trouble when they pursue the wrong source at the wrong time.

Your chances of success are improved by concentrating your energies on a source that is likely to produce results. To help you sort out what sources make the most sense at what point, I have discussed below characteristics of the most common sources of funds for a for profit child care business.

Tapping Friends and Relatives

Friends and relatives are the money source of first and last resort for entrepreneurs just setting out to make their mark in the world. When all you have is a dream, it is very difficult to attract investments from conventional sources of money. As enthusiastic as you may be about your dream, potential investors will primarily be looking at economic return. Weighted heavily against you are the all too familiar statistics showing that most new small businesses fail. As a result, those starting from scratch must turn to the people who are most likely to be supportive — friends and relatives.

Advantages:

• **Friends and relatives are most likely to be receptive** to your plans because they know you and have more reason to be confident that you will succeed.

• **The money will come with fewer strings attached.** Since people close to you will invest in you on faith, they are not likely to insist on placing formal restrictions on how you use the money — or on how you run the business.

• **Most often they will invest for equity only.** This means that you will not be encumbered by a tight repayment schedule or interest payments.

• **You will probably not suffer serious economic repercussions** if your business doesn't pan out and you don't repay the money. Friends and relatives are much less likely than bankers or investors to press for repayment.

Disadvantages:

• **The emotional pressure can be overwhelming.** You don't want to fail for the people who are closest to you. The personal embarrassment is greater if your business is failing and you are losing the money and the respect (you assume) of the friends and relatives who were counting on you. For example, if you lose $50,000 borrowed from your parents and it turns out this was their retirement fund, the emotional cost involved can be very, very high. In many cases, complete alienation results.

• **You are not likely to raise as much money** via this route as you would from conventional money sources, unless you are one of those rare individuals blessed with rich relatives who are eager to part with their money. On the other hand, while the $50,000 to $100,000

Table 1
Types of Business Financing

Child care businesses utilize outside financing for two general purposes:

To finance the business itself: Money needed for the total operation of the business in order to facilitate growth. This article explores options available for this purpose.

To purchase real estate: Financing required for the purchase of land and real property. The real estate serves as collateral. A wide range of real estate financing vehicles are available, such as conventional bank mortgages, loans from insurance companies, and investments made through limited partnership arrangements.

There are two general types of financing available:

Equity investments: Money that is invested in your business in exchange for a share of the ownership. Money is invested with the expectation that a return will be realized in the future as the value of one's share of the business appreciates.

Loans: Money advanced to a business with a formal repayment schedule. Return is realized from interest charged for the use of the money.

---

that is the most that you are likely to secure from friends and relatives will not enable you to launch a national chain, it should be sufficient seed money to start a single center.

Other Considerations:

In most cases, it is best to treat money raised from friends and relatives as an investment in the company. Give everybody stock in the company. If your business is successful, everyone will get a stock dividend or be bought out by someone else (hopefully at a nice profit). If the business fails, they will have gambled and lost.

On the other hand, if for some reason you desire to retain 100%

of the stock, you would want to treat the money received as a loan with an agreed upon repayment schedule and rate of interest. While this will place you under a stronger obligation to repay the money, it will enable you to exercise full control of the business.

Finding an Angel — A Private Investor

An angel is a wealthy individual who you persuade to invest in your business. This approach is similar to convincing a friend to invest, although — since this individual will not necessarily know you personally — your personal credibility as well as that of your business plan will be subject to much tighter scrutiny.

Advantages:

• **A private investor will be more emotionally removed** from you than a friend or relative. Your relationship can operate in a more businesslike fashion, without the emotional undercurrents of a personal relationship.

• **An angel will probably not insist on gaining control** of the business. Most likely he or she will not have the time or inclination to become immersed in everyday decisionmaking.

• **You are likely to have access to more money** from a wealthy individual than from friends and relatives.

• **An angel will not necessarily be looking for a quick return**, so you will not be pressured to generate dramatic profits immediately. More likely, the private investor will be looking for a reasonable return three to seven years in the future when you sell the business or go public.

Disadvantages:

• **A private individual will be harder to win over** than friends and relatives. You will need to prove yourself and the viability of your plan.

• **He or she will want more protection.** One way to structure a more attractive deal for a private investor is to offer preferred stock. A preferred class of stock could offer many privileges to this individual: a stated rate of return, some preference upon liquidation, some preference in terms of dividends (that he/should would receive dividends before you did, for example), the right to move from preferred stock to common stock, or the right to pick up voting privileges to more actively protect his/her investment if the business is not doing well.

• **More documentation and more legal work will be involved** in putting the transaction together.

• **The final arrangement will likely be much more tightly structured** than one with a friend or relative. There will be more restrictions on how you spend the money and run the business, such as frequent reporting on your progress, participation in approval of the budget and major fixed asset purchases, limits on expenses, and limits on your salary.

Other Considerations:

How do you find an angel? By talking to your banker (most larger banks have something akin to an executive banking section for wealthy individuals), your lawyer (particularly lawyers in bigger law firms which have contact with affluent individuals), your accountant, and representatives of trust companies and investment management services (that manage assets for other people); by going to the right business meetings and belonging to the right community organizations; and by advertising in the business or classified section in the newspaper. In all these ways you will be seeking referrals which will lead you to an individual who is willing and able to put up the kind of money you need.

Making a Private Placement

A formalized method of securing private investors is the private placement. Under this procedure, you go out to the business or investment community with a business plan and offer to sell stock in your company. Typically the purpose of a private placement is to attract money from a number of people beyond your inner circle of friends and relatives.

A private placement is a less rigorous procedure for selling stock than a public offering. The rules governing private placements are less involved, and the disclosure requirements less stringent. However, there are specific limitations on how much can be raised in this manner, and who can invest. You will need to consult your lawyer regarding rules and regulations defining these limitations.

Advantages:

• **You are spreading the risk.** By selling shares in your company to a number of investors, the degree of risk each one is being exposed to is less than if one individual was making the whole investment. People may be more willing to invest if they know that others are willing to do so also.

• **A greater amount of money can be raised**, in most cases, through a private placement than through private individuals.

• **You can retain final control.** While you are selling shares in your business in order to generate capital, you can normally retain at least 51% of the stock yourself.

• **This is a long-term investment.** Investors are typically looking for a payoff coming not from annual earnings but from resale of the company either to someone else or to the public through a stock offering (so their 3% share in a $1,750,000 company becomes 3% of a $10,000,000 sale). Normally, investors expect a return in a three to seven year time frame. Thus there will not be pressure to achieve an immediate high level of profitability. However, there will be the expectation that the company grow steadily and significantly.

Disadvantages:

• **This is not a do-it-yourself project.** You will need to hire a lawyer to prepare a form of prospectus known as a private placement memorandum. In this document you spell out for prospective investors the nature of your company and the business that you are engaged in, the key people in your company, your future plans, your past financial performance and future financial projections, and your money needs.

• **This is not an appropriate vehicle for a small business** planning for modest growth. Even if you perform most of the paperwork and legwork yourself, legal fees can run anywhere from $10,000 to $20,000. With this built in cost of raising the money, it means that for raising anything under $200,000, this would not be a practical vehicle. This is not for single centers looking to add one or two locations. It is more applicable if you are operating three or four centers profitably and can present a creditable plan for growing significantly.

• **This is not an appropriate vehicle for a new business.** Typically

---

Table 2
Financing Under Different Stages of Development

Stage of Organizational Development	Likely Financing Sources
Start-Up Stage	
• Organization is only in the idea stage.	Self, friends, or relatives
• No service is being delivered.	Private sources
• This represents a high risk investment.	
• A limited source of funds is available.	
First Stage	
• Organization is now delivering a service.	Venture capital
• It has proven that it can sell in the marketplace.	Private placement
• Profitable operations are still at least two years away.	
Second Stage	
• Organization is up and running.	Venture capital
• It is marketing its service with a degree of success.	Private offering
• It needs funds for expansion.	Public offering
	Bank
Third Stage	
• Organization is running well.	Public offering
• It is generating steady profits.	Bank
• It needs additional capital to continue its rapid growth.	
Mature Stage	
• Organization is running well.	Bank
• It is generating steady profits.	Insurance company
• It has been able to manage in both up and down business cycles.	Public offering
• It generates sufficient cash flow to handle most of its working capital needs.	
• Its services are well accepted by the marketplace.	

you need to be up and running in order to establish credibility. In some cases, primarily in the high tech arena, it can be a vehicle for start-up, but in this case you will need a strong sell on yourself.

• **This is a time consuming process.** It will require that you take time away from your business. This means that you must be able to set your business up in such a manner that it can run without you during this period. If not, you may see your business go down the drain before you get the investment to make it grow.

• **You must be prepared to lose** the time and money you invest in the process. There is a high likelihood that the deal will fall through. Therefore, the legal fees and the time you invest in the effort will go for naught.

Other Considerations:

Once your private placement memorandum is complete, you can conceivably sell it yourself by tracking down likely prospects and pitching it to them on a one-to-one basis. You are more likely to experience success, however, if you enlist professional assistance. Often you can find a small local brokerage firm, a local investment banking firm, or a local financial management firm that is willing to take on the sales effort for you. What they end up doing is placing your shares with their clients. Financial planners, who have emerged in the last few years, are a good vehicle for taking your plan and presenting it.

Keep in mind that any investment professional will expect a commission in the 5% to 10% range. In

addition, you must recognize that they see a multitude of plans. You must make yours stand out from the crowd. Finding a lawyer who is experienced in doing private placement deals will be most helpful here.

Borrowing from a Bank

Your friendly neighborhood banker is often the first person you think of when you need money. Unfortunately, you are likely to discover that this friendliness is only skin deep when you come asking for money to grow a business. While banks have tremendous assets at their disposal, they are not inclined to risk these assets on any business that is not already well established. However, at various stages in your growth, bank financing is feasible and desirable.

Advantages:

• **Banks are easy to find.** Bankers love to have deals brought to them to look over. (It's amazing how positive they are at the first interview, how difficult they are to deal with after that, and how cold they are when they turn you down.)

• **The methodology for dealing with banks is clearly defined.** From the very start, it is clear what banks will lend money for, what hoops you will have to jump through to get it, and how the deal can be structured.

• **Banks can be very helpful** to you in your business. They have trained people who look at numerous businesses and see how they perform. They routinely analyze your financial statements and compare them with other industries. If you can see these comparisons and

the financial ratios they develop on your business, this can be quite useful to you.

• **Banks have several financing vehicles** to employ: working capital loans when you need more money in your business, and have the profitability to support it; asset financing when you want to grow your business, but need money to buy new equipment, etc.; real estate construction funding when you want to construct a new facility or remodel your old center; and mortgage financing when you want to purchase or refinance your property.

• **The amount of money obtainable is limited only by your ability to qualify.** Loans can range from $500 personal loans to commercial loans for billions of dollars. Most independent banks will be limited to the $200,000 to $300,000 range, but this should meet the needs of most center operators.

• **You don't have to give them part of your company.** Banks are not equity investors, they are lenders. They will insist upon a tight repayment schedule, not a share of your business.

Disadvantages:

• **Banks are very conservative.** Banks are tightly regulated and closely scrutinized, and this forces them to be conservative. A banker is thinking at all times, "What can go wrong?" We, as entrepreneurs, think of all the things that will go well. It is important to know how a banker thinks and tailor your presentation accordingly.

• **Banks rarely give long-term loans.** You can get term loans in the three to five year range, but seldom are they willing to go beyond that (with the exception of mortgages). A common procedure is to write a loan with a five to seven year payment schedule, with a single large payment at the end of every year. This gives them the leverage to review the loan every year to determine if it should be renewed.

• **Banks will closely monitor your business.** They will periodically want to see your financial statements and, if you start falling behind, will ask for more frequent and detailed reports. This can become onerous if your record-keeping is haphazard or done in an unconventional way.

• **Banks are professionals at collecting money.** In the event you fall behind, they can make it reasonably difficult for you.

Other Considerations:

When evaluating your loan request, bankers will take a close look at the three c's of banking: *character, credit,* and *collateral.* Is the person running the business competent and trustworthy? Does the business have a solid credit history? Are there sufficient assets in the business to secure the loan? Almost always, you will be asked to provide a personal guarantee.

These criteria tend to work against businesses just starting out, or those that are struggling. In addition, the stipulation that investments be secured by hard assets can be a problem in child care where there is no inventory, no receivables, and few tangible assets (outside of property) which a bank would view as marketable.

Pursuing Venture Capitalists

In recent years, most of the glamour in venture capital has gone to high tech industries. However, now that growth in this area has leveled off, venture capitalists are looking around for other hot industries. And child care is one industry that has started to attract their attention.

Companies that venture capitalists find appealing are not yet at the bankable stage. Sometimes they are start-up companies, but more likely they are already organized and just starting to show a potential for dramatic growth. What these companies need is an infusion of money to turn this potential into a reality.

Advantages:

• **They will help you grow.** Because venture capitalists are in the business of growing companies, they have talent on hand to assist you in managing your business. They are going to be actively involved in protecting their investment.

• **Venture capitalists can make substantial investments.** Because of all the investigative work that goes into making investment decisions, they are not interested in any deal for less than $250,000. Venture capital is not a viable source of money for small companies. It is only a realistic possibility for a business with aspirations of becoming a regional or national chain with around 50 centers.

Disadvantages:

• **Venture capitalists are hard to find.** They are not on every street

corner like banks. However, lists are available from *Inc.* and *Money* magazines.

• **Dealing with a venture capitalist can be an intimidating process.** They won't know you, and won't have any confidence in what you can accomplish. You will need to convince them that you are worthy of their trust.

• **You will need to sell them on the child care industry** as well as on your business. They won't share your dream. When you say *child care,* they will say *insurance problem.* You will have had to do your homework well to make a convincing case for them to invest in a soft service industry that they won't understand.

• **You will have to give away a big hunk of your company and you will be under the gun to perform.** They will want seats on the board of directors, and they continually will want to know what is going on. You can retain control, but only if things are going as planned. In all likelihood, they will insist upon provisions that will improve their influence over the company if things don't go well.

Other Considerations:

A venture capital firm is absolutely going to want to know "How are we going to get out of this deal?" If you can't demonstrate to them, with a high degree of certainty, that within three to five years they will be able to walk away from the deal with a healthy profit, they won't even talk to you.

They are not looking for dividends paid out of profits. They're looking for the return that comes from building a company and then disposing of it. The return they expect from any one investment is in the range of 50% to 60% per year. In other words, if they put in $1 million they would expect $10 million back at the end of five years.

Approaching Insurance Companies

Insurance companies are not a likely funding source for garden variety child care businesses. The financing vehicles they prefer are suited to massive real estate investments. For the most part, insurance companies won't even talk to you if you're looking for less than $1 million. On the other hand, if you are an established regional chain needing $12 million to build 20 centers at $600,000 apiece, an insurance company would be an appropriate vehicle for arranging for that investment in one fell swoop.

While insurance companies will consider some equity arrangements, they are primarily interested in real estate deals. Like banks, they are not risk takers; but because of the size of their investments, they can sometimes offer better interest rates, and they can be somewhat more flexible in how they structure the deal.

Making a Public Offering

A public offering is a vehicle for mature companies that want to finance growth or a change in ownership. This is a route that would only make sense for regional or national chains with 50 or more centers looking to raise at least $10 million.

Investors in a public offering would be interested in a return on earnings — your profitability is going to determine what price you can get for your stock.

You could have a public offering for a start-up venture, but you would need one of the regional or national brokerage firms to work with you on it, and it is unlikely that you could sell them on the idea. On the other hand, a public offering would be an appropriate route if an individual had built up a chain of 50 centers and wanted to sell them, yet wanted to stay involved in the day-to-day management.

Keith Stephens, a CPA, is the former president of Palo Alto Preschools, once the country's largest privately owned child care chain, and past president of the National Association for Child Care Management.

Keys to Success in Raising Funds

by Roger Neugebauer

Child Care Information Exchange *has surveyed over 100 child care centers about their successful, as well as their disastrous, fundraising projects. From the experiences of these centers, the nine factors described below have emerged as keys to successful fundraisers.*

Define Your Purpose

The willingness of staff members, parents, volunteers, and members of the community to give their support to a fundraiser will be enhanced to the extent that the need for funds is clear and important. People need to know that their contribution of time, talents, or resources will make a difference.

Before launching a fundraising effort, therefore, a center should assess whether it is truly necessary and, if so, for what purpose. This purpose should then be identified at the outset of any appeals for support.

Centers have found that the more specifically the purpose can be defined the better. It is easier to generate support for "constructing an outdoor climbing structure" than for "building up the contingency account"; it is more inspiring to contribute towards a "scholarship fund" than towards "general operating expenses."

In child care, fundraisers often have important secondary purposes as well. Centers often utilize these projects to provide publicity for the center and to enhance parent involvement. These purposes should clearly be identified at the outset also, so that the project can

be organized in such a way as to ensure their accomplishment.

A common pitfall here is when a secondary purpose is really the main purpose. Centers sometimes use fundraisers as a gimmick for getting parents involved. This can unnecessarily waste the precious time of parents and can backfire when the parents realize their efforts do not accomplish anything of importance.

Set a Goal

Centers have found it beneficial to set a target amount to be raised each year. Having a financial goal helps planners to gauge the magnitude of the effort required, and to decide the type of activities which are appropriate.

A center needing to raise $500 would not establish a thrift shop, nor would one requiring $6,000 schedule a bake sale. Having a specific dollar goal also is more likely to instill confidence in potential donors that the center knows what it's about.

Once the goal is set, it can also help focus volunteers' efforts if they are kept informed about the progress toward that goal. Some centers even post a chart at the center, much like the thermometer of United Way, which shows volunteers how close they are to accomplishing the goal.

Know the Audience

Who is likely to contribute to your center? The type of fundraising projects a center implements should be appropriate to the project's potential audience.

If your center is known by individuals in your community who have abundant financial resources and who believe in what your center is doing, the direct approach may be best. Contact them, explain your need, and ask for a donation. The direct mail and membership drive described in this publication are examples of this direct approach.

If, on the other hand, your program is known and supported primarily by individuals with scant financial resources, asking for donations may not be realistic. Instead, it may be more appropriate to offer some goods or services in return for people's contributions. The **Thrift Shop** and **Retha's Carry Out** fundraisers (described in "Directors' Fundraising Hits" on page 118) are examples of this indirect approach.

In planning this type of fundraiser, the potential audience needs to be examined even more closely. Who is the potential audience? What goods or services are likely to be of real interest to them? How much are they likely to contribute? You are operating on shaky ground if

you cannot answer these questions with some certainty before planning a fundraiser.

Make It Fun

Select a project that staff and parents are excited about. Most fundraisers depend heavily upon the volunteer work of staff, parents, and board members. The amount of effort these people are likely to invest in a project relates significantly to the extent they are excited about the project.

If the chairperson of a fundraising committee decides that a raffle will be the solution to all the center's financial woes, but parents are none too eager to hustle prizes or tickets, chances are the raffle will fizzle.

Build on Strengths

Try to select a fundraiser that builds on the skills that already exist in the center. Personnel in child care centers have expertise in areas such as child development, child nutrition, children's activities, and parent education.

Examples of fundraisers capitalizing on such skills include the children's entertainment series, as well as gymnastics classes, babysitter training and referral, cookbooks for children, and parenting workshops. A child care center should be most effective and efficient in organizing fundraisers such as these. In addition, such a project can showcase the skills and services of the center to potential supporters and customers.

Look for Repeaters

Centers surveyed noted several reasons for selecting fundraisers

that can be repeated on a regular basis. First, the center can learn from its mistakes. Errors which were made the first time in planning, publicizing, and putting on a project can be eliminated in future reruns, thus saving on wasted energy and resources.

Second, the project will not need to be organized from scratch every time. Press releases, flyers, costumes, booths, or publicity strategies developed the first time can simply be refined rather than reinvented.

Third, the more often a successful project is run, the more effective publicity will be. The **Night On the Town** (described on page 118) has become such a well-known and anticipated annual event that people now rush to sign up as soon as the event is announced in the local paper.

Be Cost Effective

Centers can fall into the trap of thinking that any project that brings in money is worthwhile. However, such reasoning fails to consider the value of staff and volunteer time expended in raising the money.

People's time should be considered as a valuable resource. It should not be squandered on fundraising projects that generate a small return on time invested.

To calculate the return on time investment (R) of any project, simply deduct all expenses (E) incurred in putting on the project (including the value of paid staff time) from total income (I) of the project, then divide the remainder by the total number of hours (T) spent by staff and volunteers on the project:

$$\frac{I - E}{T} = R$$

To illustrate, consider the case of a spring fair held by a nursery school in New England. This school's staff and parents donated about 475 hours of time (T) planning, publicizing, setting up, and operating the fair — and expended $250 in center funds (E) for booths, food, and publicity in order to raise a total of $850 (I) for the center. Plugging this into the formula, it can be seen that for every hour invested in this project the center earned $1.26 in profit:

$$\frac{\$850 - \$250}{475 \text{ hours}} = \$1.26/\text{hour}$$

Even though the project was a "success" in terms of raising a significant chunk of money, the return on the investment of volunteers' time was dreadfully low. Bake sales and dinners are often equally wasteful of volunteers' time.

On the other hand, the fundraisers described starting on page 115 brought returns of anywhere from $25-150/hour. Given the fact that such cost effective projects are quite realistic, a center should certainly think twice about engaging in any project which will return less than $10/hour.

Publicize Aggressively

Centers that have the most success with fundraisers are those which have mastered the art of getting the right message to the right people.

The first step in an effective publicity campaign is clarifying what is being "sold." If the fundraising project is a direct appeal for donations, what is being sold is the cause — people are being asked to give money to a cause they believe in.

For an indirect fundraiser, such as a raffle, a bake sale, or a dinner, it is the product or service that is being sold — the chance to win, the cookies, or the meal. The "message" of all publicity should concentrate heavily on what is being sold.

This right message must also reach the right people. Often in membership drives and appeals for donations, certain professionals — such as doctors, who are deemed most likely to contribute to the center — are singled out for calls.

Likewise, a center which offers a noon luncheon in a downtown area sends flyers around to offices in the neighborhood to alert people who eat lunch out. Effective publicity has much less to do with "how much" than it does with "where."

Centers with sound ongoing fundraising campaigns also take great pains to develop extensive lists of known supporters. Included on this list should be former parents, staff, and board members; those who have visited the center; and those who have attended or contributed to past fundraisers. For every fundraiser, this group should be sent a special announcement.

Thank Contributors

After every fundraiser, the center should send out a thank you to all who contributed to the project — those who planned it and volunteered time to make it happen, as well as those who donated money, goods, or services. The thank you typically includes a final report on the results of the fundraiser — "We reached 110% of our goal," "We were able to finance remodeling of the infant room," etc. Some centers keep donors on their mailing list for the center's newsletter.

Circles of Support

by Kathy Hines

During a job interview, I was once asked how I liked being a professional beggar. The image of fundraising as panhandling permeates our world, yet it couldn't be farther from the truth. A beggar offers nothing in return for your support. A fundraiser offers concerned constituents an opportunity to invest in a cause. Chances are, a beggar won't ask you whether you'd prefer your loose change to support food purchases or bus tokens. A successful fundraiser works with donors to make sure mutual needs are met. When was the last time you received a thank you note, annual report, or donor newsletter with a return address of "corner of 7th and Main"? A fundraiser recognizes the importance of cultivating relationships, not simply to ensure a repeat gift, but rather as an acknowledgment of the donor's interest in and concern for the organization.

The constituency from which our donors are drawn is one of our most valuable organizational resources. By taking the time to properly identify and clarify who your constituents are, fundraising efforts can be maximized. A model called "constituency circles" has been developed by The Fund Raising School Center on Philanthropy at Indiana University. The following steps will help you to map out the circles for your own child care center.

Let's start with brainstorming. Write down each type of person, group, or business who has ever had any type of connection with your center. The more categories you come up with, the better. For the time being, don't concern yourself with questions about the appropriateness of your list items.

Just let your imagination flow. A sample list might look like this:

- Students
- Parents
- Teachers
- Board of directors
- Grocery store where we buy our snacks
- Playground equipment manufacturer
- Snow removal service
- Donors
- Volunteers
- People who came to open house
- Parents of alumni
- Anyone who saw the article on our center in the Hometown Child Care Newsletter
- People interested in education
- Bakery where we went on a field trip
- Store where we buy art supplies

Once you've finished your list, draw a series of four concentric circles on a separate sheet of paper. These circles will provide a map of your constituency, showing your closest connections in the very middle and radiating out as relationships weaken. Use the following guidelines to place each group on your list into a category. Each of the four circles represents a piece of your constituency:

• **Primary stakeholders.** Located in the very middle, this group represents people who have the closest relationship with your child care facility, those who are most invested in its mission and success. They will include your board of directors, staff, and current major donors.

• **Lesser stakeholders.** This category includes active participants, such as parents and families of current students, active volunteers, and other donors.

• **Casual participants.** These groups have a connection with your center but it is not as strong or as current as those in the previous categories. Examples might include parents of alumni or vendors (snow removal service, stores that you patronize).

• **Similar interests.** These people have a connection with your center by a similarity of interests which could lead them to be more closely involved. Perhaps they attended an open house, requested information, or are known to support other child care centers in the community. Your ties are not as direct, but you are aware of a common bond.

The primary stakeholders are the nucleus of your child care center. These people have the closest

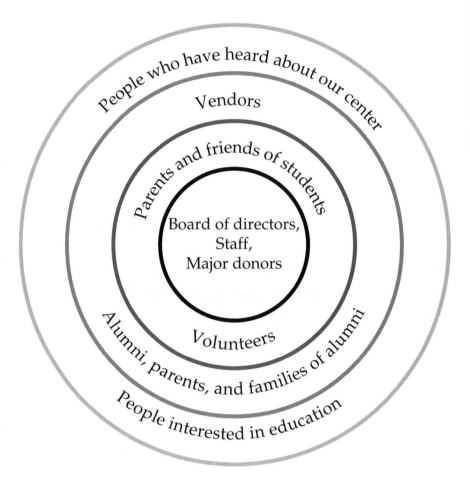

relationships, the greatest investments, and the highest level of commitment to your success. It is their responsibility to draw the outer circles in closer, whether by setting an appropriate example, providing motivation, or advocating on your behalf.

Common fundraising wisdom states that before embarking on a fundraising campaign you must have financial commitments from your board of directors. The constituency circles demonstrate that reasoning. If those who are closest to your center are unwilling to support it, how will you persuade those whose connections are weaker to get involved?

The circles are also a tool for prioritizing your efforts. With the myriad of responsibilities facing any center director, it is unthinkable that each prospective donor can be approached with the same amount of effort.

Accordingly, work from the middle out. It will be easiest to fold in those who have close, recent, and direct connections with your child care center. This is not to say that time shouldn't be spent cultivating the outer rings as well. Just be certain that you don't overextend yourself, developing elaborate schemes to entice those with minimal connections before you've secured the ones closest to you.

Similarly, choose an appropriate solicitation technique for each circle. The time it takes to meet personally with the innermost rings will be worth the effort. The numbers are smaller, the connections are stronger, and you want to focus on continuing to build those relationships.

As you move farther out, it's appropriate to reduce the level of personalization. For instance, while letters to previous donors should always be personalized as much as possible, a mail solicitation to all subscribers of a local child care newsletter can be mass produced.

It is also essential to spend time determining what motivates each circle of your constituency. Parents are looking for quality education for their children. Local businesses may be motivated by understanding the ultimate benefits this education offers to the community. The list of motivations will be as varied as your constituents.

Take the time to find out what they are. Ask your current donors why they contribute. Ask potential donors what appeals to them. And, always, talk to your colleagues about their experiences at their own centers. Don't be afraid to customize the message you put out. Your center meets many needs of many people. Use that variety to your advantage.

You'll play many roles as you raise funds. Become a storyteller while you relate tales of your center's success; a businessperson while presenting the overall financial picture; a negotiator as you determine how to match your needs with the desires of your donor; an educator as you explain child development while touring the classroom. But, as long as you have clarified your goals, believe in your mission, and respect the needs of your constituents, you won't ever be a beggar. Leave the tin cup at home and start circling.

Kathy Hines is the fund development associate at the High/Scope Educational Research Foundation in Ypsilanti, Michigan. She is a member of the National Society of Fund Raising Executives.

Have You Looked Under Every Rock? Multi-Source Funding for Child Care Programs

by Harriet Alger and Judith B. Fountain

It has never been easy to get, and to keep, the funding for good child care. The present political climate and an inflationary economy have increased the difficulty, yet the need for child care is greater than ever before. The responsibility for this problem falls chiefly on the already overburdened shoulders of child care directors.

Frequently, programs begin with one or two sources of funding. As these funding sources continue to be tapped, they can become exhausted, i.e., there is a limit to how much parents' fees can be raised. Therefore, one key to solving financial problems is to increase the number of funding sources contributing to a program — a practice known as multi-source funding.

Multi-source funding offers many advantages. It can be developed step by step over an extended period of time. By providing a broader base of support, centers are less vulnerable to cuts than when dependent on one or two sources of funding.

Multi-source funding provides for more program flexibility, since all decisions do not have to be based on rules or restrictions associated with some funds. In addition, multi-source funding can be used to add resources to programs that would be impossible or improbable under most funding available for general operating expenses.

A Multi-Source Funding Strategy

1. Build a climate of acceptance.

The first task in successful fundraising is to create a positive community understanding and acceptance of quality child care. Since such a campaign usually has to be managed by staff and volunteers, it needs to be well paced, realistic, and long range so that goals can be steadily and efficiently pursued. Efforts should not spurt heroically and then stop, leaving people exhausted and reluctant to continue.

Included in the planning should be media exposure, presentations to church and community groups, displays in community centers, and liaison with key and influential people in the community.

Good photographs of children are essential. Possible sources are local camera clubs, high school or college photography classes, newspaper photographers looking for human interest, and skillful amateur photographers among your supporters.

Slide shows that provide enjoyable informal glimpses of the many dimensions of a good program are invaluable in the effort to offset negative propaganda. Newspapers give articles better coverage if accompanied by an appealing black and white glossy picture of children. Displays in the community attract more attention and positive reaction when they feature pictures of happy children involved in interesting activities.

It is important to talk with as many politicians, educators, and business leaders as possible. Try to provide information and/or a program for every organization in your area that influences your support over a two or three year period.

One child care coalition invites local and state politicians to a cocktail party every year. They also invite politicians to lunch at centers during the "Week of the Young Child." In another community, a service organization publishes information about child care, "Finding Child Care Solutions," in cooperation with child care providers in that city, and makes it available to other organizations.

Among the most successful approaches to community leaders have been fundraising dinners held in historic or charming settings. Invitations were handwritten, china and linens were borrowed, and small round tables had informed hosts at each. Food was excellent, followed by short, well-produced slide shows. Brochures were available with more information and pledge cards.

Guests represented different segments of the community at each dinner — members of the school board and school officials, faculty of the local colleges. People not normally interested in child care came for a good dinner in pleasant surroundings. The dinners were held several times a year — and, as their reputation grew, people actually asked to be included.

The money for tickets for these dinners was almost clear profit since most of the food, wine, and help was donated. Those who were invited but could not come often sent donations. More importantly, the dinners resulted in people in positions of influence over possible funding sources being more informed about and supportive of child care programs.

2. Document the need.

As you meet with the community, well-organized factual information wins respect. General statements are not effective. In order to produce the facts readily, you need to keep very good and complete records. This will be even more important when you prepare proposals and ask for funds.

Be specific about what you are doing and why you need help. Share profiles of your families (without names or identifying characteristics).

Provide information such as the following about these families:

• How are you meeting their needs?

• Where do they live and work?

• How much do they pay?

• How much does it really cost you to provide service for them?

• How many families are on your waiting list?

• How much have costs risen?

• What do you need and why?

In order to approach businesses, industries, colleges, or universities with requests, you need to know the facts about the service you are providing (or could provide) for their employees/students/faculty. You also need data about the benefits that an organization will receive when secure and reliable child care is available.

Prepare for presentations to these and other groups by trying to anticipate questions and concerns. Agree to disagree about some things, and try to find common ground. Don't push too hard for acceptance. Keep communication open. Allow time for possible changes of attitudes.

3. Be realistic about short range goals. Keep working for quality and growth in long range goals.

Examine each possibility without optimism or pessimism. Plan time and energy; don't expect too much too soon. This year try for one piece of big muscle equipment, but plan to have a new playground in five years. Build an ever-widening pyramid of support — a broader base. Don't expect everyone to do everything.

Don't try to do everything yourself! Such dedication results in burnout. Success breeds success — try for attainable small goals that lead to measurable progress towards long range needs. This way you keep the "troops" inspired and win new friends and allies.

The amount of time spent on any one project should be somewhat commensurate with the gain. Two months of intensive effort on a rummage sale that nets $200 is not as worthwhile as the same amount of effort on an event that nets $2,000, or on a campaign to get a community development grant for $15,000.

Try to get on the regular budget of each organization you approach or try to get a long-term commitment. The establishment of regular year-to-year support makes everything easier and more secure. If an organization tells you that they will be unable to continue their support, submit a proposal anyway — and firmly, but respectfully, present the need for continued or increased support. The results are usually positive.

4. Expand coalition efforts in your community to seek broader support for child care funding increase.

There are many individuals and groups who share a common interest and concern in child care — women's groups, parents' groups, social service organizations, education associations, pediatricians and other medical groups, church groups, civic groups, and political groups. It is important to communicate your needs to them and enlist their support.

It is also important to support their efforts in areas with which you can agree and/or areas that relate to the families and children in your program. You do not have to agree on every issue to support each other. Political strength depends on the numbers of citizens who are willing to attend meetings, write letters, make phone calls, make speeches, and talk to friends and neighbors.

Expanding funding sources means more program possibilities. The process of soliciting support from many organizations can educate the community about your program and improve your status, providing more security and stability. It also makes center staff and parents more knowledgeable about, and responsive to, the community.

In a democratic society, political skills are essential. Practice may not make perfect, but it will help us to survive and to improve.

Harriet Alger is coordinator of early childhood at Cleveland State University and chairperson of the National Coalition of Campus Child Care. Judith B. Fountain is director of the child care program at Ohio State University.

Developing a Proposal: When Opportunity Knocks, Will You Be Prepared?

by Craig Boswell

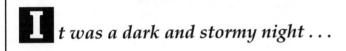

It was a dark and stormy night . . .

Suddenly, a portly, middle-aged developer burst into my office. "Are you the babysitter?" he barked.

As I stood up, graham cracker crumbs fell to the floor. "Yes. Well, not exactly," I stuttered. "We don't consider child care as babysitting," I said, surprisingly bold.

"That doesn't matter," he roared. "I'm here because I've heard you're the best in town, and I have a business proposition for you."

"Please come in and sit down," I murmured while my tongue searched for the last graham cracker crumb. "Oh, sorry, let me move that xylophone. I've been meaning to fix it for the last three weeks," I giggled, in a manner reminiscent of my seven year old daughter.

"Boswell," he said without introduction or salutation, "I'm developing the largest research park this county has ever seen. I have contractual commitments with eight out of twelve large, and I mean large, companies. But the county commissioners are demanding that I provide some amenity parks, with tennis courts and walking paths. They also wanted a day care center," he said in disgust.

"Child care," I said. "We prefer to be called a child care center, not day care."

"That doesn't matter," he roared. "I've heard you're the best in town."

"And you have a business proposition?" I interjected.

"Well . . . yes, that's right," he stumbled with his thoughts. "I'll build this center the way you want it, and CAM charges from the big boys will help pay for your rent."

I was too intimidated to ask what CAM was and who the big boys were. (I found out later that CAM stands for Common Area Maintenance Fee. I think then it should be called CAMF. The big boys referred to the research companies that would be building or leasing the property.)

"So, Boswell, I need an operations proposal with technical and management procedures with a three-year projection. The county has established a review subcommittee that will oversee the proposal review. Oh, yes, they have a consulting company to review the child care issues and the total PUD (Plan Unit Development)."

"Hold it," I bellowed. "You'll have to go a lot slower. This is new ground, and I'm used to single digits and three-letter words."

He laughed, and the corners of his mouth reached to the bottom of his ears. "I don't have time now, but here's my card. Come over to the office where I can explain in detail what I need," he said. "What time can you come next Thursday?" he asked.

"I can come during nap time," I stated without thinking. "One-thirty," I responded after realizing what I had just said.

"Great! I will look forward to discussing this matter in detail with you, Boswell. It has been nice talking to you." He left quicker than he had arrived.

I sat quietly for about ten minutes. Then I began looking for my package of graham crackers.

The developer had presented me with a unique challenge — how to write a proposal in a manner that developers, commissioners, and consultants could understand. More importantly, how would I write a proposal that I could understand?

Understanding the Proposal

RFP (Request for Proposal) usually comes in written form, ranging in length from 1 to 101 pages. It is a document that outlines a problem and solicits proposals that explain how that problem can be solved. If the problem is how, when, where, and at what cost to establish a child care in the new area, the response could have many sections, and it could take weeks to complete.

An important point to make in the "art" of proposal writing is that most RFP readers are looking for a clean, well-written document that simply tells them what they want to know.

Things You Need

✔ Space to work

✔ Uninterrupted time

✔ Typewriter/word processor

✔ Binding machine and device

✔ Copy machine

✔ Resource files

✔ Calculator or computer

✔ Independent reviewer

✔ Vision and insight

Many proposal books and seminars advocate a team approach to proposal writing. My experience dictates that team members get in the way and ask stupid questions. My recommendation, therefore, is to sit down with the door shut and have a clear outline (along with a box of graham crackers). Then go for it!

The basic elements of your proposal should stand out when the document is completed. For example:

1. The proposal should be neat, clean, and easy to read.

2. Jargon should be eliminated. Terminology should be defined so the reviewer (builder) knows clearly what you intend by using certain words.

3. Communicate your message without putting the reader in a stupor.

4. Your language should communicate your enthusiasm for this project. Be positive.

5. Use supported assumptions:

a. describe your organization clearly

b. document the need in context, by describing how the "national issues of quality child care" relate to local efforts

c. use tables and graphs sparingly and when you do employ them be sure headings clearly explain what is being presented

Outline

1.0	**Executive Summary**
1.1	Introduction letter
1.2	Board of directors' letter (optional)
1.3	History statement
1.4	Management commitment statement
2.0	**Technical Section**
2.1	History
2.2	Management team with organization chart
2.3	Administrative policy
2.4	Management challenge statement
2.5	Time line
2.6	Early childhood quality guideline

3.0   Management Section

3.1   Personal and compensation package and job description

3.2   Staffing ratios, staff supervision, and staff retention

3.3   Inservice training guidelines and professional advancement

3.4   Program information

3.5   Philosophy overview

3.6   Curriculum statement

3.7   Explanation of daily curriculum

3.8   Center/parent relationships

3.9   Health and safety

3.10   Children with disability condition statement

3.11   Food program and procedures/menu

3.12   References (at least five)

3.13   Personal resume

4.0   Cost Section

4.1   Marketing plan

4.2   Budget/item description

4.3   Equipment/supply cost

4.4   Proforma — three year projection

4.5   Sample of parent tuition, handbook, registration

4.6   Schedule for obtaining licenses and insurance with cost breakdown

5.0   Appendix

5.1   Sample of parent handouts

5.2   Sample of infant information sheets

5.3   Sample of newspaper clipping of school's program

5.4   Sample of medication authorization forms

5.5   Sample of school/teacher evaluation forms

5.6   Sample of posted preschool curriculum outline

This article does not afford me the capability to describe in detail the subtopics of each section outlined above. However, I will briefly review a few.

1.4 — Management commitment statement is a subtopic that pledges your expertise to long-term operations, realizing your past experience and future goals in early childhood education and child care operations. Furthermore, it acknowledges the tremendous challenges that lie ahead in the planning, start-up, and long-term operations.

Details and concerns can be elaborated upon — e.g., "Our experience has determined that organizations outside the scope of early childhood education have a difficult and costly time of setting up, operating, and maintaining the type of quality center they envision. A management team that is educated, trained, and experienced can cut through the problems that arise and focus their energy/resources in maintaining the elements that are associated with quality, staff training, low teacher turnover, and a low child to teacher ratio."

2.3 — Administrative policy. This section allows for explanation on multiple site operation and the manner of hiring, training, and supervision of middle management and faculty staff — e.g., "During the start-up phase, the executive director will be on site, hiring, training, and supervising the teachers. The on-site director will be trained at our nearest child care center under   current   child care management. The hiring and training will occur well in advance of children entering the school. After the school is operating satisfactorily, the executive director will maintain an inservice education, monitoring, parent-board participation schedule that is satisfactory to both the staff and the parents and the parent advisory council."

3.2 — Issues regarding **ratio**, **supervision**, and **retention** will always be foremost on a reviewer's mind. You must provide details on how your child care company can provide solutions to these significant concerns — e.g., "Although the staff turnover rate is a natural issue as it relates to child care,   our   child care has had the fortunate opportunity to retain most of the staff throughout all its center(s)." The retention is achieved through the following reasons:

✔ Higher salaries than the local average.

✔ Insurance benefits — health, life, dental, and maternity.

✔ Staff child care at a significantly reduced rate. Food is provided free while staff is working.

✔ Paid vacation and ten days for major holidays during the year.

✔ Creative expression through involvement in curriculum.

✔ Inservice training and recognition of completed tasks.

✔ Involvement with an organization where the primary directive is to provide the best learning and caring environment possible for young children.

4.4 — Proforma (budget) and three projections are critical information for any developer or banker, but most important for the financial feasibility of the new center. The proforma is used to illustrate the connection between child ratio, teacher salary, staff benefits, cost of living, and parent tuition.

Remember to factor in cost of living increase for the staff/faculty and parent tuition increases throughout the next three years.

General Proposal Checklist

1. Acknowledge receipt of the RFP to developer.

2. Determine qualification and commitments.

3. Consult informally with board of directors, trustees, owners, or husband/wife, etc. to determine your commitment to the new project.

4. Make copies of RFP (used for working copy).

5. Make formal presentation to decision makers in your organization.

6. Decision makers' — e.g., board, trustee, owners, etc. — signatures of support.

7. Plan response time and deadline.

8. Identify and allocate supplies and support.

9. Outline RFP tasks.

10. Secure work space.

11. Develop proposal writing and assembly schedule.

Proposal Writing Checklist

✔ Cover letter

✔ Letter of support from "decision maker"

✔ Table of contents

✔ Executive summary

✔ Technical section

✔ Management section

✔ Cost section

✔ Appendix

One final thought: Always use the overnight express mail (I use Federal Express). They keep terrific records on time, date, receiving signatures, etc. That doesn't mean that you need to wait until one day before the deadline. However, I've never met a time-compulsive early childhood educator. But you and I both know if it weren't for deadlines, taxes, payroll, board reports, and RFPs would all be sitting on our office floor with the xylophones.

Craig Boswell, Ph.D., has been active in child care and early childhood education for the past 20 years. He is currently an assistant professor at the University of Central Oklahoma.

Fishing for Dollars in Philanthropic Waters

by Anne Mitchell

Every child care director, at some point, has confronted the fact that parents (even well-off ones) just can't pay enough to support good child care services. The savvy director is always looking for new sources of funding and evaluating whether they're worth pursuing. If we could become a United Way agency, would the effort be worth it? What could we do as a fundraiser besides another bake sale? Is buying lottery tickets a good investment? Somewhere in this process, the idea of soliciting foundations comes up. Probably right after you hear that some national child care group just got a multi-million dollar grant from You-Name-It foundation, you think: "Why couldn't we do that?" This article is for you.

First, let's be clear that foundations are not now (or ever) going to be the direct source of funding that solves the compensation-affordability problem. Foundations are not — and never will be — the main source of funding for any child care center's operation. The direct services or general operating expenses of any organization are almost never supported by philanthropy. The role that foundations play in a field is something like what an entrepreneur does — improve, expand, and innovate. The difference is that foundations do this indirectly through the work of those organizations they fund, rather than directly as an entrepreneur would in operating a business.

Foundations are looking for innovative solutions to problems, promising approaches to improve on current methods, or expansions of successful programs that address a problem. Expanding services for families (adding or starting new programs), improving practice through professional development, linking child care services with other services families need are all examples of child care ideas foundations might consider supporting.

Foundations correctly believe their role in child care is to help the field solve problems and address current needs, not to become a direct funder of services. Given that cautionary note, foundations can and will fund child care if you approach the right ones in the right way.

The Philanthropic Landscape

Philanthropy comes in many forms, from individual donors to national foundations. This article focuses on philanthropic entities (foundations and corporations) that might support local child care projects. If you want to know how to find major individual donors, that's another story (actually, a set of unique and non-replicable stories). Understanding something about the types of foundations and their basic characteristics can help you identify the right ones to consider pursuing.

All foundations are legal entities designed to give away money for particular purposes to other non profit entities. Many were established with the funds from one individual, one family (or extended family), or one corporation. Others are collections of funds bequeathed by many different individuals and families. Some foundations are restricted to supporting certain types of work or particular geographic areas — either by the will of those who gave the money or the wishes of the current trustees.

Foundations can have a national, regional, and/or local focus in their grantmaking. Some national foundations also have a local grantmaking program to benefit the community they reside in. Community foundations are usually collections of trusts and bequests that are restricted to a specific community. Community foundations often have the word "community" or "area" in their names, e.g., the Rochester Area Foundation or the Marin Community Foundation.

Corporate foundations (or a corporation's annual charitable giving) focus mainly (or solely) on those communities where the corporation has worksites and employees. Community foundations and corporate foundations with a local focus are probably the most likely to support local child care projects. National foundations with a diverse local grants program may also be supporters.

Foundations can legally only give money to certain types of organizations — almost always a non profit corporation which has tax-exempt status (a 501(c)3 organization). Most non profit child care centers would qualify, but for profit centers generally cannot receive funds directly from a foundation. However, associations of providers such as a family child care association or a for profit directors' association can qualify if the association is incorporated as a non profit and has tax-exempt status.

Generally a foundation establishes a set of program areas, priorities, or strategies that guide its grantmaking. Child care is unlikely to be a distinct program priority all by itself, but child care easily fits into a broader area — such as child and youth development, community building, strengthening families, early education and school readiness, or prevention — which are typical philanthropic program areas.

In larger foundations, each program area is the responsibility of an individual program officer. Smaller foundations may have only one staff person who covers all the areas. In some cases, one of the foundation's directors manages the grantmaking as a volunteer. Knowing whether there is a program area where child care would fit and which foundation staff person handles the area where child care fits are essential pieces of information to have.

Foundations generally make grants based on thoughtful, well-written proposals that directly address the specified issues within a program area. Sending a proposal — no matter how brilliant

the ideas in it might be — is not the best way to introduce yourself to a foundation. Very few foundations will read and respond to proposals sent "cold." Some foundations do not accept unsolicited proposals at all — they will return them unread — because they only fund projects that are developed at their request by organizations they select.

Others only accept short letter proposals that follow a specified format. Before you make a move, you must know how each foundation approaches grantmaking and what its requirements are for applicants or grantseekers.

What Foundations Fund

Given that foundations will not underwrite your center's parent fees, what will they support? Answer: Improvements and innovations that solve child care problems and benefit the wider community. Professional development is a good example. If the community lacks infant care, a proposal from a group of centers to collectively train their infant care teachers in a manner that would institutionalize an infant care course in the community college might be a fundable proposal. Building the infant care rooms might be fundable if you could find a foundation that supports capital projects, so called "bricks and mortar."

Another example is collaborations to expand services. If the community's Head Start grantee and a child care center(s) wanted to jointly provide comprehensive all-day early education, a foundation might fund the planning and start-up phase of such a venture.

Fundraising — no matter whether it is selling raffle tickets or writing a grant proposal — is not begging. You are offering someone an opportunity to support a worthy organization or project and, in the case of a foundation, an opportunity to give away money that the foundation is required by law to give away. Successful fundraising is the combination of four elements:

• a credible, trustworthy person

• with good ideas for feasible projects,

• that match the foundation's goals, and

• will be carried out in an organization that is financially solid and well managed.

Technically, grantmaking is the act of one organization making a grant to another organization. Actually, successful grantmaking is the result of positive human interactions — the foundation officer and the grant seeker establish a working relationship based on good communication and mutual trust that leads eventually to the approval of a grant.

Foundations fund people — people they know, people they trust, people with good ideas. Child care center directors who are active in their community are more likely to encounter potential funders in situations where relationships can be established — such as at community meetings or events — than directors who only venture out to attend an occasional conference with their early child-hood colleagues.

Getting Started

Many people think the first step is to make a list of all the geographically appropriate foundations that have any history of "giving to early childhood." On the contrary, the place to start is with ideas (although research on funders may be needed later). The goal is to make a match between your good ideas and a foundation's goals. Matchmaking is done by people — your ideas will be shaped and changed (improved, hopefully) through your interactions with the foundation officer.

Begin by developing some ideas for projects that would benefit your organization and the wider child care community. This can be done alone, but often goes faster in a small group (if everyone is clear on the task). You might get the local directors' group to brainstorm ideas. After you get a list, pick out the three or four ideas that seem most feasible and write a one-page description of each idea. The "who, what, where, when, why, how" approach used by newspaper reporters is a good way to start. Write down what the project is, why it is needed, who will do it, how long it will last, what results it will have, and what it will cost.

Because human relationships are important in philanthropic fund raising, another good method for getting started is to think about your own networks and contacts in terms of potential funders. Are any of the people you already know potential funders — that is, connected in some way with corporations or foundations? What about your board — who do they know? Some of your board members may well know philanthropic leaders and be willing to discuss child care with them and introduce you to them directly.

Finally, think about your staff and parents. Some of them may have networks that include potential funders. Don't underestimate your parents. One source of corporate funds for child care is the AT&T Development Fund. A child care provider must be recommended by an AT&T employee to access these funds, which are available for child care improvement and expansion in AT&T communities.

Chances are, if there's a community foundation in your area, you've heard of it. If not, look in the phone book or go to the library. There are a number of published sources of information about foundations that can help you find those in your geographic area that might consider a child care related request.

Your local library may have the current year's *Foundation Directory* published by the Foundation Center, an information clearing-house on foundation and corporate giving headquartered in New York City. This directory contains entries for close to 12,000 foundations, giving brief descriptions of their mission and history, total assets, annual grant total, size of an average grant, types of organizations supported, contact information, and any restrictions. *The Directory of Corporate Giving* has similar entries for over 2,000 corporate grantmakers.

If your library does not have these directories, you can contact The Foundation Center directly at (800) 424-9836. They will refer you to the nearest Foundation Center Library or to a Cooperating Collection.

Another way to access information about The Foundation Center is on the Internet (http://fdncenter.org).

The process of seeking and receiving foundation funding takes time and effort. Think carefully about whether the process is worth the reward before you start. If it were easy, everyone would be doing it. In fact, some child care center directors have successfully negotiated the foundation waters and are willing to share their lessons. A follow-up article will chronicle the actual experiences of child care center directors who have received foundation grants, including their tips, advice, and pitfalls to avoid.

Anne Mitchell is the president of Early Childhood Policy Research, an independent consulting firm specializing in policy research and planning on child care/early education for government, foundations, and national nonprofit organizations. She can be reached at awmitchell@aol.com via the Internet.

Keys to Maintaining a Good Banking Relationship

by Keith Stephens

> **A** *bank is a place where they lend you an umbrella in fair weather and ask for it back again when it starts to rain.*
> — Robert Frost

Many child care operators probably share Robert Frost's cynicism about banks. They may remember with bitterness how when they were getting started every bank in town turned down their loan requests. Now that they have a profitable venture going, these same bankers are eagerly soliciting their business. But if times get tough, they may just disappear.

While such cynicism may well be warranted, in the long run, it is not productive. A bank can be such a valuable asset for a small or growing business that it is in every operators best interest to invest time in developing a positive working relationship with a bank.

Selecting the Right Bank

Not all banks are the same. You should shop for a bank that best meets the special needs of your business. Some suggestions:

• **Find a bank that specializes in your business**. Different banks specialize in different areas: real estate, small business, international lending, service industries, capital goods industries, etc. You will get much better service from a bank that is used to doing business with your type of business.

Advertisements by banks in your local newspaper's business section often spell out the types of business they are soliciting. A bank's annual report will contain a statement of purpose and lists of offices, departments, and board members. This can yield insights into a bank's specialties. And finally, by talking to other local child care professionals and small business operators, as well as to your accountant

and lawyer, you can benefit from their experiences in dealing with a variety of local banks.

• **Look for a small local bank**. Unless you manage a large or growing child care business that is looking for a multi-million dollar loan (banks typically are prohibited from making loans in excess of 10% of their total capital — thus a small bank will not be able to handle a multi-million dollar loan request), your interests will probably be best served by a small bank.

Small banks offer a number of advantages. In order to remain competitive with larger banks, they must try harder to attract customers, i.e., they strive to excel in their service. In addition, they can be more flexible in putting together financial packages. And finally, you will have more clout in a smaller bank where your account will be more important to the success of the bank. You will get to know more of their key decisionmakers.

• **Find a bank that is close by**. As a matter of sound internal controls, a child care business should be making deposits on a daily basis. In that case, the proximity of the bank will be an important factor.

That is not to say that the nearby branch bank is always your best bet. When checking out a nearby bank, be sure to ask these questions: Does it have a commercial lending department? Do its hours fit your needs? Are its fees competitive? Will it provide immediate credit on your deposits?

• **Consolidate your banking**. Some business people spread out their banking at a number of banks. Their theory is that when it comes time to ask for assistance, they will have a number of ready alternatives.

I am much more inclined to recommend focusing on one bank. A bank will price your transactions based on how much business you do with them. You want to be as important a customer as you can possibly be.

Developing a Positive Ongoing Relationship

Banks' decisions are made by people — not by computers, formulas, and financial statements. When the time comes that you need help from a bank, you are much more likely to get a fair hearing if you know the decisionmakers on a personal basis than if you are a stranger.

This not only applies if you are looking for a loan, but also when you encounter little difficulties. For example, let's say you make a mistake that causes your account to be overdrawn. If you are only a number to the bank, chances are they will bounce the overdrawn checks, thus aggravating those you made

the checks out to. On the other hand, if you have a friendly representative at the bank, she may call you up and give you some time to cover the overdraft before taking action.

It takes time to build personal relationships at your bank, but it is time well invested. To start with, introduce yourself to the bank president, the branch manager, and/or the head of the commercial lending department. Keep them posted from time to time on how your business is doing. There is a lot of turnover at banks, so the higher up your personal relationships, the better.

It is especially important to build a good working relationship with your account officer, the bank official who is in charge of your business at the bank. This person represents your company within the bank to other officers and loan committees, as well as outside the bank when creditors call for references. Therefore, you want this person on your side as an advocate.

There are many steps you can take to improve relations with your account officer. Use your daily deposits as an opportunity to keep in touch with her. Put her on the mailing list for your center newsletter. Send her announcements when you pass important milestones, receive positive press coverage, open a new center, receive center accreditation, or hire key new people.

Devote some time to helping your account officer better understand your organization, as well as the overall child care business. Share with him articles (from trade

journals as well as business publications) that support the strength of this growing industry. Invite him out to see your center or centers in action. Enlighten him on your organization's niche in the child care market.

Show your appreciation for her hard work by introducing her to other business persons who may be interested in opening accounts with her bank. If your account officer has been especially efficient in handling your needs, you should send a letter to the bank president conveying your pleasure.

On the other hand, if you are having difficulty with your account officer, you may consider asking for a new one before decisions are made about your account that are difficult to reverse. This can be risky because you may alienate your current officer. But if the relationship is deteriorating, it may be necessary.

Getting a Loan

When the time comes that you need money, you will want to present your case well. Keep in mind that your account officer will not be reviewing your request in isolation, but along with many other requests competing for the bank's money.

Since a banker, like anyone else, is likely to take the course of least resistance, you can increase your chances of success if you make his work easier — if you present him with a proposal that is thoughtful and complete. Presenting a complete proposal not only makes the bank officer's work easier, it also shows that you have thoroughly researched what you propose to do.

Likewise, when he inevitably asks for something that was not included, your fast response will demonstrate the urgency and seriousness of this request, and will convey the impression that you are organized. If he has to call you every day for information, and you are slow to respond, you will create the impression that you have something to hide.

You should expect that the bank will review your proposal carefully. If there are any problems or discrepancies, point them out and provide explanations up front. Don't cross your fingers and hope that they won't be found, because when they are, your credibility will suffer.

Your loan request package should answer the following basic questions:

How much money do you need?
Don't go in with an inflated figure, hoping to negotiate down to a satisfactory amount. Start with what you want exactly. All your documentation should support your request for this amount. This will demonstrate that you have done your homework and are not making a frivolous request.

How will you use the money?
The clearer you can be about what you will do with the money, the better the banker will understand your proposal. If you can spell out that his money will be used to purchase tangible assets such as computers or playground equipment, all the better. If the money will supplement general operating funds during an expansion phase, be as clear as possible about how this extra operating capital will insure increased profitability in the future.

When and how will you repay the money? In the final analysis, a bank will lend you money not because you are a good person, nor because your business looks good, but because they are confident they will recoup their money with interest. A vital part of your proposal, therefore, will be to demonstrate that you have the ability to pay them back.

You will need to supply a current income and expense statement, a balance sheet, and a cash flow projection for the duration of the loan. If you are a small business, a sole proprietorship, a partnership, or a closely held corporation, you will need to supply personal financial information as well.

While banks will accept financial statements that you prepare in house, they tend to give more credence to statements that have some third party seal of approval. Their first choice would be CPA-audited statements, their second choice CPA-reviewed statements, and their third choice CPA-compiled statements (where a CPA takes the numbers that you provide and compiles them into standard financial statements).

No matter how complete a package you provide, the bank will take your numbers and put them through their own financial statement analysis. Some banks will give you these results if you ask. This will help you understand your own numbers better, and will give you some idea about what the bank considers important.

For example, a bank may analyze such factors as *margin management* (what are your controllable expenses, what does it cost in addition to your fixed costs); *working investment* (the rate at which you collect and pay bills); *solvency* (how liquid your assets are, what kind of cash flow you are generating); *debt capacity* (how much debt your business can reasonably carry); and *sources of equity* (how much trade credit, bank credit, and personal credit you have).

After You Get a Loan

Bankers hate surprises. After they have loaned you some of their money, they want to hear (1) that you are doing what you said you were going to do and (2) that your financial projections are coming true. Keep them posted on your progress with at least quarterly updates. Don't make them come to you for a status report.

If your numbers are not working out, or if something is going wrong with your plans, your banker will want to know about it early. You may be reluctant to share bad news, but it is better to be up front about problems. If you are, the bank may be willing to reschedule your payments to help ease you through the tough time. If the first they know of your problems is when you fail to make a payment, they will be considerably less conciliatory.

With an investment of a little time, your banker might hand you an umbrella just when you need it most.

Keith Stephens, a CPA, is the former president of Palo Alto Preschools, once the country's largest privately owned child care chain, and past president of the National Association for Child Care Management.

Fundraising Success Stories

"Nothing gets your creative juices flowing better than learning about others' success stories."

Directors' Fundraising Hits

Ideas from center directors

The following is a representative selection of the best fundraising ideas which have been contributed to **Exchange** by child care directors.

Auctions for Fun and Profit

Jan Silverman (Lucky Lane Early Childhood Center, St. Louis, Missouri) shares how her center plans an auction which has been their most successful fundraiser. The auction is planned and implemented by a committee of board members. It is held at a local hotel and those attending pay $40 each to participate in the evening's festivities.

The evening begins with a silent auction of small items, valued at less than $100. The excitement builds with dinner and a live auction.

A catalog listing the 300 items — including trips, dinners, and other things donated by the community and parents — goes home with the children a week before the auction. Trips, condos, and autographed sports equipment stimulate high bidding. Each board member is encouraged to bring a full table of guests. In past years, the center has netted close to $16,000.

The **YWCA Drop-In Children's Center (Watsonville, California)** raised over $5,000 with an auction. The auction was organized by a committee of ten volunteers which started working five months before the event. Most of their time was spent on canvassing parents, friends of the center, and local merchants for the several hundred items donated.

The auction was held outdoors on a Sunday. Participants were allowed to view the items from 10 am to 1 pm, and the auction itself lasted from 1 pm to 6 pm.

A wide range of items are big hits at auctions. At the Watsonville auction, the big item was a wedding package which included a minister's services, a place for a reception, a photographer's services, a cake, and a honeymoon in San Francisco.

The **Summit Child Care Center (Summit, New Jersey)** raised $11,000 with a "Vacation Auction." A parents' committee sent out requests to over 1,000 resorts around the world. Seventy-five vacations were donated, ranging from hotel rooms in Europe and Hawaii to weekends at private summer cottages.

A center in New York City raised $18,000 auctioning off gift certificates for up to $500 to department stores.

The **Brownie Preschool (Alexandria, Virginia)** featured season tickets to the Washington Redskins and a catered dinner for eight in the bidder's own home. Other less sensational, but highly popular, items include babysitting services, meals at restaurants, food, furniture, antiques, housecleaning services, and hairdressing.

All centers agreed that the key ingredient to a successful auction is a lively auctioneer to keep it entertaining and to loosen people up. Most centers used a professional auctioneer (some of whom donated their time).

Several centers had a dinner or party in conjunction with the auction. The **Brownie Preschool** held the auction during a buffet luncheon for which $4 per person was charged. Several centers noted that providing free wine and beer during the event had a positive effect on the size of bids.

Another essential ingredient is recruiting enough volunteers to handle all aspects of the auction. Considerable time and energy is required before the event to solicit items; to collect and transport them to the auction site; and to label, catalog, and display them. The day of the auction people are needed to direct traffic, to haul items back and forth, to collect money, to assist the auctioneer, to serve refreshments, and to answer questions.

Mary K. Parker, from the **YWCA Drop-In Center**, reported that about 20 parent volunteers were needed for their action. She stated that without the support of these parents before and during the auction it would not have been possible. **Dr. Lois Ferrer**, from the **Brownie Preschool**, also recommends having center people on hand to provide activities for children of attendees.

A variation on the typical auction is the silent auction. Items in the auction are displayed, either at the center for a week or during a social event. Bidders write out their bids

and submit them in a sealed envelope. When the envelopes are opened, the item is awarded to the highest bidder.

Raffles! Raffles! Raffles!

Raffles have been utilized by child care centers to raise anywhere from $400 to $18,000. Regardless of the scope of the raffle, there are two essential ingredients to success: attractive prizes and an aggressive sales force.

Most centers try to have at least one big prize to catch people's attention and a number of smaller prizes to increase participants' chances of winning something.

The **Fallbrook Child Development Center (Fallbrook, California)** had a raffle with 32 prizes — the top one being $100 worth of gasoline.

The **Sweatt-Winter Day Care Center (Farmington, Maine)** raffled off a wood stove at a county fair.

The **John E. Boyd Center (Fall River, Massachusetts)** has found handmade wooden toys and color televisions to be popular items at its annual raffle. Other big draw prizes include quilts, afghans, getaway weekends (free babysitting, free resort hotels, free meals), and three-minute supermarket dashes.

A 50/50 raffle is one of the easiest fundraising ideas used by **Jennifer Ramey (Turtle Mountain Head Start, Belcourt, North Dakota)**. The center prints tickets that include a space for name, address, phone number, and the date of the drawing. The tickets are sold for $1 each. Parents and staff find it easier to sell and keep track of

tickets in books of 10. Before the raffle, decide on a goal, say $500. When the goal is reached and the drawing is held, the winner gets half — $250 — and the center gets half — the remaining $250.

The **Androscoggin County Head Start** operates a "20-20 Club Raffle." A limited number of participants contribute $1 per week for 20 weeks. Each week a name is drawn and $20 is awarded. At the end of 20 weeks, a party is held at which $850 in additional prizes are awarded.

Getting parents, staff, and board members to sell tickets is probably the hardest aspect of a raffle. Some centers offer incentives to ticket sellers. The **Fallbrook Center** offered a free automobile tune-up to the parent selling the most tickets.

Other centers offer incentives to ticket buyers. The **Fallbrook Center** made an arrangement with a local pizza house whereby anyone buying a $1 ticket received $1 off on a pizza of their choice.

Before setting a raffle in motion, centers need to take care of two administrative issues. First, a check should be made with local and state authorities to be sure the proposed raffle complies fully with all relevant laws. Second, a sound system for distributing tickets and collecting stubs and money needs to be set up. Tickets should be given directly to the parents and not sent home with their children.

Annual Membership Drive

For the past several years, the **Ossining Children's Center**

(Ossining, New York) has held very successful direct mail membership drives. The first year, the drive raised $4,000 for the center; by 1980, the proceeds had increased to $7,000.

The project was launched the first year by sending letters to 12,000 community residents selected from the phone book. The following year, letters were sent to all residents who gave money the first year. In addition, all parents, teachers, and board members were asked to submit names of additional prospects.

Now the letters are sent out to about 1,000 residents each year — including all doctors in the area. This letter is sent out in April, with a follow-up mailing in early December (timed to coincide with the end of the tax year.)

The mailing package consists of a form letter and a return envelope. The letter is signed by the president of the board, and it lists the names of all board members. It briefly describes the center and explains why it operates a deficit each year. Their support is requested in making $5, $10, $25, or $50 donations. The bulk of the donations are for $10. Donors are sent thank you letters which invite them to attend the annual meeting.

Sally Ziegler, the center's director, believes that a key to the drive's success has been active maintenance of the mailing list. Every year, anyone who has not given in two years is culled from the list. In addition, board members and parents are asked every year to contribute new prospects' names for the list.

"Friends" Donate to Center

Church of the Saviour Day Care Center (Cleveland Heights, Ohio) has organized a donation fund and named it "Friends of the Day Care Center." Staff members and parents give to the director, **Alice Licker**, the names of individuals who they think might be willing and able to give money to the center. She sends them a two-page letter which describes the program, lists the items that donations are used for (equipment and scholarships), and invites them to become "friends." This letter tends to be most effective at the end of the year when wealthy individuals often need to increase their tax deductions. Ms. Licker writes a letter of thanks back to each contributor and often encloses a piece of children's artwork.

Previously, this fund has brought in about $750, with the largest single contribution being $250. Other centers have received gifts of as much as $5,000 and have found that they can go back with success to the same contributors year after year.

The Whateverathon

Capitalizing on current interest in endurance-type events, many centers have successfully employed marathon spinoffs for fundraisers.

The **Spanish Educational Development Center (Washington, DC)** sponsored a ten-mile jogathon. Staff, parents, and friends who agreed to run in the race went to their friends and collected pledges to donate a certain amount for every mile they completed in the race. After the race, the runners collected over $1,000 from these pledges for the center.

There are many variations on this theme. The **Pinewoods Center** and other schools associated with the **Association for Retarded Citizens (Troy, New York)** raised $20,000 with a swimathon; the **Parent Child Center (La Salle, Colorado)** sponsored a walkathon; the **Refreshing Spring Child Care Center (Schenectady, New York)** held a bikeathon; and **Indiana County Head Start (Indiana, Pennsylvania)** undertook a 24-hour danceathon.

The directors of these programs had several recommendations to those interested in attempting whateverathons. First, the event itself should be carefully prepared for. If there is a course to be traversed, it should be laid out very clearly, with rest and refreshment points, distance markers, course officials, etc. Advice from local athletic associations may be valuable here.

Second, emphasis should be placed on actually collecting on pledges. One center was able to collect less than one-third of its pledges. This director suggested collecting the money at the time the pledge is made.

Third, make provision for all eventualities. Have medical personnel on hand, clear the route beforehand with the police, and set a rain date.

Evenings with Experts

From **Betsy Newell** of the **International Play Group (New**

York City) comes the idea of offering evenings with experts. For example, an authority on antiques could offer a session to which participants could bring their own antiques for identification and appraisal.

Other possibilities include presentations by experts on restoring furniture, wine tasting and selection, identifying and appraising china, making bagels, investing in gold or stocks, using make-up, treating back problems, making Christmas decorations, jogging, and self-protection for women. Sessions could also be held at noon, with sandwiches provided.

Presenters would be asked to donate their time, so the major costs would be for providing sandwiches at noon or for renting a room if free space is not available. Staff time would be required for recruiting speakers, arranging space, and securing publicity.

Tickets could be sold for a single session or at reduced rates for a series of sessions. If an average of 50 individuals paid $5 per session to attend four sessions, the center would realize $1,000, less expenses.

Thrift Shop Yields Big Results

A profitable thrift shop has been operated for several years out of a storefront in downtown Boca Raton, Florida, by the **Florence Fuller Child Development Center**. The shop's inventory is primarily donated by the center's 700 members in the community who send in a steady flow of furniture, clothing, jewelry, and

antiques. In addition, manufacturers are asked to donate their seconds.

The shop is operated and staffed by volunteers. The volunteers are trained in advance and are required to visit the center so they know what they are working for. On a yearly basis, about 60 to 75 volunteers work in the shop.

The expenses of the thrift shop for rent, utilities, transportation, and one part-time staff member average about $1,000 per month. **Harry Lippert**, the center's director, initially devoted a great deal of time to setting up the shop. Now that it is operational, it requires less than two hours a week of his time.

The gross monthly income of the shop has been averaging $3,500, with a profit after expenses of $2,500. In addition, the 60 to 70 weekly customers are encouraged to visit the center. Many do and end up making donations to the center. In 1980, the thrift shop exceeded $100,000 in sales for the first time; and, after expenses, it yielded $72,000.

After reading about the thrift shop in *Exchange*, **Jan Lucas** had the **Westend Day Care Centre (Portage la Prairie, Manitoba)** set up a thrift shop. With the profits, the center was able to buy its own building.

Night on the Town

The **Summit Child Care Center (Summit, New Jersey)** raised $20,000 in 1980 from a unique dinner and dance fundraiser. About 60 "hosts" throughout the

community invited from 4 to 40 couples to have dinner at their houses. Those invited included the hosts' friends as well as other couples recruited by the center.

After dinner, a theme dance (disco last year) was held at the child care center. For the full evening's entertainment, couples were charge $30.

As an added feature, hosts submitted their menus in advance to be published in a "Night-on-the-Town" cookbook which was sold that night and thereafter. The event has been held annually for several years.

Most arrangements are handled by an eight-person (non-board members) volunteer committee. This committee starts nearly a year in advance recruiting hosts, recruiting couples, and assigning them to hosts, planning the dance, cookbook, etc.

The hosts contribute their hospitality as well as the food (sometimes over $500 worth) for which they can claim a charitable tax deduction. Last year, the total cost to the center for running the event was $750. Staff time involved in the planning was minimal.

Retha's Carry Out

Patty Siegel reports that one of the best fundraisers for her children's day care center, **Pacific Primary (San Francisco, California)**, is the cook, **Retha Green**. She has enabled the center to purchase much of its kitchen equipment, including a freezer, by operating a unique carry-out service for parents.

Every Friday, Retha bakes chocolate chip and oatmeal cookies and sells them to parents when they pick up their children. The cookies sell for $1.50 per dozen. About 50 families take advantage of this offer every week. Once every three months, she makes complete homemade chicken dinners and sells them to parents for $3 per person. Parents are required to order these dinners in advance.

In response to the reputation Ms. Green developed for her exceptional cooking, the center also compiled for sale at $3 each a cookbook of her most popular offerings. Because of what the center's children commonly asked their parents at mealtimes, the cookbook was entitled "Why Can't You Bake It Like Retha Does?"

Children's Entertainment Series

A number of centers offer a children's entertainment series as an ongoing fundraising activity. Some centers run movies for children in the center on four consecutive Saturdays, or one Saturday a month during the school year. Other centers offer them during school vacations when parents are often most eager for ideas on what to do with their kids.

As a variation, centers could offer puppet shows, skits, gymnastic lessons, dance classes, swimming, field trips, story hours, craft sessions, or any combinations of these.

Tickets to the events could be sold singly or at a reduced rate for the entire series. The advantage of offering a series instead of single events is that nearly the same amount of time and energy would go into preparing and publicizing

one event as would go into a series. Tickets could also be sold at the door.

One or two volunteers could be put in charge of setting up and running each event, while a separate committee would be in charge of publicity and advance sales.

No-Cake Bake Sale

The **Jewish Community Center Preschool (Tampa, Florida)** netted $300 with little effort by holding a no-cake bake sale. In lieu of asking parents to buy supplies, bake cakes, and staff a booth for a bake sale, parents were asked to send in a donation of $5 or more.

Trip to Bermuda

A successful raffle of a trip for two to Bermuda for four days and three nights — air fare and hotel included — added to the fundraising efforts of **Mt. Hope Day Care Center (Providence, Rhode Island)**. **Elizabeth Adams** reports that a board member knew of a local travel agency that gives away two trips a year to a community agency.

Last year, they received the trip to Bermuda. After a two month effort of selling tickets for $1 each or six for $5, a drawing was held and the center was $2,500 richer. The only cost involved was buying the raffle tickets.

Special Lunches

Olga Scharninghausen (Oak View Nursery School, San Rafael, California) adds variety to the daily routine and raises money at

the same time. Before the school year begins, several special lunches are scheduled throughout the year — about one a month. The school does not serve lunch, so this is a special treat. The typical menu is hot dogs, chips, orange juice, and ice cream for $2.

Parents sign up and pay for the lunches at the beginning of the year. Parents are reminded of the special lunch a week before — so that if they did not purchase it, they can include something special in their child's lunch. A few days before the lunch, a mother is recruited to buy the food. You could also vary the menu with pizza or tacos. Almost 100% participation raises $1,000 and provides lots of fun, too.

Mini Fiesta

Judy Morris (First Presbyterian Child Care, San Antonio, Texas) combines fundraising and fun for children, parents, and teachers. Every spring, they hold a mini fiesta for the children — two hours one evening.

All activities are planned with the children in mind — pony rides, an obstacle course, the renting of a space walk, throwing pennies in a jar, etc. The center closes one hour early, and families come to eat dinner and try all the activities. Tickets are sold — 25¢ each or five for $1 — to be used for activities and food. Examples — pony rides for four tickets or juice for two tickets.

Parents and teachers supervise all activities and the cooking. The menu includes food that children like — fajitas, nachos, chalupas, fruit, and juice or soda. The door prizes are contributed by local businesses. The center posts a list of needs for the evening — food, paper products, or balloons to decorate the center. All parents sign up to contribute something.

Judy reports that the fiesta is lots of work, but lots of fun for all involved. The families and friends of most currently enrolled children come, in addition to some former families and church members (150+). The money raised — $2,000 — is used for the needs of the center or staff enrichment.

Car Smash

Anyone who has ever had car troubles has probably had the urge to smash a car. Many centers raise funds by giving people the opportunity to take their aggressions out on automobiles. A junked or about-to-be-junked car is towed to a field or vacant lot near a busy street or to the booth area of a fair. A big sign is put up offering passersby the opportunity to take two whacks at the car with a large sledge hammer for 50¢. Aggressors must pay a premium ($1 or more) if they want the first swing at the windows or headlights.

A variation on the theme used by one center was to have people pay to paint graffiti, designs, or whatever on an operational VW. At the end of the day, the painted car was sold to the highest bidder.

Usually it is possible to get a junk car donated. The major problem is the clean up. A center will need to have a flatbed truck available to haul the car away at the end of the event. In addition, volunteers will be needed to clean up the broken parts.

If 200 individuals pay 50¢ to violate the auto, the center will net about $75 after expenses.

Haircutting

In **Chapel Hills, North Carolina**, a group of hair stylists gave haircuts at a city street fair and turned the proceeds over to the **Warrenton Child Development Center**. **Faith Becker**, the center's director, reports that the hair stylists were recruited months in advance, and posters plugging the event and the stylists' business were put up city wide several weeks in advance. The haircutting took place for ten hours on a Sunday. Refreshments were provided by the center to those waiting to be served. There were also hair products on display which customers could purchase.

The cost to the center was minimal as the hair stylists paid for the posters and the parents donated the refreshments. Staff time in organizing the event and setting up the booth was estimated to be about 30 hours.

The customers were charged the going rate in Chapel Hill of $15, or a lesser rate if they could not afford this. The center netted $250 from the event. Ms. Becker reports that they could have raised more if they had had more than the two stylists to service the long lines that waited throughout the day.

Kids' Calendar

Many nursery schools and child care centers publish and sell calendars. The **Parent Child Center (La Salle, Colorado)** prints a calendar with the pictures of the center's children on their birthdays. The **New England Home for Little Wanderers (Boston,**

Massachusetts) prints full-color paintings by children on every page of their calendar. Other centers feature pictures of children engaging in center activities, drawings by young children from different countries, pictures of various scenes in the community, recipes for each month, and children's activities. Some centers also sell advertising space to local businesses. Others list on the appropriate dates coming events of community organizations.

Designing, laying out, and printing calendars can cost anywhere from 25¢ to $2 per calendar. The actual cost will depend upon the amount of copy design that has to be paid for, the quality of paper used, the number of colors used, and the number of calendars printed. These costs can be reduced if the center lays out the calendar itself and if it can get local technical schools or insurance companies to donate the printing.

If 300 calendars costing 50¢ each are sold for $2 each, the proceeds would be $450. On the other hand, if 25 business ads are sold for $50 each and 100 community events are listed for $2 each, the 300 calendars could be distributed free and the net proceeds would be $1,300. In either case, having the calendars in 300 homes would provide considerable publicity for the center.

House Tours

Mt. Zion Presbyterian Child Care Center (Mt. Zion, Illinois) raised $1,200 by selling 500 tickets, at $2.50 each, for a tour of five local houses. On the tickets was printed a map showing the location of the five houses along with a brief description of each house. On the day of the tour, ticket purchasers were free to visit these houses in any order between the hours of 2 and 5 pm. They were asked to take off their shoes upon entering the houses. No guided tours were offered — rather, people were free to explore the houses on their own.

The houses selected represented a variety of styles and features. The tour was held in December so that the families' Christmas decorations were also featured. Other organizations have pursued specific themes in their selection of tour houses.

For example, solar houses, renovated old houses, or houses with creative children's rooms or kitchens have been highlighted.

Owners of the homes were given the opportunity to stay and keep an eye on their homes or to go out and leave volunteers from the center in charge. In either case, **Elsie Mills**, Mt. Zion's director, recommends having one person stationed in each open room in each house to handle problems and answer questions.

The center provided free babysitting for participants at their center while the parents were touring the houses. After the event was over, all the homeowners visited each other's houses and then went to a potluck organized by the center. At the potluck, an instant evaluation of the event was made to help in planning the event for the following year.

Costs to the center for the project were less than $50 — for tickets and publicity. Since this was taken on by the board as their project, little staff time was expended on

the project except on the day of the event. One person on the board took charge, but many board members volunteered considerable time — selecting and recruiting homes, developing informational publicity releases about the homes, and selling tickets. The day of the tour 20 to 30 volunteers were required to staff the houses and the center.

International Food Feast

A new twist on the standard dinner fundraiser is an evening with an international flavor. The basic format is to have a series of booths set up around a central eating area. Each booth offers desserts and entrees from different countries. Participants at the feast can move from booth to booth selecting a meal with samplings from any variety of countries. Cheeses and wines from each country could be offered as well. Recipes for all the foods could be made available for sale.

To add to the festivity, periodic performances could be given featuring music and dances from the various countries. For excitement, there could be a raffle or door prize for a trip abroad. The trip could be donated or offered at a reduced rate by a local travel agency which might also be persuaded to provide travel posters to decorate the booths and to use in advance publicity in return for permission to set up a booth at the event.

Tickets could be sold to the event which entitle the purchaser four free "samples." The profitability of the event would depend upon the food being donated by parents, staff, and friends. An organizing committee would need to prepare

for the event about six months in advance. The night of the event 20 to 50 volunteers would be required to set up, maintain, and clean up the booths. Major expenses would include rental of a hall, purchase of plates, tableware, etc., and payment for entertainers.

Fairs! Fairs! Fairs!

The following is a collection of ideas on running successful fairs submitted by **Exchange** *readers:*

Organizing Ideas

Fairs are often inefficient as fundraisers because they require so many hours of volunteer time to organize and put on while yielding only a modest income. To avoid continuing an ineffective event year after year, a center should keep reasonably careful records of income, expenses, and volunteer hours expended for the event. One nursery school kept such a record and found that 65 individuals had invested over 500 hours in order to net $625 from a fair. If each volunteer had instead contributed only $10, they would have raised more money with no labor.

• In planning activities, care should be taken to provide a mix of activities which appeal to adults and children of all ages. If the fair is going to be aimed more narrowly at adult interests, thought should be given to providing child care during the event.

• Centers have found that fairs tend to be most successful if they are held outdoors since they can attract the interest of passersby.

• To begin developing a fundraising mailing list, have people register for a drawing at the fair.

Compile the names and addresses of those registering and send them notices of future fundraising events.

• Don't forget the publicity value of the fair. Be sure to have big signs clearly identifying your center and describing your services, and have plenty of your brochures on hand for interested parents.

Activity Ideas

• **Dunking booth.** Local celebrities are perched, one at a time, on a seat suspended over a water tank or swimming pool. People pay to throw baseballs at a target which, when hit, triggers a mechanism to dump the celebrity into the juice.

• **Used toy sale.** Parents and the center itself donate used but usable toys for resale at low prices at the fair.

• **Marble racer.** Using V-shaped corner boards and blocks, a parent constructs a marble racer on which two marbles pursue separate but equal twisting crisscrossing paths downhill to the finish line. Due to the amount of work involved, this should be constructed sturdily for reuse in future fairs as well as by children in the school.

• **Craft booths.** One area is reserved for tables for craftspersons to sell their wares. The center makes its money by charging a $15-25 fee for rental of each table. Crafts sold should be screened beforehand to ensure that goods offered are varied and of good quality. Some centers also rent tables to local merchants (such as florists and book dealers) to peddle their wares.

• **Miniature golf.** A challenging nine hole course is set up for junior and senior golfers. The object is to hit golf balls over, around, and through a variety of obstacles to hit nine targets. Obstacles could include drain pipes, ramps over children's swimming pools, old tires, bricks, string fences, chairs, and balloons.

Children's Style Show

For the past several years, **Kingsley House** in **New Orleans, Louisiana**, has held a style show in which all the center's children participate. Each year, two teachers and an aide are appointed to coordinate the event. They choose a theme (such as "King Tut"), plan appropriate decorations, and recruit parents to help decorate, sell tickets, and bake food for sale at the show.

Children can wear anything — swimsuits, shorts, nightgowns, etc. The parents write up a description of the outfit, which need not be handmade, and one mother reads this description as the child walks down the walkway during the show. Children also become involved by drawing some of the murals for the show.

Since the food and most of the decorations are usually donated, expenses are few. The three staff coordinators spend a good deal of time in preparing the show, and parents volunteer considerable time.

Margaret LaBlance, the center's child care director, reports that the original purpose of the event was to have an enjoyable social event for the families. Now it not only

provides a fun event that all look forward to but it also raises some money (approximately $450) for special classroom activities.

The Christmas Gift Wrap

From **Nancy Travis** at the **Southern Regional Education Board** comes the suggestion of operating a gift wrap service. Secure permission from a large department store or, better yet, a shopping mall to set up a gift wrapping booth on their premises during the weeks prior to Christmas. In setting up the space, be sure to use tables which are high and wide enough to provide a comfortable work area and to put up highly visible "gift wrapping service" signs which state clearly who the proceeds are for.

During store hours, have two or three workers on duty for a four or five hour shift basis. Charge customers a set rate on the basis of package size, but leave the door open to charge a negotiated rate for oversized or odd-shaped items. Be sure to make arrangements with the store owner on a safe overnight storage area for your materials.

Sufficient wrapping paper, pre-tied bows, and scissors would be needed to wrap 100 or so packages per day. The cost of these materials could be reduced by buying paper in bulk (on rolls with a cutter bar) or by seeking to have items donated (boxes from a bakery or department store, for example). The major commitment would be in terms of volunteers to plan the event and staff the booth — for a two-week stint, a total of 260 to 280 person hours could be required. If on the average ten packages were wrapped an hour during a two-week period, the net proceeds would be between $750 and $1,000. In addition, the center could receive considerable publicity by giving the center's brochure to every customer.

Community Scholarship Fund

Utilizing a $4,000 United Way grant, the **Day Care and Child Development of Tompkins County (New York)** has established a cooperative day care scholarship fund. Families experiencing short-term financial distress are potentially eligible for scholarships on a sliding fee scale basis to enable them to keep their children in child care during their crises. Applications, which are accepted from any of the Council's 11 centers or 200 family day care homes, are screened initially by a Council staff member who also checks to see if the person would be eligible for alternative forms of assistance. Qualifying applications are then reviewed for final approval by a committee of participating child care directors.

While expenditures are minimal, considerable Council and providers' staff time is required to solicit funds and screen applicants.

Parents, children, and centers all benefit from there being a continuity of care, instead of disruption, during crisis periods. Although it is too early to tell whether the Council will find it beneficial as well as possible to expand the scholarship fund, it would seem that such a collaborative project focusing on the needs of families should be of interest to a number of funding sources (unions, busi-

nesses, civic groups, and wealthy individuals).

Ice Cream Social

The **First United Methodist Day Care Center (Erie, Pennsylvania)** raised $1,200 by sponsoring an ice cream social. Most of the money was raised by sending out two tickets, selling for $1 each, to the 600+ families of the congregation of the church in which the center is housed. Many church members sent in money for the center even if they did not plan to attend. Most sent in donations of $5, although one $100 donation was received. Since the social was timed to coincide with a local arts festival in a park one block away, there were also some tickets sold at the door.

The event was held on a Wednesday in June from 6 to 8 pm. About 350 individuals attended in person. Many sales were also made on a carry-out basis. Parents brought home sundaes after picking up their child at the center. Elderly persons from a nearby senior citizens' high-rise brought home ice cream for their friends who were unable to attend. The event was advertised on the radio, in the local newspaper, in the center's newsletter, and in church.

The center's director, **Karen Morey**, reported that minimal resources in terms of time and money were required. Less than $100 was spent for the ice cream, tablecloths, disposable dishes, and refreshments. Cakes were donated, and five people spent one hour picking strawberries for topping. About 50 to 60 person hours were required for the entire project — about half for staffing the event while in progress and half for planning and setting up.

Challenge Grants

Many child care centers have been able to double their fundraising income by having businesses and foundations provide grants to match the monies the centers raised locally.

For example, a child care center in Pennsylvania raised about $500 with a fundraising event and then went to a local business and got it to contribute an equal amount to the center. Many foundations utilize this matching strategy in what are often referred to as "challenge grants." The Kresge Foundation provided a grant of $75,000 to the **John E. Boyd Center (Fall River, Massachusetts)** to construct a new facility with the condition that the center raise a matching $75,000 through their local fundraising efforts.

The intent of challenge-type grants is to maximize the impact of scarce charitable funds, as well as to ensure the commitment of and support for the recipient agencies. Generally, organizations making these grants require that the recipient agencies raise their matching funds primarily from donations and pledges from individuals and organizations in their own communities. Funds from government agencies and foundations usually do not qualify.

In some cases, funding sources have required that centers raise their entire matching share before the challenge grant is made. Other centers have received funding on a dollar-for-dollar basis. For example, a funding agency might reserve a specific amount of money for a center; and for each chunk of money the center raises, the agency makes a matching contribution until the reserved funds are exhausted.

Centers have found that a commitment to a challenge grant can be helpful to their local fundraising. They find that people are more inclined to make pledges or donations when they know the center will, in effect, receive $2 for every $1 they contribute. The reverse may also be true. Local businesses that do not have formal challenge grants may still be more inclined to give money to a center if that center asks the business to match whatever they can raise rather than asking for a flat 100% grant.

A Weekend with Buchwald

The **John E. Boyd Center for Child Care and Development** in **Fall River, Massachusetts**, raised about $10,000 when Art Buchwald donated his services for a weekend. **Kathleen Harrington**, from the center, set this in motion by writing a personal letter to the humorist describing the current needs of the center, the history of the center, and some of the crazy incidents which were part of its history (such as when the center was temporarily housed in an armory and they had to convert a military latrine into a Raggedy Ann bathroom). She concluded that if he would let her share with him the story of the center, there would be parts he could make hay with.

As a result, Buchwald offered to come to Newport, Rhode Island (near Fall River), for a weekend to do what he could for the center. The center took full advantage of this offer. Into the weekend they

packed a press conference, an appearance on a radio talk show, a dinner, a "lecture" at an historic mansion owned by Salve Regina — Newport College followed by a cocktail party at another of Newport's famous mansions, a sail on Ted Turner's yacht "Courageous," and a tennis match between Buchwald and local celebrities. All proceeds from these activities were donated to the center, as Buchwald waived his normal $6,000 speaking fee and the use of the mansions was donated.

Exchange does not recommend that centers bombard Buchwald for repeat performances but offers this as an example of how to secure support from local, area, or national celebrities.

Weekly Bingo Game

The **Shelley School**, a child care program serving 18 mentally retarded children in **Raleigh, North Carolina**, has raised as much as $27,000 in one year for its building expansion fund by operating a Bingo game. For two years, the school hired an outside Bingo operator to run the games five evenings a week. The school received a percentage of the profits from these games.

Lately, under new, stricter state legislation, the school has recruited volunteers to operate the game one night per week. Under the new rules, the school has been raising about $500 per month from Bingo.

To oversee the game, the school has set up a Bingo committee. This committee registered the game with the local sheriff as required. An initial investment of about $1,000 was made to purchase

Bingo equipment. Space, tables, and chairs to accommodate 100 to 125 players per evening were rented in a community building. A separate account was set up to maintain solid financial records on the project. Once the game was organized, little time has been required from center staff and parents for the ongoing operation.

Evelyn M. Turner, the school's director, observed that, while the benefits to the program have been invaluable, there have been drawbacks. Some organizations in the community ceased or lessened their support to the school either because they objected to the gambling aspect of Bingo or because they believed the school needed less support considering its Bingo revenues. She stresses that any program considering Bingo as a fundraiser must weigh this potential lessening of community support.

Warning: Bingo games are strictly, but diversely, regulated in every state. Check applicable laws and procedures in your state before launching a Bingo fundraiser.

Annual Tag Sale

Everything from pianos to tennis rackets is sold at a tag sale by the **Day Care Center of New Canaan (Connecticut)**. According to director **Margaret Easley**, the center has netted over $2,000, plus a great deal of publicity. Planning started four months before the event with a parents' dinner prepared by the center's children. At the dinner, parents signed up to work on one of six tag sale committees. Two parent/board member co-chairpersons, recruited to oversee the project, met periodically with representatives from the committees to plan and coordinate activities.

• A publicity committee (3 people) distributed posters as well as placed a newspaper ad appealing for donations of furniture, appliances, clothing, glassware, toys, books, and other salable used items. It also contacted, with great success, local real estate agents and professional tag sale promoters for leads on large scale donations.

• A heavy moving committee (2 people) collected heavy items donated.

• A set-up committee (10 people) brought in and set up tables donated by a church.

• An understaffed tagging committee (12 people) spent five long evenings putting price tags on all donated items.

• A selling committee (8 people) ran the sale and collected the money.

• And last, but far from least, a clean-up committee (10 people) spent several days cleaning out unsold items.

The event took place on a Saturday from 9 am to 3 pm in a gymnasium which the public school board allowed the center to use free of charge. The center also held a bake sale and a plant sale in conjunction with the sale and raised an additional $200 to $300.

Current Stationery Sales

Current, Inc., a mail order stationery company, offers a 45% discount on all its products for agency fundraisers. The **Cal Poly Children's Center (San Luis Obispo, California)** has found this a simple, yet productive, way of raising money.

The center distributes Current catalogs, provided free by Current, to the 40 families it serves, as well as to friends of the center. Twice a year it collects orders from everyone and sends them to Current. Those ordering pay the full catalog price, but when the center places the order, it gets the 45% discount. It collects abut $500 in orders each time from which it raises $225. **Missy Dannenberg**, the center's director, reports that it only requires two volunteers about an hour to fill out the order and then to sort the items when they arrive.

Gymnastics Program

The **Groton Child Development Center (New York)** runs a gymnastics program for children aged 2½ to 12. Up to 200 children can enroll for $2 per week for 10-week fall and spring sessions. The center employs a gymnastics director and four instructions (at $4 hour) to run two one-hour sessions weekday evenings and Saturday mornings.

Children are grouped by age and ability with a ratio of one instructor per group of five children. The program is operated in the gym of the local elementary school. In return for the use of the space, the center buys the school additional gymnastics equipment. **Brenda Benson**, the center's director, reports that the program raised about $1,000 for the center.

Concert Tickets

Elizabeth Adams (Mt. Hope Day Care Center, Providence, Rhode Island) has been successful in bringing several groups together to raise funds for her center. A local retirement home donated refreshments and the use of their large dining room for a concert by the Brown University Glee Club (which appreciated an opportunity to perform).

Tickets were sold to the residents of the home and the parents enrolled at the center. The only cost involved was printing the tickets. The $1,500 raised assures that this event will be repeated again.

Fundraising Ideas That Work

by Roger Neugebauer

Fundraising is often looked upon as a necessary evil in child care. Centers engage in fundraising to bring in the extra funds needed to ensure a basic level of quality.

But fundraising need not be a burden. A survey of **Exchange Panel of 200** members disclosed many fundraisers that are not labor intensive, that are fun, that build team spirit, and that provide positive visibility.

This article will share a variety of panel members' successful fundraising ideas. In addition, it will provide some tips for success that you can use as guidelines in developing your fundraising plans.

Sales

The most common form of fundraisers is the sale of products or services to parents and community members. Such fundraisers can range from a thrift shop bringing in profits approaching $100,000 a year to a bake sale netting less than $100. However, no matter how large your project, you need to take care to secure all necessary permits and pay all applicable taxes.

• **Consignment sale.** The **Harmony Schools** in Hopewell, New Jersey, raised $500 in a consignment sale. Parents brought in good condition items of need for young families, such as clothes, strollers, and cribs, and the center earned a percentage of each sale.

• **Paper cut-outs.** As a fundraiser for the Child Abuse Prevention Fund, the **Ebenezer Child Care Centers** in Milwaukee, Wisconsin, sold paper cut-outs of children. Families included their name on each cut-out they purchased, and the cut-outs were displayed like paper-doll chains around the centers.

• **Class pictures.** A professional photography company took pictures of the centers' children, and **Rainbow Chimes** in Huntington, New York, realized 50% of the profits of the sale of the pictures to parents and grandparents. The organization raised $4,000 with this project.

• **Spa days.** As Mother's Day gifts, the **Beginnings Child Care Center** in Lake Worth, Florida, sold "A Day at the Spa" for $90. The spa day included a Swedish massage, mineral pools, saunas, and a deep cleansing facial, all donated by a local resort.

• **Gourmet coffee.** The **Willow Woods Child Development Center** in Kansas City, Missouri, made $400 by selling gourmet coffee to parents. The center purchased 22 flavors of coffee wholesale in single pot packs and sold them prior to the holiday season in their centers with a minimum purchase of 50 packets.

• **Supermarket coupons.** The **Children's Learning Center** in Yardley, Pennsylvania, earns from $100 to $200 per week from the sale of supermarket certificates to parents. The center pays $950 for every $1,000 in certificates it buys from two local supermarkets.

• **Candy sales.** Every March, the parents at **Children's Discovery Center** in Toledo, Ohio, sell candy in time for Easter. In 1995, candy sales resulted in a profit of $9,500.

• **Book/toy store.** Every October, the **Harper Learning Center** at William Raney Harper College in Palatine, Illinois, holds two book and toy sale days at their center. Parents recruit local vendors and sales representatives for national companies to set up tables in the center's lobby. The center receives from 15% to 40% of each company's sales, resulting in a profit of from $1,000 to $3,000 per year.

• **Plant sales.** Twice a year, **Smoky Row Children's Center** in Powell, Ohio, earns $1,000 from the sale of plants. In November, the center sells poinsettia plants; in the spring, it sells bedding plants and hanging baskets.

• **Art auction.** The **Monadnock Community Day Care Center** in Peterborough, New Hampshire, raised over $10,000 with an art auction. The center approached local artists and asked them to donate one piece of art. The art was sold in a formal auction at the city hall.

• **Hoagie sales.** Periodically, the **Crafton Children's Center** in Pittsburgh, Pennsylvania, raises money by selling hoagies to parents. The staff prepares the sandwiches in their own kitchen and realizes a profit of 50% on all sales.

Events

Events can combine pleasure with profits. They can be fun, but they also can be a lot of work. Centers have experienced success with fundraising events as ambitious as golf tournaments and as modest as a morning tea.

• **5K run.** This year, the **Hi-Hello Day Care Center** in Freeport, New York, raised over $9,000 by sponsoring the second annual Waterfront 5K Run/Walk. A professional race organizer took care of managing, measuring, and timing the race. The center was in charge of promotions, registrations, refreshments, and prizes. In addition to the 5K run and the non-competitive 5K walk, the center also organized short fun runs for children.

• **RockerThon.** An annual event of the **Great Beginnings Christian School** in Canoga Park, California, is the RockerThon. Staff members secure pledges and try to rock for up to 24 hours (one year, five teachers lasted the whole time). The center has raised from $1,000 to $4,000 a year with this event.

• **Children's concert.** The **Good Samaritan Hospital Child Care Center** raised $500 by sponsoring a concert by Hugh Hanley. The center paid the performer's minimal fee, booked an auditorium, and sold tickets in the community.

• **Gala dance.** By holding a dinner dance for two consecutive years, the **Springfield Day Nursery** in Springfield, Massachusetts, has been able to raise over $55,000 for a scholarship fund. The black tie affair is held in the ballroom of a local hotel.

• **Fashion show.** For five years, the **Samaritan Child Care Center** in Troy, New York, has sponsored a children's fashion show. The event is held in the auditorium of a local community college. Children from the center, walking with their parents, model clothing provided at a discount by a local store. Local businesses pay for ads in the program. The event generates proceeds of around $4,000 a year.

• **Wine/food tasting.** In Fremont, California, **Tri-Cities Children's Centers** has sponsored "Tri-City Treats" for eight years. Area restaurants and wineries set up tasting booths at the local Hilton hotel. Mayors of area towns act as judges for the food and wine and award plaques to the winners. A newspaper provides all the publicity, a community college provides musical entertainment, and other businesses underwrite all other event expenses. As a result, the child care organization makes 100% profit on ticket sales, with this year's proceeds exceeding $10,000.

Games of Chance

Lotteries, bingo, and raffles raise large amounts of money for educational and charitable activities in this nation. Early childhood organizations often have difficulty justifying participation in these high stakes ventures. However, centers have found many creative

Tips for Fundraising Success

1. Make sure it's time efficient. People's time is a valuable resource and should not be squandered on fundraising projects that generate a small return on time invested. Successful projects generate anywhere from $25 to $150 per hour of time invested. Any project that generates less than $10 an hour should be viewed as a poor investment. For example, a few parents at the **Bethany Early Childhood Learning Center** in Highland Park, Illinois, raised over $2,000 wrapping gifts at holiday time with a minimal investment of time.

2. Sell what people already plan to buy. It is easier to sell someone something they already intend to buy than to create an interest. **Brooklyn Heights Montessori School** in Brooklyn, New York, for example, sells Christmas trees and clears between $10,000 and $12,000 per year. The **Gresham Heights Learning Center** in Gresham, Oregon, sells take-home spaghetti dinners. Parents pre-order the dinners, and then the staff makes spaghetti, sauce, garlic bread, and salad and packs it in to-go boxes.

3. Make it an annual event. There are several advantages to turning a successful fundraiser into an annual event. Usually the second time you do a project you can benefit from all the organizing that went into the initial effort — it will take less time and you won't repeat your mistakes the second time. In addition, if an event becomes an annual tradition, people will look forward to it, and set aside time and money for it. For example, **St. Rita's Child Care Center** in Dayton, Ohio, has held its auction every year for the past 11 years. Probably the longest running benefit for an early childhood program is the Westport Handcrafts Fair, an annual benefit for the **Westport Weston Cooperative Nursery School** in Westport, Connecticut, this year being held for the 30th consecutive year.

4. Build on your strengths. When thinking of a fundraising idea, you should think first about sticking to your knitting. Think of a project where you can use the skills and experience your organization already possesses. For example, the **Illinois State University Child Care Center** in Normal, Illinois, organizes and sells first aid travel kits for cars. **Children's for Children** in Cincinnati, Ohio, sponsors a one day early childhood conference for local caregivers which brings in about $3,000 per year.

5. Team up with other organizations. Sometimes a small child care organization can participate in a large fundraising project by joining forces with other local organizations. In Colorado Springs, the city, the library district, the park department, and the **Care Castle** intergenerational child care center are developing an intergenerational garden where flowers will be planted in memory/honor of grandparents, parents, and grandchildren. In Lansing, Michigan, several community organizations, including **St. Vincent's Home for Children** and the **Community Nursery School**, cooperate in sponsoring an annual raffle. By joining forces, they are able to offer prizes as big as automobiles.

6. Make it unique to your organization. To make for an appropriate and memorable fundraiser, tie the project into a unique feature of your organization. The **Fruit and Flower Day Nursery** in Portland, Oregon, for example, sells "Fruit and Flower" holiday baskets as a fundraiser.

7. Tie it to a celebration. Major events in the history of your organization present high profile opportunities to raise funds. For example, the **Early Childhood Enrichment Center** in Shaker Heights, Ohio, used the occasion of its 20th birthday to set up a 20th Anniversary Endowment Fund for scholarships. **St. Michael's Day Nursery** in Wilmington, Delaware, used the celebration of its 100th anniversary to raise over $300,000.

8. Capture the PR value of your fundraiser. Fundraising projects can increase the visibility of your organization in addition to generating funds. In the long run, the heightened recognition from a fundraiser may be of more value than the funds raised. For example, when the **Fairfax-San Anselmo Children's Center** in Fairfax, Virginia, conducts its annual fundraiser, it hangs a banner over a city street announcing "Annual Back to School Haircut Marathon" along with the center's name.

ways to raise funds with fun, low key games of chance.

• **Chinese auction.** The **Children's Space** in Salem, New Jersey, had a fun evening with a Chinese auction. Parents and staff solicited donations from local merchants. At the event, these donated items were displayed on tables with a bowl for each one. Participants buy tickets and place them in the bowl for each item they would like to win. At the end, one ticket is drawn from each bowl to determine the winners. Last year, the auction netted over $1,500.

• **Raffles.** Many organizations use raffles as fundraisers, either separately or as part of other activities. For example, the **Marriott Child Development Center** in Bethesda, Maryland, raised $2,500 by raffling weekend hotel packages donated by their corporate sponsor. The **Euclid Avenue Preschool** in Cleveland, Ohio, holds an annual Mother's Day Raffle in which "gifts for mother," such as dinners at nice restaurants, manicures, a dance cruise, and a night of babysitting, are the prizes.

• **Egg hunt.** The owners of a jewelry store came up with a creative way to help the **Fairfax-San Anselmo Children's Center** in Fairfax, California. The store filled 1,000 plastic Easter eggs with jelly beans. In 20 of these eggs, they also inserted gemstones. In one egg, they inserted a 21 carat diamond (in honor of the center's

21st anniversary). The eggs were displayed colorfully in the jewelry store's front window. The center mailed invitations to 3,500 people on their mailing list and that of the jewelry store encouraging them to join the egg hunt by buying an egg for at least a $3 donation.

Appeals

Sometimes the easiest way to raise money is to ask for it directly. What you are selling is the value of your service to the community. Success depends as much upon the reputation of your organization as it does on the means of making the appeal. Before launching a major appeal, be sure to check out all applicable rules and regulations.

• **Letter/phone appeal.** In Madison, New Jersey, the **FM Kirby Children's Center** raised $10,000 for a playground through an appeal for donations. A letter was mailed to all parents. Then one parent in each classroom called all parents who had not responded and reminded them that any donation, no matter how small, would be welcomed.

• **Care shares.** When the local Kiwanis Club in Cannon Beach, Oregon, adopted the **Cannon Beach Children's Center**, it came up with the idea of selling local residents "Care Shares for Quality." Shares were sold for $20 donations. Donors received official looking stock certificates.

• **Annual letter.** For 24 years, the board of the **Calvin Hill Day Care Center** in New Haven, Connecticut, has been sending out an annual appeal for donations. Each board member mails anywhere from 5 to 15 letters asking for a donation in any amount. This letter brings in about $5,000 a year.

• **Deposit donations.** One way **Early Childhood Options of University Circle** in Cleveland, Ohio, raises money for its scholarship fund is to ask parents to donate all or part of their deposit when they leave the program. Most parents have forgotten they made the deposit and gladly donate it to the fund.

• **Newsletter appeal.** The board newsletter of **Long Beach Day Nursery** in Long Beach, California, is used as a fundraising as well as a communication tool. The newsletter, which is mailed four times a year to 2,800 individuals, includes a progress report on the organization's three centers, a list of recent donors, a wish list of items the centers currently need, and a reply envelope for sending in donations.

• **Adopt an item.** In Fort Worth, Texas, the **St. Stephen Presbyterian Day School** periodically displays pictures of items the center needs along with their prices. Center parents and church members "adopt" an item by donating the price of a specific item.

Ask and Ye Shall Receive: A Primer for Large-Scale Fundraising

by Patricia Berl

In the past, large-scale fundraising activities went hand in hand with non profit organizations. Today, in an increasingly competitive and challenging business environment, every center, whether large or small, non profit or proprietary, single or multi-site, can benefit from a well-orchestrated fundraising campaign.

For child care directors, executing a successful fundraising plan can generate needed funds for daily operations or program expansions. Equally important, effective fundraising strengthens a center's image in the community and expands its market presence.

Fundraising in the 1990's will be a significant factor in maintaining the economic viability of many child care centers. Escalating costs of quality child care services necessitate supplementing income from parent tuitions and state and local subsidies.

Many centers are already turning to private individuals, corpora-

tions, and foundations who give over $10.5 billion annually to charitable causes. As the child care industry expands, competition for the funding sources will intensify. Directors must be prepared for the fundraising challenge ahead.

Before you embark upon a fundraising campaign, consider the primary axiom of fundraising:

Successful fundraising lies in blending your organization's goals with the interests and needs of the community.

An effective fundraising plan takes into account six key elements. These are:

• Gifts — the amount of money you are seeking to raise

• Prospects — the people in your community who have both an interest in and a potential for contributing to your cause

• Opportunity — the benefit that is directly bestowed upon the donor as a result of giving

• Appeal — the urgency, immediacy, and inherent attraction of your proposal

• Timing — the time frame within which you seek contributions or make an appeal

• Resources — the financial and human potential you have available to commit to fundraising activities (this includes planning time and management time for board, paid staff, and volunteers)

Much has been written about the psychology of fundraising. Professionals carefully consider three basic questions: who to ask, when to ask, and how much to ask for. A simple analogy of cookie jar economics illustrates the basic elements of strategic fundraising.

Successful fundraising lies in blending your organization's goals with the interests and needs of the community.

Think back to when you were a child and desperately wanted a cookie. Unfortunately, at three years of age, you could not independently obtain the cookies (gift) which were safely tucked away in a container on the top cupboard shelf. To fulfill your need, you naturally sought any family members (prospects) who could deliver the cookies to you.

If you went to your father, who was absorbed in the Sunday afternoon football game, your request fell on deaf ears (poor opportunity). If you approached your older brother, you were apt to run into more disappointment since, out of sheer sibling rivalry, he would choose not to grant your request. If, however, you approached your mom (favorable prospect who could derive personal satisfaction, i.e., benefit from meeting your request, since she baked the cook-

ies), you would likely meet with success providing that you met the following conditions:

• you did not ask right before dinner (timing)

• you were not greedy

Naturally, your petition emphasized how much you needed those cookies to the one person who would feel the most fulfilled in having met your request (appeal). Having successfully obtained your cookies, you came again and again to that generous donor (resources) for additional cookies.

What's true in cookie economics is true in all organized fundraising programs: First, identify your organization's needs; second, translate these needs into financial goals; third, determine your prospects; fourth, approach potential donors being mindful of the timing and immediacy of your appeal; and fifth, package your request in ways that match the donor's needs, style, and level of giving.

There are many activities from which to choose when drafting a fundraising plan. In selecting the *right* activity, begin by determining your center's financial needs. Then, balance your fundraising goal against the financial and human resources you have available to commit to the task of raising money.

Effective fundraising takes planning and time, not only from the director, but also from paid staff and volunteers. Finally, whatever activity you choose, whether it be an annual fundraiser or a gala special event, be certain that it is

consonant with the goals and values of your center and is acceptable to the community.

Below are several effective approaches for large-scale fundraising.

Annual fund drives. Annual fund drives are the bread and butter of professional fundraisers. These drives solicit donors annually by letter to contribute funds for the continued operation of the organization. Annual fund drives work because they capitalize on the fact that donors already believe in their cause and will support the organization. It is a fundraising fact that if people give once they will usually give again. Annual fund drives are institutionalized and occur year after year, thereby expanding exponentially the number of donors and gifts that can be realized.

Before you can reasonably expect a corporation to make a contribution to your center, you must first demonstrate your organization's viability and the community needs which you serve.

Capital campaigns are used to raise large amounts of money for capital improvements or program expansion. Capital campaigns selectively target donors who are capable of giving large contributions and have already demonstrated an interest in and willingness to donate to the organization. Capital campaigns are one-time events and focus 80% of available time on 10% of the potential donors who are most capable of giving 90% of the money needed.

Special events are particularly attractive to for profit centers since they focus the community's attention on the organization and expand its community image.

Generally, special events such as house and garden tours, auctions, dinners, lecture series, etc. require an outlay of cash to produce the event and are time and labor intensive. Expenses to put on a special event can eat voraciously into the event's proceeds if not carefully monitored. Special events require a six to eight month lead time. Nevertheless, they can enhance an organization's image in the community and expand business presence.

Corporate philanthropy. Before you knock on corporate doors, remember that corporate giving is not just altruism. Corporations give because they realize tax benefits or see potential to expand their markets, e.g., McDonald's sponsorship of the Special Olympics. When making an appeal to corporate donors, consider how you will provide donor recognition.

Before you can reasonably expect a corporation to make a contribution to your center, you must first demonstrate your organization's viability and the community needs which you serve.

Finally, have clearly stated goals, long-range plans, experienced leadership, a competent staff, an involved and resourceful board, and a fiscally sound budget in place before corporate solicitation begins. Corporations expect their investments to pay off both in terms of donor recognition and community needs fulfilled.

Before outlining your center's fundraising strategy, define the organization's mission and programs, identify funding goals, allocate available financial and human resources, select an approach, plan well, start early, and think positively.

Ask and ye shall receive.

Patricia Berl is a regional manager for CorporateFamily Solutions, an organization managing work site centers for employers.

People Giving to People: Executing an Annual Giving Campaign

by Patricia Berl

Increasingly, child care centers are seeking ways to expand financial resources beyond parent tuition. Toward this end, fundraising strategies are taking on a greater significance in enhancing the economic survival of non profit centers.

While in the past fundraising was synonymous with flea markets, car washes, and door-to-door candy sales, today it requires a highly disciplined and managed process. Its success lies in:

• a thorough understanding of the center's goals and objectives;

• knowledge of the potential bene-factors;

• rigorous planning and follow up.

Most child care directors recognize the need for fundraising. Yet, they are reluctant to initiate fund development programs, lacking experience as well as understanding of well established professional techniques for executing a successful campaign.

Gearing Up

Before you embark on a fundraising program, consider the first axiom of fundraising: *people give to people*. Since 1985, individuals have been contributing 90% of all private philanthropic dollars in the United States. Corporations and foundations give less than 10% of the total charitable giving. Clearly, the major source of philanthropy is the individual contributor. The fundraising challenge to directors is to tap the individual giver.

An effective fundraising campaign cannot be undertaken solely by the director. It must have the full understanding and support of the board of directors and the knowledgeable commitment of dedicated volunteers. The quality of this commitment among participants will define the scope of the fundraising campaign that can be realistically executed.

Annual Giving Campaigns

Fund drives known as *annual giving campaigns* are the most effective way to raise significant and supplemental operating funds for schools and centers. Because these campaigns directly target the current and potential families in your center, there is a strong incentive for donors to give. Furthermore, the inherent recurring nature of the annual giving campaign format reinforces the donor's connection with the center over time.

For the past seven years, I have conducted annual giving campaigns at two centers, raising an aggregate of over $150,000. In the course of conducting these campaigns, I have identified eight essential points for managing a successful fund drive. These are:

• Know why you are raising the money.

• Set a financial goal.

• Target the message.

• Tailor the appeal.

• Draft the letter.

• Cultivate donor response.

• Implement donor response.

• Evaluate the campaign.

Know Why You Are Raising the Money

Before you initiate an annual giving campaign, stop and consider why you wish to raise the money. To answer this question, begin by defining what your center is: how it communicates its needs, goals, and objectives to the community. In fundraising circles, this exercise of introspection is a *case statement*. It includes the following: your statement of purpose, list of current goals and objectives, history, statement of current needs and future needs, financial resources, list of previous donors, and an analysis of the market. In preparing the case statement, define your center in concise terms that will help gain consensus among the board of directors.

Next, consider how your center fits into the broader community — its market. Unfortunately, the *do good mentality* of most non profits is not sufficient justification for donors to give to your cause. Successful fundraising depends upon fundamental marketing principles.

Barry Nicholson, consultant to the Funding Center in Washington, DC, sees it as the process of understanding and responding to the exchange relationship between the community and the non profit organization. According to Nicholson:

"Centers usually emerge in response to perceived needs in the environment. But the environment is constantly changing; and, therefore, non profits must remain sensitive to these changes or market requirements. Non profits must recognize that they are something more than do good entities, that they do not live in a vacuum. Market sensitivity requires that organizations continually look at their role in the community."

Summing up Nicholson, environments tend to dictate what people need, and this in turn dictates what organizations do. With an awareness of marketing principles, child care centers can examine their mission in light of the real (versus perceived) needs of the community.

Set a Financial Goal

Having identified your mission and needs, set a financial goal. Think realistically but think big, at least 50% more than you expect to raise. It is helpful to suggest a contribution amount sought from the donor. Left on their own, donors will frequently underestimate the amount of contribution needed. By specifying the size of the donation needed, chances are increased that the financial target will be attained.

Emphasizing 100% participation is also important, although personalized follow-ups are most effective when focused upon specific donors who have the greatest potential for giving significant contributions. In fundraising, as well as in business, the 80/20 Paretto rule applies — 80% of the funds you receive will come from 20% or fewer of the donors solicited.

Concrete objectives stated with clearly understood price tags — for example, "the addition of a $3,000 piece of climbing equipment to improve the playscape for the two year olds" or "the creation of a continuing education fund for staff to pursue graduate education" — are appeals that attract donors. These goals have a visible and more lasting effect on your program and services.

Generally, avoid appeals aimed at improving administrative support. Computers in the office, while necessary, do not generate the same degree of interest as computers in the classroom.

Finally, determine the length of the campaign. Generally, six to eight weeks is a good rule of thumb since most responses will be received within 10 to 14 days of the appeal. Fund drives that extend beyond three months rarely justify the investment in time.

Target the Message

Identify potential donors and target the funding appeal to specific populations that share a mutuality of interest with your organization. Obviously, those who benefit most directly from your services — the families of the children in your center — are the primary donor base. But parents of current students are just one group within the universe of donors to whom you appeal.

Parents of former students who once benefited from your center, parents of children yet to come, and grandparents of presently enrolled students expand the potential donor base.

Secondarily, community service groups, vendors, and contractors who perform service for your center can also be considered as donor prospects. All have a stake in seeing that your center remains a viable and contributing organization in the community.

Tailor the Appeal

Tailoring a fundraising appeal can be one of the most challenging and creative aspects of the development process. It involves matching the donor's interests with the needs of your organization. Because people give to people and not to causes, the more you know about the donor's personal history, values, education, interests, and investment in your community, the greater your success at appealing to the mutuality of interests between your center and the prospective donors.

Each appeal should be designed around the profile and interests of the donor. Appeals to parents of current students can stress the urgency of receiving money now to enrich a specific program that directly benefits their children.

Appeals to parents of former students can remind the donor of the important start their child received from your school, and the value in supporting the center in its mission to others. Parents of younger sisters and brothers who will attend the center in the future can be approached from the perspective that future viability depends upon the availability of the resources now.

When approaching the grandparents of children in your center as prospective donors, two considerations should be given: (1) gain the parents' permission before soliciting grandparents for contributions and (2) send some form of communication such as a newsletter or program brochure to the grandparents before mailing the appeal letter. Providing these guidelines are followed, grandparents can become a substantial donor group.

Finally, businesses, contractors, and all others who routinely provide services to the center can be approached from the perspective of the value your center adds to the community. When soliciting these groups, consider the length of time of the relationship, playing on the strength and continuity of that relationship.

Draft the Letter

The solicitation letter is the most direct way to reach donors. It consists of three parts: the letter; donor response card; and a return, school addressed, stamped envelope. Inserting a fact sheet, newsletter, or brochure of the school is also helpful to donors who are not currently parents in the center.

The length of the letter should be limited to a page and a half, single spaced, with a large signature block. The addition of the names of your board of directors in reduced type in the upper left hand margin contributes to a professional look.

In constructing the letter, do not exceed eight paragraphs. For the opening, identify your center, its goals, and student population. You also may include a few sentences of brief history about your center. In the following paragraph, define your needs and announce the fund drive. State the financial requirements needed to achieve your goals. Emphasize the urgency of the need, the necessity of the annual giving campaign, and budget constraints.

Next, restate the financial goal of the campaign, specify the amount of individual contribution needed, and stress everyone's participation. Explain the donor response card, time frame for making the response, and any follow up planned.

In the closing paragraphs, reaffirm your need and reiterate the importance of the campaign's success. Express gratitude for the donor's consideration and participation.

Cultivate Donors

Many annual giving campaigns include a preappeal telephone contact with targeted donors to introduce the program and to entice special interest. Other campaigns send out solicitation letters, then follow up with a call to answer questions about the campaign, thereby encouraging each donor's careful consideration of appropriate levels of giving.

Social events such as receptions, dinners, and home-school events can provide a forum for introducing the annual campaign. Peer solicitation from parents to parents is most effective, as their common interests are integrated with the challenges and benefits of the campaign drive.

Implement Donor Response

The donor response card will help you track your donor and follow up pledge contributions. It will also provide you with the information necessary to update your mailing lists for subsequent fund drives.

The response card includes donor name, status (parent of current child enrolled at the center, grandparent, friend of organization, board member, etc.), address, and contribution amount or pledge amount with date specified when pledge will be made. This card accompanies the donor's contribution, serves as the record, and becomes the future base for next year's donor list.

Respond to donors with a prewritten thank you note that contains a blank for filling in the contribution amount. Add a written word of thanks at the end and personally sign all acknowledgments. A carboned letter is useful. The top copy is sent to the parent and the carbon is your record.

Evaluate the Campaign

Be sure to correct your donor lists against information provided

from the return donor response card. Analyze your campaign results and establish next year's goals on the basis of your experience. If donors give once, they will give again, so continually follow up.

Remember, people give to people: believe in your organization and, above all, believe in yourself. Ask confidently for what you want, do not settle for less, and begin now!

Carefully executed, your annual fund campaign effort will not only generate ongoing financial support but will, additionally, and of equal importance, enhance your center's presence in the community.

Patricia Berl is a regional manager for CorporateFamily Solutions, an organization managing work site centers for employers.

Step by Step to a Successful Annual Giving Telephone Campaign

by Jane Ewing and Susan Morris

Fundraising is a part of life in any non profit organization. A telephone campaign allows you the opportunity to personalize it. Ideally, you would be able to talk to each constituent face to face, but that isn't realistic with many potential donors and limited numbers of volunteers. The solution is a personal phone call to people that we know and that know us. At The Little School, we have had successful phone campaigns for nine years now, resulting in close to $200,000 in donations. With careful planning, telephone campaigns can be a source of much needed funds for any organization.

Step #1 — Rallying Board Support

Make sure that your board of trustees understands their responsibility to make annual giving successful. It is first and foremost the responsibility of the board to ensure the financial stability of the organization. The development committee needs to present information about the campaign to the board, well in advance of when the campaign is expected to start. If you have never done one before, you will need several months of preparation/explanation time. Often, there is resistance from board members who don't understand that this is part of their responsibility. They need to acknowledge the responsibility and then become enthusiastic about it. Information about annual giving campaign responsibilities should be given to prospective board members during the recruitment process.

Board members also need to know that they have a responsibility to contribute themselves. We don't tell our board members how much to give, but we do tell them that we expect everybody to give something. You can't expect your constituency to participate if your own board does not participate.

Step #2 — Preparing Your Constituency

If your organization has never had a formal organized annual giving campaign, in any form whatsoever, it would be realistic from the time that the board decides to have one, until you begin the campaign, to give yourself at least six months for low key explanations to your constituency. Information could be in your newsletter or in a preliminary letter that goes out over the signature of the president of the board. Tell people why — annual giving campaigns are needed because tuition or fees do not cover the cost of providing the services you offer. You are trying to keep these costs as low as possible but the time has come for an organized campaign. Let people know that you would appreciate all comments and questions. Let people know that the campaign is coming.

When people enroll in your program, inform them that fundraising is part of the life of the institution. We don't tell people a fixed amount or percentage to give, but we tell them that we do have an annual fundraising campaign and they will be asked to contribute. When a family enrolls, we request from them all of the information that is pertinent to their child, but we also want to know who they work for and any other demographic information that would give us a picture of what their capacity is as a donor. All of this is kept in the confidential files, accessible only to the development committee for the purposes of extracting pertinent information.

It is important to know who people work for, particularly when it comes to employees of a company like Boeing, where a gift matching program exists. For a list of companies who offer gift matching programs, consult the Development Officers Association or a large non profit organization.

One of the disappointments is that the vast majority of companies will not support educational programs below the secondary level. A few years ago, Boeing would not match gifts made by elementary level families; now they do. Get your constituency to be more and more aware of what their employer is willing to do.

Step #3 — Setting Your Sights

You need to establish a very specific monetary goal for budgeting purposes. Establish a realistic goal — one that you can and will achieve. The sense of accomplishment, success, and pleasure in achieving your goal is very important to all involved. Establish your goals far in advance of beginning the campaign. Inform all prospective donors of the amount.

To figure the goal, look at the recent history of fundraising at your organization — note that, hopefully, the amount of funds raised has been steadily increasing over the years, look at the number of families enrolled in the school (or members or constituents of the organization), consider your current tuition or fees and how they might affect fundraising. The first year we had an established goal, it was roughly the equivalent of a 10% increase over the previous year's actual donations. Work with the finance committee in setting a realistic goal.

Step #4 — Maintaining Your Files

The development committee should keep its own complete files on all current families, all alumni families, all current and previous donors, and friends of the school who have been donors, or anyone who could have some interest in or connection to the school.

At the time of the annual giving appeal, go through these files and segment or divide them into relevant categories, such as their current association with the school. We also break the donors down into giving categories — donors who have given anywhere from nothing (if they are new families) up to $100, then $100 and over.

Review all of this information on an ongoing basis — keeping phone numbers and addresses up to date and noting separations, divorces, remarriages, births, deaths, and changes in employment status. If someone has had a big promotion or is now unemployed, you need to know that sort of thing.

A complete donor history is also included. It's very useful to see that somebody started out as a new family giving $25, increasing steadily until now, after being with the school for five years, they are giving $250. This information helps you know what kind of gift to ask for.

Step #5 — Getting the Timing Right

We find that fall is the best time of year to do annual giving, after school has been in session six to eight weeks. Try not to conduct a campaign close to Christmas or right after the first of the year. For tax purposes, there may be advantages to completing the campaign before the end of the year. In some cases involving the matching funds, you may not want donors to actually make their payment before year end if timing affects how the gift is matched.

Step #6 — Establishing a Time Frame

It is impossible to contact everybody in one or two nights. Spread the campaign out over a period of several weeks so people who are unavailable on specific nights of the week can be reached. Do not call after 9:00 pm or on a Friday night. If there is something going on, like the election last year, don't call on that night. If a big sports program is being televised, you can weigh whether or not they would be more annoyed at being interrupted or more likely to be at home. Think about the logistics of the timing.

Step #7 — Making the Appeal: The Letter

The appeal really matters! At least two weeks before the phone-a-thon, send a short personal letter to all of the people who will be contacted. It should go out over the signature of the chairperson of the development committee and the president of the board of trustees. It should be a combination of emotional appeal and factual information. Explain briefly that annual giving supports the annual operating budget, it covers a variety of different programs at the school, and we need to do fundraising because we attempt to keep tuition as low as possible. Let your constituency know that the phone calls will be coming; give them the dates and even the times so they know when you will be calling. Communicate in a positive, very upbeat way without the faintest whiff of an apology.

Send out the mailing so that it looks like first class mail but is really bulk mail. To do this, you need to use fairly decent stationery and get bulk mail stamps from the post office, instead of using an imprint. People are more inclined to read mail if it doesn't look like junk mail. DO NOT put a pledge return envelope in this mailing. You might elicit donations that are a smaller amount than what you would get from making a personal phone call. Sending out this preliminary mailing reduces the amount of time you need to spend making your pitch on the telephone.

Step #8 — Making the Appeal: The Call

Look for donated office space so that you have access to many telephones and perhaps many separate offices. Privacy allows for more personal conversations and less awkwardness while callers are warming up.

Let all of your volunteers know well in advance what your dates are so that they can make commitments on their own calendars. Send reminders at least four to seven days before their night to call and include specific driving directions. Provide a light supper during the training.

We train our board members and other volunteers early in the first evening they work. Begin by acknowledging the importance of the volunteers to the campaign and that everyone is nervous and finds it difficult to ask for donations, but they will be effective after training and practice. We show a video on how to make solicitation phone calls.

Guidelines are very specific: be enthusiastic, supportive, and convincing. Ask the prospective donor for a specific amount. We give very clear guidelines of how to go about this. If somebody has been giving $25 a year for the last five years, try to move them up, either increase it by 10% or move up to a round number. This year, because it was the 30th anniversary of the school, we asked people to give $30.

Be creative but realistic! If somebody has been giving $25 a year, it would not be realistic to ask them for $500 unless you have very specific information about their financial circumstances having changed. If a family has been giving generously but is no longer in the program and they appear reluctant to give, the appeal might be that we are asking all supporters of the school to continue to be supporters and would they consider giving a token gift. The language is very specific. Always ask WOULD you consider giving a gift of a certain amount. Let the person think about it briefly.

Inexperienced callers should call people who are in the modest gift giving range. Experienced callers should call major givers. If possible, have the same person call the same group year after year. There is a real advantage to this because a relationship is established. People who currently have children in the program are very effective in calling new families and other currently enrolled families because they have something in common. It is especially successful to have someone who was a new parent last year call people who are new parents this year.

Step #9 —
Documenting the
Response

When we make our phone calls, each solicitor has a loose leaf notebook with the printout — one sheet per person — of donor information. They record directly on the printout the results of their phone call — the person wasn't home, the person was home and declined to make a gift, the person was home and agreed to make a pledge of a specific amount or agreed to make a pledge of an unspecified amount. All of this needs to be noted, dated, and initialed.

Phone solicitors have a choice of three different form letters that they fill out after each phone call, depending on the results:

• One letter is a thank you for your pledge — the specific amount is filled in.

• The second one is a thank you for your pledge of an unspecified amount.

• The third one is a thank you for giving me the time to talk to you: I understand you don't wish to make a pledge; we hope that we can count on your support. Although this third letter is rarely productive, it is a gracious thing to do.

The volunteer notes on the donor's record the results of the phone call and fills out the form letter, personalized with the donor's name and a very brief personal note at the bottom. A pledge envelope accompanies this confirmation

letter. The letters go out the next day by first class mail. It is very, very important to have an immediate follow up of the telephone call.

We have become much more skillful in capitalizing on matching gift potential, which has had a tremendous positive effect on our goal. We've been very successful in increasing the percentage of participation of the current families and in renewing donors who hadn't been giving in recent years. We have been able to go back to people who had given consistently but who hadn't been actively giving in the last couple of years and make an appeal to them to simply elicit a modest gift which brings them back into active giving. Effectiveness comes from getting your files in order — knowing who these people are, why they were giving in the first place, and why they stopped — and tailoring your appeal in a way that makes sense.

Step #10 —
Following Through

Toward the end of the calendar year, we put a reminder in our newsletter: "For those people for whom it's important to make their pledges before the end of the calendar year for tax purposes, this is a reminder."

We tell people when they make their pledge that they have until June 30th, which is the end of our fiscal year, in order for their pledge to count for that year's budget. Some people will tell us specifically they will make their pledge in February, etc. or will ask for a specific reminder.

To people who have not made their payment by the end of April, we send out a personalized reminder: "We are coming to the end of our fiscal year and the end of our school year. Our records indicate that you made a pledge of $75. This is just a reminder. We hope we can still count on you. If you have already sent in your pledge, please let us know so that we can make sure our records are accurate and up to date." This elicits the vast majority of pledges that have not been paid up until that point.

Before December 31st, we mail a letter to all of those people who received the initial appeal letter whom we were not able to reach by phone: "We are sorry we could not reach you. We hope that we can still count on you. We're at 70% of our goal and 70% of our participation." Give them a little update. DO include a pledge envelope. If these people do not respond to this letter, we usually don't contact them again.

The acknowledgment of pledges is very important. Our goal is to have an acknowledgment in the mail the same day each gift is received. We have preprinted acknowledgment cards that need to be filled in with the donor's name, the gift amount, and the date. When donations are received, the name and the amount are recorded in our donor receipts book and on their donor record file. We make a photocopy of every check as another form of back-up information about who the donors are and as a resource for updating addresses and phone numbers. All volunteers are thanked in writing.

When we print our annual report, the names of ALL donors are included unless somebody requests anonymity. It is essential to make sure that you include everybody who should be included in the annual report and that their names are listed in the way in which they wish to be acknowledged.

To conclude, the annual giving phone campaign is a way to keep your constituency giving. A personal phone call assures them that every contribution is valuable and appreciated. Be grateful for $5 gifts and for $500 gifts! Annual campaigns put you in the business of receiving gifts and acknowledging gifts, in the way you would acknowledge a birthday present. You want to be gracious and efficient about how you do it. This is important! If people are giving you their money, they want to give it to somebody who will manage it efficiently and gracefully.

Jane Ewing, at the time this article was written, was director of development at The Little School and a board member of Northwest Development Officers Association. Susan Morris was a member of the board of trustees of The Little School.

Losing Money/ Making Money

by Lynne Meservey

Where have all the dollars gone? You were so sure that the tuition rate you established was competitive, yet fair. You've controlled your expenses. So why isn't your center earning what you expected? It may be that two important factors have not been considered. The first factor is discounting and the second is ancillary programs.

Discounting

Most child care programs offer discounts for employee children, multi-child families, vacations, and/or absenteeism. Often these discounts are deducted from tuition fees prior to recording income. When this bookkeeping procedure is used, the center's financial statements will not contain important information concerning the actual cost of discounting. A $65 tuition fee may result in $57 of actual income after discounting. It's best to have your profit and loss statement show the full tuition amount and to account for each of the discount categories.

Ancillary income programs can help recover losses due to discounting.

Ancillary Income

Centers that lose $8 to $10 of income to discounting can recover the loss *and actually improve on it* by offering well planned ancillary programs. Ancillary income is the money centers generate from sources other than normal tuition fees. These programs add diversity and enrichment to educational programming. The added value of ancillary activities can also keep families from withdrawing prematurely.

The working parent prefers programs that provide activities for their children that they have difficulty providing. There aren't many extra hours in a working mom's schedule to take children to dance classes, get haircuts, or to visit the circus when it is in town. Because parents want the best for children, dance, gymnastics, music appreciation, or other enrichment lessons are among the most popular of these programs. Children are also looking for fun and interesting things to do. School-age children respond especially well. Some projects can also be promoted to the public. These may be fundraisers for a charitable organization or promotions that help sell services.

There are four categories for child care ancillary programs — service, enrichment, product sales, and fundraisers. A well-balanced program will appeal to many family needs.

Service programs. Ask yourself, "What services could reduce the demands on busy working parents?" The most effective services will be those that save parents time and money. A survey of parents often produces a list of needs. The programs you choose should have value for a relatively large group of parents. The less staff time to oversee and implement the service, the better. Continually monitor and evaluate the quality and appropriateness of the service, and be sure that it does not detract from normal operations. Typical service programs include: breakfast, parent coffees, developmental testing, vision/hearing/speech assessments, occasional Saturday or evening care, birthday parties, tutoring, or mailing services.

Enrichment programs. Directors are most familiar with ancillary programs like dance, art, music, sports, field trips, movies, speakers, and computer lessons. They appeal to a relatively large number of children and have definite value. When consistent with a center's educational philosophy, they successfully relate to other learning in the center. There should be no pressure on families to participate and, whenever possible, these activities should occur out of view of children who are not part of the enrichment activity.

Product sales. Books, tote bags, t-shirts, and children's photographs are typical products centers sell to parents. Other creative items like toys, pre-made Easter baskets, or letters from Santa may be popular. It's wise to limit product sales in your ancillary program planning. The greatest risk is having a surplus inventory of an item that you can't unload on anyone! On a more positive note, a terrific, creative item can be a very effective money maker. Choose carefully and wisely and you'll be a winner. Volume purchasing will reduce the cost per item but watch out for overstocking. Inventory each piece and store carefully.

Fundraising. Fundraisers can be a great way to increase income. They require more pre-planning, organization, and lead time, but the returns can be good. Depending on the activity, manpower demands can affect the success of the project. Consider the types of money raising activities that are popular in your community and try to come up with a fresh approach. Be cautious. If a particular organization is already well known for having a big annual bazaar or carnival, you may be wise to develop a completely different idea. People expect to be entertained and to spend money — give them as many opportunities as possible to do both.

Choose dates carefully to be sure they don't compete for participants with another activity. A weekend following a holiday is often a good time. Always plan on an alternate rain date for outdoor functions, or have an indoor facility available. Involve as many others as you can; not only will the extra hands be helpful, but the more people you have, the more the word will be spread about the venture.

Projected Earnings

What kind of return can you realize? Let's face it, some projects are more fun to do and may be less work. Before you choose any program, consider:

• How much of your time will the project take?

• How much staff time will it take?

• What effect will the project have on the day-to-day operation of your center?

• How interested will the participants be in the project?

• What kind of return will you expect for the time and money invested?

• What are the risks involved?

• Can the parent afford the expense?

A mark up of at least 25% should be expected from any ancillary activity, but don't let that limit you in negotiating or setting prices. Supply and demand will guide you in determining the price and the program offered. When considering a project, carefully estimate the time it will take. Is it better to have several smaller, easier projects or one or two large ones? What effect will it have on the operation of the center, teachers, and children if special projects are continually changing routines, room arrangements, and employee workload?

Often a simple, easy-to-administer program produces a better return than one that is more complicated. For example, breakfast programs are fairly easy to administer and provide regular additional income while swimming or dance programs typically offer a much smaller return.

Planning Is the Key

Good ancillary programs require good planning. Compare programs and providers before you choose the ones you will use. Ask for written bids and check references carefully. Try to see instructors in action.

Give careful consideration to staffing needs beforehand. Staff must "buy-in" before they can be expected to support your plans and be enthusiastic about them. Involving your staff in the selection process will increase receptivity.

Balance the program carefully. Avoid scheduling two programs at the same time if they are likely to appeal to a wide market. Consider other events, activities, or timing that might affect participation. Perhaps holidays, vacation days, or public school schedules will have an impact on the program. Summertime is often a good time to plan a program for the up-coming school year. Outline the program and make contact with potential providers. Ask others for referrals. Require providers to be bonded and to produce insurance certificates.

Promotion

Use every resource at your disposal to promote all of your ancillary projects. Parents and children are a captive audience, so get their attention and support early to build enthusiasm. Several reminders will encourage action — at least three reminders seem to be the key. Use center newsletters, separate invitations, posters, banners, ancillary brochures, and bulletin boards to promote the program internally. Pre-selling tickets or requiring deposits encourages commitment and assures participation.

To promote your projects to the general public, send notices to local papers for placement in community bulletin boards. Contests may draw interest prior to the event, as will drawings for attractive prizes.

Repeat business is important. Be sure everything is prepared ahead of time and is organized. Nothing hurts a program more than confusion. It's always wise to ask participants and workers to evaluate each project so that improvements can be made.

And, lastly, have fun. Ancillary projects add variety to daily routines and play a major role in successful child care operations.

Lynne Meservey is vice president of operations for CorporateFamily Solutions in Nashville, Tennessee.

Long Range Planning

*"While day-to-day survival
sometimes feels like
a major accomplishment,
you really shouldn't
pat yourself on the back
until you are able to be working
on where the organization will be
two or three years into the future."*

How to Prepare a Business Plan

by Keith Stephens

> *"Cheshire-Puss," said Alice, "would you tell me, please, which way I ought to go from here?"*
>
> *"That depends a good deal on where you want to get to," said the Cat.*
>
> *"I don't much care where . . ." said Alice.*
>
> *"Then it doesn't matter which way you go," said the Cat.*
>
> *". . . so long as I get somewhere," Alice added as an explanation.*
>
> *"Oh, you're sure to do that," said the Cat, "if you only walk long enough."*
>
> — Lewis Carroll, ***Alice's Adventures in Wonderland***

Whether you are running General Electric or ABC Child Care Center, you will not succeed for long operating like Alice in Wonderland. Every business needs to know where it wants to go, and how it plans to get there.

For most child care operations, if there are any plans at all, they only exist in the head of the owner or the director. I am a firm believer in taking time to formally think through the directions for your child care business, and then committing the results to writing in the form of a business plan.

Having a business plan in place provides you with a starting point, a set of directions to guide your actions and decisions along the way, and a target to work towards. Having a specific goal is what drives most of us to accomplishment.

In addition, having thought through your business, set priorities, and documented your thinking, you will have a convenient vehicle for communicating with the people — staff, business advisors, bankers, etc. — who will help you accomplish your goals.

There is no set formula for writing a business plan. No matter how it is formatted, however, it should provide answers to five key questions:

Where are we?
What threats and opportunities do we face?
Where are we going?
How do we plan to get there?
What do the numbers say?

Where are we?

Just like when you use a road map, before you can determine how to get to where you want to go, you have to start by identifying where you are. The description of your current status should address the following points:

• **What business are we in?** What is the service we are selling? (Is it child care, education, family support?) Who are our customers? (Spell out as specifically as you can a profile of your current customers in terms of where they live, how much they earn, where they work, and what they want for their children.)

• **What is our philosophy?** Not only is it important to spell out your philosophy for other people to understand but it also helps each of us to go through the process of making a clear statement about what we are trying to accomplish: what our attitudes are about the needs of children, about the process of education, about the needs of parents, and about our role in terms of the families and communities we serve.

• **What is our track record?** Where are we coming from? How did we get started? How successful have we been to date? What major changes have we made along the way? In putting together your historical data, it can be very helpful to use charts and graphs to depict your progress visually.

• **Where are we now?** This should be a snapshot of the status of your business: assets, locations, enrollments, organizational structure, key personnel, main competitors, and current financial position.

What threats and opportunities do we face?

Answering the first question will cause you to take a hard look within your organization. This second question will force you to look outside, at forces and trends that may impact your program's future.

• **What threats do we face?** What factors could interfere with the development of our program? Is our lease about to expire? Are any new centers opening up within our service area? Is the availability of

qualified staff becoming a problem? Are the demographics of the neighborhoods we serve changing? Are parents being attracted to centers with different philosophies or lower fee scales? Are pending changes in licensing requirements going to increase our cost of doing business?

• **What opportunities are there?** Is there new residential growth taking place that will increase the demand for child care? Are local employers exploring child care options for their employees? Is the developer of the community's new business park interested in having a child care center as an amenity for the development? Could we build a new structure that is a better facility, yet more economical? Are there nearby neighborhoods or communities where the demand for child care is going unmet? Are any national chains interested in buying our business?

• **How do we rate with the competition?** You may find it helpful to analyze your relative competitive position by completing the chart entitled *Competitive Position*. In the left hand column, "Bases of Competition," list the characteristics that customers use to choose a child care center. These might include location, service, staff, program, reputation, facilities, and pricing, among others. In the second column, assign a relative weight to each characteristic on a scale of 1 to 5 (5 being the most important, 1 being the least). Now, list your major competitors across the top, beginning with your organization. For each characteristic, rate each competitor — including yourself — relative to each other with a rating of +1, 0, or -1. For example, if one competitor is relatively strong in terms of *location*, you would place a rating of +1 in

the upper part of the box for *location*. If another competitor is average in terms of its pricing, you would place a rating of 0 in the upper corner of the *pricing* box.

Determine a score for each characteristic by multiplying the individual rating by the weight for each characteristic and writing that score in the lower corner of the box. For example, if an organization was rated +1 for location, and you have assigned a weight of 5 to location, the resulting score would be +5. Now, sum up all the scores for each organization to arrive at total score. Finally, rank each of the competitors in terms of their total scores.

Where are we going?

This is the focal point of your business plan. After reviewing the current status of your business, set goals for your organization.

There are many ways to express the goals of your organization:

• **Customer objectives**. You may set specific goals for generating new customers, or for reducing customer turnover. Alternatively, you may decide to shift your customer base ("We will increase the share of families enrolled in the center with incomes above $35,000 to 50%").

• **Staff development objectives**. You should take a look at what objectives you need to achieve in terms of recruiting and training staff. For example, such goals might include, "Each staff member will attend one seminar or class on child development each month," or "A gymnastics person will be added to staff by September 1."

• **Program enhancements**. This encompasses any plans to upgrade the operation of your program — such as adding a new playground, remodeling the interior of your center, or equipping your center with a new computer program.

• **Market share**. You should take a look at where you are going to be in the market. For example, if you are in a major city, one of your goals might be to increase your share of the market from 1% to 2% in order to solidify your business base in that community.

• **Growth rate**. Your goals for growth may be expressed in terms of *units* ("We will add two new centers a year for the next five years"); *enrollments* ("We will increase the number of children enrolled by 100%" or "We will increase the utilization rate of our center to 90%"); or *stability* ("We will maintain the utilization level of our current center").

• **Income objectives**, articulated in terms of *gross revenues* ("We will increase revenues at the rate of 20% per year for the next five years") or *profits* (We will increase center profits by 15% per year"). Since the revenue you collect is a function of the number of customers, the programs, and the rate charged, you may want to establish goals for each of these items ("We will increase the number of children served to 160 by September 30," and "We will add an after-school program serving 25 children by September 1," and "Our rate will be increased 5% on July 1").

• **Business ratios**. These can become useful as another means of measuring your progress. For example, you might state as your goals "reducing accounts receivable to less than one week's tuition" or "keeping my investment in proper-ty down to 50% of my total investment in the business." Expense ratios can be particularly helpful in the month-to-month management of your business. For example, such a goal might be "maintaining supply expenses at 5% of total program cost."

• **Personal objectives**. If you are the owner of the business, you need to be thinking about how the business fits into your own plans. Do you plan to run the center until your children are old enough to take it over? Are you grooming someone else to run the center for you when you are ready to retire? Or are you planning to build up a sound business and then sell it to a national chain? None of these will just happen. You need to recognize these personal issues in setting goals as well.

How do we plan to get there?

Having written your goals is a major accomplishment. But it is not enough. You need to translate these goals into results by developing and implementing specific *strategies* or *action plans* for making them happen.

If your goals call for considerable expansion, you will need to develop strategies for securing financing, for locating suitable sites, for designing appropriate buildings, and for accelerating your marketing efforts. If your goals call for working more closely with employers, you will need to develop strategies for identifying and making inroads with employers likely to be interested in child care as a benefit.

People. No matter what your goals are, however, one area you will cer-tainly need to look at in developing your action plans is people. Having the right people on board at the right time is crucial to the success of nearly anything you want to accomplish.

You need to look at your goals and ask: "Will we need to add people to accomplish what we plan to do?" "Will the types of people we need be readily available?" "What kind of training will be necessary to prepare people for what they will be doing?"

Structure. An organizational chart is a necessary part of analyzing your people requirements. Not only does it depict for you how your organization fits together, it also helps you identify key people you will need to bring in and when, or who will need to be upgraded by when, and when their training will need to start if they are going to be groomed from within.

In the business plan you may include more than one organizational chart — one for how your structure looks today and one for how it will look a few years down the line if you are to accomplish your goals.

Critical elements. A final step in analyzing your goals is an examination of elements critical to your success — things that absolutely have to be in place in order for you to accomplish your goals. Your business plan should include a listing of the three to five most critical elements. For example, if your intention is to locate new centers on fringes of development, then a critical element for your success will be infill — continued economic growth in communities you will be serving.

What do the numbers say?

After you have defined your goals and strategies, it is time to assign numerical values to these plans. It is important to convert the plans to cash because cash is what drives the machine. However, it is important to recognize also that the numbers are only one part of the business plan — really the last part. Your budgets and projections are just a numerical statement of goals. If you do everything up front well, the writing of the budget will come easy. All you are doing is taking the thought process you went through and assigning numbers to what you plan to do.

A standard business plan will forecast financial statistics for three to five years. These statistics typically include:

• **Annual income and expense statements**. Forecast the revenues and expenses that are likely to be generated as a result of the goals you have established. Don't forget to assign a cost to training and promotional activities that will be required to implement your goals.

• **Cash flow projections**. These projections are important to do in tandem with your annual budgets because they give a running view of the ebb and flow of income and expenses. They can help you identify points in time when your plans will result in cash surpluses and cash deficiencies. In doing these projections, it is helpful to separate out the cost of doing special projects (such as a major staff training effort or a one shot marketing campaign).

• **Balance sheets**. A balance sheet allows you to take a snapshot of what the business is worth at any point in time. It is a numerical assessment of how much the business owns (how much its assets are worth), how much it owes (how much its liabilities are), and what its net worth is (the difference between its assets and liabilities).

By projecting balance sheets on an annual basis, you can see the strength of the business and how it is changing from one year to the next — you don't really see that if you look only at your income and expense statements or at cash flow projections. They allow you to see when your cash balances are large so you can use this cash to do something else.

• **A statement of assumptions**. In making cost projections, you have to make certain assumptions. For example, you will have to make estimates about interest rates, food costs, and insurance costs. These assumptions will need to be spelled out in your business plan so that someone reading the plan can interpret your numbers.

A final caution: Developing a business plan is not a simple process. After you develop your goals and work out the numbers, you may find that you will end up losing money. You may have to go through the entire process several times in order to develop goals that are in line with your resources.

Q & A about Doing a Business Plan

Does every center really need to do a business plan? Without a doubt, every center can benefit from developing their own business plan. This is true whether you operate a chain of six centers or a single center for 40 children, wheth-er you are seeking outside financing for a major expansion effort or you are content to remain at your current size. Every business needs to think through in a formal way where it is going and how it plans to get there. Without such a plan, your business will drift from year to year in no particular direction.

How far in advance should you forecast? The standard for business plans is three to five years. That is a reasonable time period for most larger centers. A smaller center not looking to expand can probably do just as well with a one or two year plan. In any case, the farther into the future your plans and projections are made, the less reliable they will be. Therefore, while your projections for the coming year can be, and should be, quite specific, there is no point in pinning activities down dollar for dollar or month by month for distant years. For example, your cash flow projections could be done on a monthly basis for the first year, on a quarterly basis for the second year, and on an annual basis after that.

How often should the plan be updated? Every year. Very seldom will what you write in your plan today be what you actually implement when you get there. Inevitably, many changes will occur. But annual updates are not too burdensome. Once you have done all the hard work developing the initial plan, tinkering with it to reflect changes should not be too difficult. This is particularly true if you perform this work on a computer. If major changes occur, however, you may have to update it more than once a year. If you start veering off course significantly, you may find that your business plan is not at all reflective of reality — in which case you may need to chuck it and start all over again.

Would you do a plan differently if you were using it as a tool for raising money outside? No! Your basic business plan should be developed just as thoughtfully if you are going to use it to raise money outside or if it will only be used internally. If you do a good job on your business plan, you should only need to add two or three pages to have a package to deliver to outsiders. For example, if you are presenting the plan to your banker, you would probably want to include an initial statement of the kind of money you are looking for and how you plan to use it. If you are looking for investors, you would have more of a sales presentation at the front of your plan, and you might include some analysis of what their return would be.

Even if you do not plan to send your plan outside, you should still package your final product well. The better job you do on the packaging, the more important the document (and the thought processes behind it) becomes. If you have a handwritten, two-page plan with one 13-column scratch pad, this product is probably not something that you would treat as significant for very long.

Your business plan needs to be a working document that you review, access for information, and monitor your progress against on a regular basis. I'm a firm believer in putting it into a good enough format that it takes on some significance to the writer and to other people who should use it.

Who should be involved in developing the plan? You will probably

need an accountant to help you with the income projections. If you have any other business advisors, you should show them your plans to see if they make sense. In a small organization, board members who are involved in running a center need to be part and parcel in developing the plan.

It is also very important to involve employees. They can be particularly helpful in the evaluation of opportunities and threats — and in coming up with recommendations about what should be done.

Once the plan is completed, you should distribute it widely. My personal preference is to share all the information, even the financial information, with all officers and staff members. Your people are going to make the thing come about and they need to know what is expected and where the organization is going.

One reason to share information is that if the prospects are good, staff members already think they are better, and if prospects are bad, then they think they are good. It is a great asset for the people to know what the facts are, for them to know where the business is going, and what the opportunities are for them.

How should the final plan be formatted? The manner in which you commit your plans to print should first and foremost make sense to you. You can simply follow the format that was described above, with sections on the history and status of the organization, threats and opportunities, future plans, and financial projections. Or you can organize the information

as a series of goal statements, with background information and action plans spelled out for each one.

However, no matter how the plan is organized, its first page should be your mission statement. While you will not be able to develop this until all other parts of the plan are completed, this statement should be up front as a capsule summary of what is to follow. The mission statement should briefly state: who we are (your markets), what we provide (your services), where we operate (your service area), where we are heading (your goals), and why we are going to be successful (your competitive advantage).

How pessimistic or optimistic should you be with your financial projections? When you initially do your cash flow projections, you should strive to be as objective as possible. Try to be realistic in estimating revenues and expenses. Then, since none of us project the future with 100% accuracy, go back and say, "What if the revenues we project are not as great?" or "What if the projects that we want to undertake cost more than we expected?" In other words, go back and take a very conservative look at the cash flow.

Your business plan should include both of these projections — the realistic and conservative one. Chances are, you will end up somewhere in that range.

Keith Stephens, a CPA, is the former president of Palo Alto Preschools, once the country's largest privately owned child care chain, and past president of the National Association for Child Care Management.

Guidelines for Selling Your Child Care Business

by Keith Stephens

My partner and I recently sold our child care business. Fortunately, we prepared for the process and got some good advice along the way. As a result, we were able to strike a deal that gave us an excellent return on all the money, time, and ideas we had invested in our business.

In retrospect, I can see that had we not been so well prepared and well informed, we could easily have thrown away a substantial share of our investment. So when **Exchange** invited me to share my insights from this experience, I jumped at the chance. I am eager to share with those of you who may be thinking about selling your child care businesses, either today or in ten years, some pointers I learned along the way.

The time to prepare for the sale of your business is now. In order to secure a satisfactory sale price, you need to do your homework. How you organize and manage your business today determines its salability tomorrow.

Have a sound record keeping system in place.

When it comes time to sell, potential buyers will be interested in not only what your bank balance is today but also how your business has performed over time. If you want to get a good price, you have to be able to make the case that you have a growing business with a solid track record. Without sound records, you have no case.

Keep financial information in standard formats.

In the sale of your business you need to communicate serious financial information to potential buyers. You need to present your information in a format that can be quickly understood by the recipient. Most buyers will not have the time, or the desire, to learn how to interpret information presented in a new or unusual way.

Keep the components of a financing package on file.

At Palo Alto Preschools, because of our ongoing need for capital for expansion, we always had a package of information about our business on file to present to bankers, mortgage brokers, and venture capitalists. Having the components of this package on file enabled us to respond quickly to unexpected needs and opportunities. Information you may want to start accumulating in your files will include:

• Overview on the status and trends of the child care industry;

• Current structure of your organization;

• Profiles of your key management personnel;

• Key strengths and unique features of your business;

• Detailed financial information;

• Enrollment records; and

• Summaries of mortgages and leases.

Build a management team.

Many child care businesses have prospered due to the toil and talent of the owners. However, even if these businesses are extremely successful, potential buyers may be scared away, fearing that the business will fall apart once the original owners leave.

The development of a management team in a closely held business cannot be left to the last minute. It is a slow, sometimes painful, process. First, you must adjust to the idea that you do not need to do it all. You must be willing to let others make some of the decisions. Second, you need to identify people with management talent. Finally, you need to bring them along slowly but steadily by giving them increasing amounts of responsibility.

Develop relationships with potential buyers.

In looking back, I find one factor about our sale to be especially interesting. All the companies that in the end were seriously negotiating with us were companies with whom we had a long-term relationship. All our other efforts to attract buyers produced nothing.

I cannot stress enough the importance of being visible in the industry. Building relationships now

will pay off when the time comes to sell your business. If potential buyers already know who you are, who your people are, what your strengths are, and where your business is heading, you stand a much better chance of attracting their interest. Otherwise, you are just one of many faces in the crowd vying for their attention.

Know Where You Stand

Before you start actively promoting the sale of your business, it is vital to determine what you hope to accomplish. Once you start negotiating, you can easily lose control of the process if you aren't clear in your own mind as to what constitutes favorable terms and conditions.

Set a value on your business.

Once we decided to sell Palo Alto Preschools, we sat down and worked out a sale price that we believed accurately reflected the net worth of our business. This was not a value that we plucked out of thin air, but one that we arrived at through a set of standard calculations for determining the value of a business. It was a price that would provide us with a favorable return on our investment, but also one that we could reasonably defend.

In dealing with potential buyers, we gave out this price right away. Serious buyers, of course, ended up generating their own numbers, based on their own calculations. But having our numbers on the table gave us a position to negotiate from, rather than forcing us to respond defensively to their numbers and their method of calculation.

In setting your sale price, you've got to be reasonable. You should expect a reasonable return on your investment, not a windfall. If your expectations are too high, you will be engaging in a futile effort.

Determine how you will respond to various offers.

In addition to determining what your business is worth, it is also important to decide in advance what position you will take on various terms and conditions a potential buyer may propose. For example, the buyer may agree to your price, but recommend that payment be made over a period of years. Or the buyer may propose implementing the transfer of ownership by swapping stock in their company for stock in your company. To intelligently respond to alternatives such as these, you will need to consider your personal cash needs as well as to investigate the tax implications of each of these alternatives, both for the buyer and yourself.

During negotiations, the nature of your involvement after the sale will undoubtedly become an issue. From the outset, you should have a position that covers under what conditions, if any, you will continue working for the business after the sale, either as a long-term employee or as a short-term consultant.

Prepare for the Process

The process of selling your business can be a draining experience, both physically and emotionally. If you are not fully prepared, your bargaining position may erode as your energy and emotions wear down.

Make an irrevocable decision to sell.

If you enter into the sale process only partially committed to doing a deal, you will not be as aggressive nor as effective a negotiator as you should be. You must be committed to following through until a deal is done or you will find too many excuses to back out, or equivocate, when the going gets tough.

Decide how much to inform staff and parents.

Once you have made the decision to sell, you need to decide when and how to inform the staff and parents. Some would argue that you should tell them as little as possible until the deed is done. The argument here is that if staff and parents know the center is on the blocks, they will become apprehensive and start abandoning ship.

We decided to take this approach with parents and did not officially inform them until after the sale was completed. Inevitably, of course, parents started finding out via the rumor mill. However, there were no serious repercussions.

With the staff, we chose to be completely open from early on. Shortly after we started receiving serious offers, we held a meeting of all the center directors to discuss what was taking place. We told them who we were negotiating with and how we thought things would change for them under each of these companies. We tried to stress the career opportunities they would have in each case.

We decided to be up front about all this because we figured that,

with all the visitors going through taking pictures and asking questions, the staff would soon put two and two together, but would come up with the worst possible interpretations. Staff members accepted the news surprisingly well, and in the end no one quit over this issue.

Set up your business to run without you.

Don't underestimate the demands that will be placed on you from the day you decide to sell your business. Much of your time will be consumed with preparing reports, meeting with your accountant and your lawyer, meeting with potential buyers, giving tours of the center, and tracking down endless pieces of information. In order not to frustrate potential buyers, you will need to drop whatever you are doing and find answers to their many questions.

Meanwhile, your business needs to keep operating in top form. If your business falls apart while you are preoccupied with making a deal, you may lose the deal and your business, too.

Therefore, you need to delegate, in an orderly fashion, the day-to-day operation of your business during this period. If you are a small child care operation owned by a husband and wife, possibly one spouse could take over the operation of the business and one the sale negotiations. In a larger operation, you will need to entrust operations to your management team.

Be prepared for the extreme emotions of the process.

One day you will be sky high about the prospect of receiving a

high return on your investment, and the next you will be depressed because you are giving away your baby. One day you will be as proud as can be showing your excellent facility off to a prospective buyer, and the next you will be down in the dumps when they call back and say they're not interested in what you consider to be your centers' strengths, or that your centers aren't big enough, or they cost too much to operate.

You've got to be prepared for this emotional roller coaster. If you've cared enough about your business to make it a successful venture, inevitably you will have a difficult time letting go, and a difficult time accepting negative assessments of your business.

This is all very natural — there's nothing wrong with you if you experience these emotions. But you can't let these emotions preclude you from conducting the negotiations effectively.

One of the hardest issues to deal with will be when potential buyers start proposing changes they will make. For example, they might observe that they will have to bring in a new director to replace someone you have worked closely with for many years, someone you care about deeply. Or they may propose tearing out some walls to make the classrooms bigger, or doing away with the infant component, or closing your favorite center.

Your reaction to such proposals may well be one of anger — "They're going to tear apart in months what it has taken years to build up!" But you have to keep in mind that once you sell your business the new owners will inevitably want to put their stamp on it, to make changes to fit their goals, their style, their mode of operations. If you cannot accept such changes, you should not be selling your business.

Negotiate Openly and Knowledgeably

Now it's time to get serious. In actively seeking to sell your business, you need to find the most likely candidates, to give them a clear picture of your business, and to maintain your energy until the deal is done.

Hire a broker and a lawyer experienced in the sale of businesses.

You will want the best possible players on your team. The lawyer who has been handling your real estate deals and writing your contracts may not be capable of representing you properly in negotiating the sale of your business. You need a lawyer who is experienced in handling mergers and acquisitions, who is knowledgeable about the legal and tax questions you will encounter, and who is familiar with the up and down emotions of the acquisition process.

Next you need to find a good broker. You may be tempted to try to save some money by selling it yourself. But selling a business is a complicated process. You need to turn it over to someone who is trained to do it right. You also need someone on your team whose only interest is in keeping the deal moving. You will want a business broker, not a real estate broker. Selling a business is vastly different than selling a piece of property.

Aggressively approach potential buyers.

Sit down with your broker and draw up a list of any and all parties who may be interested in buying your business. This list will include child care chains known to be operating in or interested in your community, as well as any individuals and organizations that have expressed an interest in educational ventures in recent years.

Organizations looking to jump into the child care business in a big way may also be worth pursuing. These will, of course, be harder to locate; but contacts you have established through state and national organizations may help give you some leads.

Be open.

Don't be afraid to give people information. You're not going to make a deal unless you give the buyer a complete picture of what you are selling. A natural tendency is not to give away your company secrets. But in this industry there aren't that many secrets — it's really a matter of who works the hardest.

In selling Palo Alto Preschools, we gave out detailed information to all interested parties. In one case, a company looking to expand in the child care business came back to us over and over again with requests for more information. In all, we devoted over 100 hours to educating them about our company. And we never heard from them again. I felt that we had been taken advantage of. But this was a risk that we decided we needed to take. If we hadn't been completely open with everyone, we wouldn't have

maintained the interest of the three potential buyers.

Be honest.

Don't try to fudge the facts. Companies that are in the business of acquiring other companies have better accountants, better lawyers, and better business people at their disposal. There is no advantage in trying to make your numbers look better than they really are because they are going to uncover this. And once they do, the deal is off. All you are doing is raising a red flag to mistrust all the information you are supplying.

Be persistent.

Even in the smoothest of sales, it's going to take a long time from start to finish. In our case, it took seven intense months. There will be many times when you get frustrated, angry, or discouraged. There may be times when you feel like bagging the whole deal, or settling for a lesser deal just to get it over with.

However, if you have invested 10 to 20 years of your life building up your business, you don't want to throw this away because you can't hang in there to the finish. Your mental toughness in the final weeks of negotiating will pay dividends that you will appreciate the rest of your life.

Keith Stephens, a CPA, is the former president of Palo Alto Preschools, once the country's largest privately owned child care chain, and past president of the National Association for Child Care Management.

Selling Your Child Care Business: Determining Its Value

by Roger Neugebauer

You invested a substantial amount of time and creative energy into building your child care organization. You carefully selected your staff, and are proud of the services you provide for children and families. To you, therefore, the business has substantial value!

The $64,000 question is: Would a prospective buyer of your business agree with you about this value?

This article is designed to help you project your organization's potential sale price. We will review the factors to be considered in valuing a "closely held business" — a business which is privately owned by relatively few shareholders or owners. The factors discussed are based on the guidance from CPA, and frequent *Exchange* writer, Thomas Lukaszewski from Naperville, Illinois, as well as on the insights of child care profes-

sionals with extensive experience in buying and selling centers. This article is not intended to serve as a substitute for utilizing competent valuation professionals.

Preliminary Considerations

Before you get your calculator out to tabulate your bottom line, here are a few points to take into account:

• **Be prepared.** Your ability to sell your business for its best price will be dramatically impacted by how well you prepare for the sale process. Make sure you pay attention to the first article in this series by Keith Stephens (see article beginning on page 152).

• **Have your number.** You should always have an accurate fix on the current value of your business. From a strategic point of view, it is to your advantage to enter into negotiations with your own number already in mind. From a tax perspective, it is also important to arrive at a realistic value for your business. If the ownership of the center is impacted by a divorce or death, the IRS can impose serious penalties if your organization's value has been significantly overstated or understated on tax returns.

• **Recognize there can be more than one number.** Estimating the value of a child care business is not an exact science. As this article details, there are many factors that enter into the valuation process, and many of these factors rely on subjective interpretation. Inevitably an owner will experience reverse sticker shock when his number ends up being dramatically higher than a potential buyer's. Clark Adams (CEO of Mulberry Child Care Centers, headquartered in Needham, Massachusetts) comments that the first buyer to approach an owner is often the "agent of disappointment" — the one who first alerts the owner to the fact that his expectations may be unrealistic.

• **Separate business from real estate considerations**. Many current buyers in the child care market are not interested in acquiring property. To make their limited resources stretch farther, they will want to purchase your business and lease the real estate (either from the center owner or a third party).

• **Beware of multiple-think**. Henry C. Tiberi, (director of acquisitions and asset administration for Children's World Learning Centers out of Golden, Colorado) cautions, "It is dangerous for owners to rely upon simple multiples in gauging their value." Sometimes owners are led to believe that all they have to do to determine the sales price of their business is to multiply their earnings by a magic number. In fact, most buyers today do use multiples in developing their offer. However, before applying the multiple, a large number of adjustments are made to the earnings, and a wide range of factors are weighed in arriving at the multiple itself.

Steps in Calculating Value

In interviewing child care professionals for this article, it was interesting how most active center buyers follow a similar approach to determining center value. This does not mean that all buyers would arrive at the same value for a center — the different weights buyers assign to all the variables result in differing offers. However, most buyers rely upon a valuation approach known as the "multiple of discretionary earnings" method.

The object of this method is for the buyer to estimate what return it would generate on an investment in a center. To do this the purchaser must project the future cash flow of a center after its purchase based on its current performance.

Step 1. Determine current pre-tax earnings. A buyer may simply accept the tax return for the most recent tax year, average earnings over a period of years (if earnings fluctuate from year to year), or project annual earnings based on year-to-date performance.

Step 2. Calculate add-backs. A new owner of a center may not incur all the expenses of the current owner. For example, a husband and wife owning a center may run certain personal expenses through the business for such items as travel, insurance, or an automobile. If these expenses can be documented, they might be added back into the earnings of the center. Likewise, if the owner functioned as the center director and will be replaced by a director at a lower rate of pay, the differential in pay would be an add-back. Richard Goldman (who recently sold Another Generation

Preschools in Fort Lauderdale, Florida, co-owned with wife Renee) recommends that a seller be proactive in identifying add-backs by developing "a matrix comparing her costs to the buyer's projected lower costs for an array of items."

A stickier point concerns undeclared earnings. An owner might argue that the center is actually much more profitable than the tax returns show because he regularly takes cash out of the business without reporting it. This is difficult because (a) unreported income is impossible to document and reliably calculate, and (b) since the owner was dishonest in not reporting all income, this casts doubt on the veracity of all the information he supplies.

Step 3. Apply discounts. On the other hand, a buyer may find certain changes will negatively impact future earnings. For example, a new owner may not be able to capture depreciation allowances which helped the current owner reduce his tax liability. Likewise, accrued expenses, such as vacation and sick pay, could detract from future earnings.

More dramatic would be a "key person discount" which is an attempt to factor in the impact of the owner not remaining in the business after the sale. In child care centers, an owner's personal efforts and charisma may have a major impact on the success of the business. If she departs, enrollments may decline and key staff may leave. Some buyers attempt to factor these losses in by applying a discount to earnings projections. Other buyers account for this risk in setting the multiple.

Step 4. Determine discretionary earnings. This is the easy part — take the pre-tax earnings, add any add-backs identified, and subtract all discounts.

Step 5. Determine the appropriate multiple. This is the hard part. In child care, multiples tend to run in the range of 3 to 5. Where in this range the multiple for a particular center will fall will depend upon factors such as the following:

• **Value of the market**. The value of the market a center is located in may impact the multiple. David Gleason (COO of CorporateFamily Solutions in Nashville, Tennessee) observes, "If a buyer is trying to get into a new market, or to increase position in a hot market, they may be willing to pay a higher multiple for child care business in this area."

• **Security of position**. When the buyer only buys the business, an important consideration will be the length of the leases for the real estate. The multiple will be lower when the buyer can only negotiate a short term lease (less than five years). In the employer child care arena, where the buyer is often taking over a management contract not a lease, the security is even shakier since these contracts are usually of short duration. This higher risk will drive the multiple down.

• **Growth potential**. According to Harold Lewis (CEO of Childtime Children's Centers, headquartered in Farmington Hills, Michigan), "Growth oriented buyers may well be willing to pay a premium to acquire centers with a significant upside." For example, the buyer may project boosting earnings by

---

Negotiating Tips for Sellers

Dick Richards, who has brokered the sale of more than 200 centers in the past 15 years under the umbrella of Childcare Center Brokerage & Development, offers these suggestions to potential sellers:

• **Don't sell yourself short**. While it is true that center owners sometimes have inflated perceptions about the value of their centers, just as often sellers leave money on the table when they accept buyers' low valuations. A buyer purchases much more than a cash flow stream with a quality acquisition. The strong practices of an acquired company can be spread among all the buyer's centers, causing the entire company to become more productive.

• **Recruit a strong team**. What chance does a once in a lifetime seller have against a buyer who exercises his talents by purchasing centers on a day-to-day basis? To realize the maximum results from your investment, you need to assemble a top-notch team of an accountant, a lawyer, and a broker — all experienced in this type of sale. You, the seller, should not negotiate directly with the buyer until such time as a definitive agreement has been acknowledged.

• **Don't disclose your price**. It is nearly impossible for a seller to know how much a ready, willing, and able buyer will pay, exactly what motivates him to buy, or what impact the buyer believes the purchase will have on the buyer's overall financial and operational position. While it is critical that you have an idea how you expect to benefit from a sale, there is little advantage for you in disclosing your bottom line. The first offer should come from the buyer.

• **Hold out for a creative offer**. While it is true that most buyers initially follow a similar approach to determining value, the more successful, aggressive ones will deviate from these formulas. They will become far more creative in order to meet the objectives of a seller when pursuing a sale which they believe to be in their best interest.

• **Be organized**. It makes a difference not only being organized, but also convincing the buyer that you are organized. Organization generates confidence in the buyer. It helps a buyer to appreciate those things that cannot be readily seen.

---

adding an after school component, expanding the center to meet growing demand, or simply by upgrading marketing efforts to increase enrollments.

For example, Linda Nash, a business consultant with Child Care Services, Inc., was able to sell her five centers at a high multiple by convincing the buyer to factor in the projected earnings of a center under construction as well as the value options on several pieces of property.

On the other hand, success can be a negative. If a center is operating at nearly full enrollment and is charging the highest fees in the area, this may leave a buyer with no where to go but down. This may result in a lower multiple.

• **Deferred maintenance**. Often when an owner is getting ready to sell he may be tempted to cut corners on maintenance. If the buyer must invest a significant amount of capital to upgrade the facility, this will drive the multiple down.

• **Transition risks**. If there is likely to be a rocky transition, this will lower the multiple, Jon Jacka (president of Bright Start Children's Centers out of St. Paul, Minnesota) points out that "when you buy a child care business, not only are you acquiring its assets, you also are inheriting the owner's mistakes."

For example, the buyer may determine that several key staff members should not be retained after the sale. This may cause some short term disruption. Likewise, if the owner departs with the sale, she may not have paved the way for her exit, so that many parents and staff will leave with her.

A common transitional difficulty occurs when the staff benefit package of the purchased center is much more generous, or at least totally different, than that of the purchasing organization. Bringing benefits into line can cause staff turmoil.

Step 6. Compute the center's value. Multiply discretionary earn-

ings determined in Step 4 by the multiple factor determined in Step 5. Your number here may not be your bottom line. Several other factors may impact your net proceeds from the sale:

• **Lease arrangements**. If you own the real estate, and the buyer wants to lease this from you, rather than purchase it, these payments could represent a significant portion of the value you receive from the sale. You will want to devote as much attention to negotiating the terms of the lease as you do to pricing the business. Make sure the rate you receive covers all your costs and allows for appropriate increases in the future.

• **Non-compete compensation**. Dick Richards of Childcare Center Brokerage & Development in St. Louis, Missouri, observes that after you sell, your greatest asset may be the expertise you possess in growing a child care business. Even though by the end of the negotiating process you may be burned out, the fact remains that you may be in a position, combining your expertise and the cash you now have available, to explore future child care business opportunities. If the buyer fears you may become a competitor, he should be willing to either compensate you for signing a non-compete agreement, or offer you a development agreement for you to help the buyer with its own growth.

• **Selling costs**. Don't forget that you will be paying your lawyer, and probably an accountant and a broker, to help you make the deal. Unless these services are being provided to you by Uncle Frank (which will probably cost you in other ways), they will bear a

significant price tag. Richard Goldman suggests that you should calculate these known costs and then add 30% to cover unexpected, yet inevitable, additional costs. To avoid unpleasant last minute surprises, you should insist that all the professionals you employ spell out their fees at the outset.

After you have negotiated the sales price, there are still two important stages remaining in the sales process: structuring and closing the deal.

Structuring the Deal

When you are years away from selling your center, you may imagine some day being handed a fat check by a buyer and then flying away to your new condo in Florida. In reality, it is possible that you may not even receive half of the sale price in cash up front. It may be in the buyer's best interest to offer you a combination of cash and deferred payments. And, depending on your tax needs, it may also be in your best interest not to take all the money up front.

Most center purchases today involve a combination of four components:

1. Cash at close

2. Debt (promissory notes)

3. Equity (shares of the buyer's business)

4. Earn-outs (limited profit sharing)

Companies that are in the acquisition mode typically will want to maximize the number of centers they can acquire by limiting the amount of cash they offer up front for each individual sale. Most commonly, sellers will offer a combination of cash and debt (with payments, including interest, spread out from five to fifteen years). Occasionally a combination of cash and equity will be offered.

On rare occasions, earn-outs will be added to the mix. These come into play when the seller is convinced that profits from his business are due to soar. If the buyer is not convinced about the growth potential enough to factor it into the multiple, he may compromise by offering the seller a share of future profits generated by her centers above an agreed upon level.

Dick Richards observes that most sellers come to regret earn-outs. "It is a carrot that in most cases the seller should ignore. If the seller wants to remain involved in the future of the business," argues Richards, "I suggest postponing the sale."

Linda Nash points out that another way to structure the deal is a stock-for-stock transfer. "This is a way for the seller to avoid paying taxes on the value of the stock received until that stock is actually sold,"

observes Nash. However, she cautions that stock received may come with restrictions such as only being sellable in regulated increments at certain times. These restrictions reduce the flexibility of the stock, so Nash recommends that the value of the stock received should be adjusted upwards to compensate for this.

In all structured deals, the seller is gambling on the future performance of the buyer. If the buying organization falls on hard times, this could hinder its ability to generate profits and to pay off its debt. In addition, the value of its stock could decline. For these reasons, it is as important for the seller to investigate the financial standing of the buyer as it is for the buyer to check out the seller. Likewise, the seller should expect to receive a higher sale price if a significant portion of this price will be paid in debt or equity to compensate for the risk involved.

Closing the Deal

Possibly the most agonizing stage of the sales process takes place after the deal is structured. Nurturing the transaction to a success-

ful conclusion often seems to drag on forever, while a myriad of parties — buyers, sellers, bankers, licensing officials, investors, landlords, lawyers, accountants, brokers, and auditors — are convinced to sign off. During this time much can go wrong, unexpected problems may develop with center operations or the business climate, or one of the parties to the sale may get cold feet. Not surprisingly, some deals break down at this late stage.

A Final Word

Since so many of the steps in valuing a child care business involve judgment calls, it is difficult to project exactly what a buyer would offer you for your center. However, by knowing the factors that buyers consider in setting a price, you should be able to evaluate the strength of your position and get a general fix on your center's value. If you are in no hurry to sell, you can also use this knowledge to focus your preparations for the day you do sell. You can identify those areas where you should concentrate your energies to ensure that you build top value for your business.